Consumer Protection in India

About the Editors

Prof. Suresh Misra is Chair Professor (Consumer Affairs) and Coordinator, Centre for Consumer Studies at IIPA. He holds his Masters in Political Science from Jawaharlal Nehru University, New Delhi, Masters in Human Resource Management from Pondicherry University and D.Phil. from Allahabad University. He had his advance training in Corporate Management at AOTS, Japan, TQM at U.K. Civil Service College and in Training Techniques and Methodology from the Thames Valley University, U.K. Dr. Misra has authored/edited 16 books and contributed several papers in journals of repute. His major areas of interest include Consumer Welfare, Administrative Reforms, Development Administration and Local Governance

Dr. Sapna Chadah is working as Assistant Professor (Administrative and Constitutional Law) at IIPA. She has done her LL.B. and LL.M. from Delhi University and Ph.D. from Jamia Millia Islamia University, New Delhi. Dr. Sapna has organised a number of capacity building programmes in the area of consumer protection and administrative law. She has been associated with the consultancy project on 'Involvement of Universities and Colleges in Consumer Protection'. She has two books to her credit and published several papers in journals of repute. She has also completed a number of research projects.

Dr. Mamta Pathania holds her Masters, M.Phil. and Ph.D. in Public Administration from Himachal Pradesh University, Shimla. Currently she is working as Assistant Professor, Consumer Studies at IIPA. Before joining IIPA, she worked with the Department of Public Administration, H.P.U., Shimla and later on with the Department of Public Administration, Regional Centre (H.P.U.), Dharamshala, (H.P.) as a Lecturer in Public Administration. She has authored a book and contributed papers. Her major areas of interest include Public Sector Undertakings, Consumer Studies, rural and urban administration.

CONSUMER PROTECTION IN INDIA

Policies and Case Studies

Editors
Suresh Misra
Sapna Chadah
Mamta Pathania

CONCEPT PUBLISHING COMPANY PVT. LTD.
NEW DELHI-110059

ISBN-13 : 978-81-8069-874-3

First Published 2012

Published and Printed by

Concept Since 1974

Concept Publishing Company Pvt. Ltd.
A/15-16, Commercial Block, Mohan Garden
New Delhi-110059 (India)
T: 25351460, 25351794, *F*: 091-11-25357109
E: publishing@conceptpub.com W: www.conceptpub.com
Editorial Office: H-13, Bali Nagar, New Delhi-110 015, India.

Cataloging in Publication Data--*Courtesy:* D.K. Agencies (P) Ltd. <docinfo@dkagencies.com>

National Seminar on "Consumer Protection in India : Lessons Learnt and Future Challenges" (2009 : New Delhi, India)

Consumer protection in India : policies and case studies / editors, Suresh Misra, Sapna Chadah, Mamta Pathania.

p. cm.

Includes bibliographical references and index.

ISBN 9788180698743

1. Consumer protection—Law and legislation—India—Congresses. 2. Consumer protection—India—Case studies—Congresses. I. Misra, Suresh. II. Chadah, Sapna. III. Pathania, Mamta, 1978- IV. Title.

DDC 343.54071 23

भारतीय लोक प्रशासन संस्थान
इन्द्रप्रस्थ एस्टेट, रिंग रोड, नई दिल्ली-110 002 • दूरभाष : 23702400 (15 लाइन)
INDIAN INSTITUTE OF PUBLIC ADMINISTRATION
INDRAPRASTHA ESTATE, RING ROAD, NEW DELHI-110002 (INDIA)

Rakesh Hooja Ph.D., IAS (Retd.)
DIRECTOR

Tel.: 011-23702434 (Off.)

Foreword

In today's era consumer satisfaction is the focal point of any business, as any business starts with consumers as targets of its products and services and has to end with consumer satisfaction. Consumerism is not consumers' war against business, but a collective consciousness on the part of consumers, business, government and civil society to enhance consumers' satisfaction and social welfare which will benefit all of them and make the society a better place to live in. In protecting the consumers, the governments should develop or maintain a strong consumer protection policy and set its own priorities for consumer protection in accordance with the social, economic and environmental circumstances. The nature of consumer protection is such that policies, laws and regulations must have support from the government, business and the consumers, if they are to be effective.

In India consumer justice is a part of social and economic justice enshrined in the Constitution of India. Following the constitutional mandate a number of legislations have been enacted dealing with various aspects of consumer protection. Of all these, the Consumer Protection Act, 1986 is the most benevolent piece of legislation providing simple, speedy and inexpensive redressal of consumer grievances. The goal of consumer protection laws is to place consumers, who are average citizens engaging in business deals such as buying goods or using services, on an even par with companies or those who regularly engage in business. Historically, consumer transactions—purchase of goods or services for personal, family, or household use—were presumed fair because it was assumed that buyers and sellers bargained from equal positions. However, this thinking changed and soon after independence the Parliament began to respond to complaints by policy-makers and consumer advocates that consumers were inherently disadvantaged, particularly when bargaining with large corporations and industries. Several types of agencies were set up and statutes enacted to protect the consumers. Since then consumer protection has largely focused on government agencies, their efforts and attempts to develop and maintain a competitive market environment.

The existing network of legal and institutional mechanisms set up by the government to protect the consumers and promote their welfare needs to be reviewed and may be new mechanisms put in place. It would be appropriate to look at the effectiveness of the consumer related legislations and the existing redressal mechanism. Various programmes and policies also need to be examined, both in terms of their utility and effectiveness in protecting the consumers. With the technological advancements markets are becoming more sophisticated and complicated. New issues and problems are posed before the consumers. In such a scenario there is a need to create new systems and structures which will empower the consumers to a greater extent. The goal of consumer protection against substandard products and unethical and unfair trading will be achieved only when all the stakeholders work together and there are appropriate policies and safety mechanism in place.

The present book is significant in the above context. Of course, the consumers also need to be reminded about their duties, which are equally important as the rights of the consumers. But that is a subject that would merit a separate volume.

I am happy that the Centre for Consumer Studies at IIPA has been working in this direction. It has been promoting consumers interest through a variety of activities and also providing policy inputs to various agencies particularly to the Department of Consumer Affairs, Government of India by organizing seminars, conferences on topical issues and also bringing out publications on various critical issues confronting the consumers. It is in this endeavour that the Centre had organised a National Seminar on "Consumer Protection in India—Lessons Learnt and Future Challenges" in November 2009, which was sponsored by the Department of Consumer Affairs, Government of India. The present book is an outcome of the papers presented at the Seminar.

I would like to thank the editors, Prof. Suresh Misra, Dr. Sapna Chadah and Dr. Mamta Pathania, for bringing out this volume in its present form. It is an important contribution to the existing literature on consumer welfare and will prove useful to all those who are interested in strengthening the consumer movement in the country.

Rakesh Hooja

Date: March 7, 2011
Place: New Delhi

Preface

Global marketing promises to provide many benefits to consumers, however, it also presents some difficult consumer protection issues. Globalization of trade has also made it possible for dishonest marketers to harm consumers and competition by using various methods including new technologies to deceive the consumers. The objective of governance is to advance consumer protection. Often it is done through legislation and other public policy instruments as these are the most effective ways of sanctioning offenders. In a complex market place governments must remain open to different ways to address the problems of the consumers, presented both by traditional marketing and also by the new mechanisms which are largely technology driven. Therefore, new rules and guidelines should aim at protecting the economic and legal interests of consumers and also redress this imbalance by providing protection to consumers through appropriate laws and regulations.

The foundations of democracy lie in protecting the powerless consumers and holding the corporations accountable for their actions. Consumer literacy is an essential tool for consumers trying to navigate today's world, where they engage in a myriad of transactions in an increasingly complex marketplace. Consumers require literacy to make decisions related to safety, choice, managing financial transactions and resources. Just like the fundamental skills of reading and writing, consumer literacy is a key ingredient for economic success and consumer welfare. It is in this context that policy makers need to equip consumers with enough knowledge and skills to make them capable of effective consumer decision-making. Consumer protection is a two-way process: it requires not just regulation and oversight of businesses but also ensuring consumers are adequately equipped to confront the array of choices available to them.

The United Nations Guidelines as expanded in 1999 states that governments should adopt or encourage the adoption of appropriate measures, legal systems, safety regulations, national or international standards, voluntary standards and the maintenance of safety records to ensure that products are safe for either intended or normally foreseeable use. Appropriate policies should ensure that goods produced by manufacturers are safe and those responsible for bringing goods to the market should ensure that while in their care these goods are not rendered unsafe through improper handling or storage. It further states that governments should where appropriate, adopt policies under which, if a product is found to be seriously defective and unsafe for use the manufacturers should recall it and replace or modify it or substitute another product for it and if it is not possible to do this within a reasonable period of time, the consumer should be adequately compensated. Therefore, it is clear that government policies should seek to enable the consumers to obtain optimum benefit from their economic resources. They should also seek to achieve the goals of satisfactory production and performance standards, adequate distribution methods, fair business practices, and effective protection against practices which could adversely affect the economic interests of consumers and the exercise of choice in the marketplace.

In India we have adopted a number of legislative instruments to protect the consumers and promote their welfare through various policies and programmes. The Consumer Protection Act, 1986 is the most important legislation aimed at better protection of the consumers. The Act has been in existence for almost twenty-five years and the need was felt to review our achievements and various policy initiatives to draw up future strategies. Towards this endeavour the Centre for Consumer Studies, IIPA organized a National Seminar on "Consumer Protection in India: Lessons Learnt and Future Challenges" in 2009 and the present volume is an outcome of the papers presented in the seminar. It contains papers by eminent academics, researchers and consumer activists on various themes relating to consumer protection. The papers review the current scenario, policies as well as programmes and through case studies draw lessons for developing a strategy to empower the consumers.

We are grateful to the authors for their contributions. We are also grateful to Shri T.N. Chaturvedi, Chairman, IIPA for his guidance and to Shri B.S. Baswan, Former Director, IIPA for his valuable inputs and support in organising the Seminar. We would also like to thank Dr. Rakesh Hooja, Director, IIPA for writing the Foreword and for his encouragement in bringing out this volume. Our thanks are also due to the Department of Consumer Affairs, Government of India for their continued support to IIPA. Our colleagues in the Centre for Consumer Studies, especially Dr. Amit Kr. Singh and Ms. Deepa Bisht, have been of immense help in many ways and they deserve a special mention. We are also thankful to Shri Ashok Kumar Mittal of M/s Concept Publishing Company Pvt. Ltd. for bringing out this volume in a record time.

Date: 4.3.2011
Place: New Delhi

Suresh Misra
Sapna Chadah
Mamta Pathania

Contents

Foreword by ***Mr. Rakesh Hooja*** v
Preface ix
Contributors xvii

1. Introduction 1

Section I
CONSUMER POLICY AND LAW

2. Consumerism and Consumer Protection Act 31
Himadri Phukan

3. Working of Consumer Disputes Redressal Agencies 42
P.V.V. Satyanarayana Murthy

4. Perception of Presidents and Members of the District Forums in Jharkhand 59
Sapna Chadah

5. Emerging Issues in Consumer Protection: An Interface between Consumer Protection Act and the Competition Act 73
Madhav Sharma

6. Alternative Disputes Resolution and Consumer Disputes Redressal Machinery 94
Ramesh Kumar

7. Consumerism in Manipur: An Overview 108
G.P. Prasain

8. Strengthening Consumer Movement 118
G.C. Mathur and *Gauri Modwel*

9. Food Standards in India: Need to Integrate with International Standards 128
Megha Neelakshi Katheria and *Pragya Singh*

10. Expanding Media Market, Shrinking Consumer Choice 145
D.S. Poornananda

Section II
CONSUMER PROTECTION: CASE STUDIES

11. Protecting the Rural Consumers: Need to Reorient Policies 161
Suresh Misra and *Sapna Chadah*

12. Package Labelling in India: Impact on Consumer Welfare 182
Savita Hanspal and *Sri Ram Khanna*

13. Grievance Redressal Mechanism: A Study of Insurance Sector 200
Sheetal Kapoor

14. Consumer Participation in Electricity Regulation 215
Y.G Muralidharan

15. Endangered Consumers: A Case Study of Bank Lok Adalat in Delhi 226
Som Raj Choudhury and *Anu Sharma*

16. Education as a Service under Consumer Protection Act 243
Ashok R. Patil

17. Consumer Protection and Electricity Services: A Case Study of Delhi 260
Eqbal Hussain

18. Fake Products Menace: A Case Study 280
D.Y. Chacharkar

19. Role of VCOs in Consumer Protection: A Case Study of GOACAN 293
Renji George Amballoor and *Anu George*

20. Consumer Rights Awareness among Women: A Case Study of Navi Mumbai 301
Durga Surekha and *Swati Kulkarni*

21. Media Literacy and the Consumers: A Critical Study 307
Mayuri Tiwari and *Varun Thomas*

Index 319

Contributors

Anu Renji George, Visiting Faculty—Mathematics, AIS, Margao, Goa-403601, Tel: 09420218837 (M),
Email: *anuamballoor@gmail.com*

Anu Sharma, Research Scholar, Centre for the Study of Law and Governance, Jawaharlal Nehru University, New Delhi, Tel: 0674-2541608 (R), 09871884998 (M),
Email: *anuharitharit@gmail.com*

Ashok R. Patil, Associate Professor in Law, Chair on Consumer Law and Practice, National Law School of India University, Nagarbhavi, Post Bag No.7201, Bangalore-560242, Tel: 080-23397926(O), 09480000148 (M), Email: *ashok1patil@gmail.com*

D.S. Poornananda, Professor, Department of Journalism and Mass Communication, Kuvempu University, Shivamogga District, Shankaraghatta-577 451, Karnataka, Tel: 08282- 256320(O), 08282-257520(R), 09448571678 (M), Email: *poornananda@yahoo.com*

D.Y. Chacharkar, Associate Professor, Deptt. of Business Administration and Management, Sant Gadgebaba Amravati University, Amravati-444 602. Maharashtra, Tel: 0721- 2661213, 09422159818 (M), E-mail: *chacharkar@rediffmail.com*

Durga Surekha, Faculty, SIES College of Management Studies, Plot 1E, Sector-V, Nerul East, Navi Mumbai-400 706.Maharashtra, Tel: 32459007 (R), 9820043509(M)
Email: *durga.surekha@rediffmail.com*

Eqbal Hussain, Associate Professor, Faculty of Law, Jamia Millia Islamia, New Delhi–110025, Tel: 011-26841143 (O), 09811944938 (M), Email: *ehussain2006@yahoo.co.in*

G.C. Mathur, Convener-Trustee Treasurer, Binty, (A voluntary consumer Organisation) Regd. Office: H. No. 9 & B/9, Ist Floor, Kishengarh, Vasant Kunj Post Office, New Delhi-110 070, Tel: 26136232(O), 26132420(R), 09910338312 (M), Email: *gcmbinty@yahoo.com*

G.P. Prasain, Professor, Department of Commerce, Manipur University, Imphal-795 003, Manipur, Tel: 0385- 2435960(O), 0385-2435072(R), 09612158167 (M), 0385-2435145 (Fax), Email: *gpprasain@yahoo.co.in*

Gauri Modwel, Managing Trustee, (A voluntary consumer Organisation) Regd. Office: H. No. 9 & B/9, Ist Floor, Kishengarh, Vasant Kunj Post Office, New Delhi-110 070.

Himadri Phukan, Assistant Professor, Department of Management, School of Management, College of Engineering Roorkee (COER), Roorkee–247667, Uttarakhand,Tel:01332-285479, 09411111997 (M). Email: *himadriphukan@rediffmail.com*

Madhav Sharma, Student, (4th year, Business Law Group), Rajiv Gandhi National University of Law, Punjab, Mohindra Kothi, The Mall, Near Fountain Chowk, Patiala, Punjab-147001, Tel: 91-9417536878 (M), E-mail: *madhavsharma2006@gmail.com*

Mayuri Tiwari, Student, Gujarat National Law University, E4 GIDC, Old NIFT Building, Sector-26, Gandhinagar-382 026. Gujarat, Tel: +919632203212 (M), Email: mayu.268@gmail.com

Megha Neelakshi Katheria, Student, NALSAR University of Law, Room No. 308, Girls Hostel-II, NALSAR University of Law, Shamirpet, Hyderabad (Andhra Pradesh) Tel: 09000535675 (M), Email: *megk490@gmail.com*

P.V.V. Satyanarayana Murthy, Hon. Professor, Deptt. of Business Administration, Montessori Mahila College, Vijayawada, Andhra

Pradesh,Tel: 0866-2474148 (O), 0866-2474148(R), 09849082333 (M), Email: *pvvs_murty@yahoo.com*

Pragya Singh, Student, NALSAR University of Law, Hyderabad, Andhra Pradesh, Tel: +91-9618053751 (M), Email: *pragyasingh12@gmail.com*

Ramesh Kumar, Secretary, Haryana Upbhokta Chetna Manch, Tel: 124-2336984(O), 9810887134 (M), Email: *ramesh58@yahoo.com*

Renji George Amballoor, Officiating Principal and Associate Professor, Government College of Commerce, Borda, Margao, Goa-403602, Tel: 0832-2700555 (O), 0832-2751563 (R), 09421247960 (M), Email: *amballoor@yahoo.com*

Sapna Chadah, Assistant Professor, Centre for Consumer Studies, Indian Institute of Public Administration, New Delhi–110002, Tel: 23468348(O), 9810657989 (M), E-mail: *sapnachadah@yahoo.co.in*

Savita Hanspal, Associate Professor, Kamala Nehru College, University of Delhi, Khel Gaon Marg, Tel: 09891986391 (M) Email: *hanspal.savita@gmail.com*

Sheetal Kapoor, Associate Professor, Department of Commerce, Kamala Nehru College, University of Delhi, Tel: 26494881 (O), 25259404 (R), 09810751903 (M), Email: *sheetal_kpr@hotmail.com*

Som Raj Choudhury, Advocate, Orissa High Court, Shaktidhar Das & Associates, Senior Advocate & Assistant Solicitor General of India, Cuttack, Orissa. Tel: 0674-2541608(R), 9437189742(M), Email: *som.raj@aol.in, lexrex.som@gmail.com*

Sri Ram Khanna, Professor, Department of Commerce, Delhi School of Economics, University of Delhi, Delhi – 110007, 09891081399 (M), Email: *sriramkhanna@yahoo.co.in*

Suresh Misra, Chair Professor and Coordinator, Centre for Consumer Studies, Indian Institute of Public Administration, New Delhi–110002, Tel: 23766136 (O), 09312413955 (M), Email: *drsureshmisra@gmail.com*

Swati A. Kulkarni, Residence: 201, Shreyas Apartment, Sector 23, Plot C-1, Nerul(E), Navi Mumbai-400706, Tel: 9820992990, Email: *malavika.swati@gmail.com*

Varun Thomas, Student, Gujarat National Law University, E4 GIDC, Old NIFT Building, Sector-26, Gandhinagar-382026, Gujarat, Tel: 079- 40034591(R), 9904481212 (M), Email: *varun.thomas@gmail.com*

Y.G. Muralidharan, Director, CREAT, 239, 5th C Main, Remco Layout. Hampinagar, Bangalore-560104,Tel: 09448145170 (M), Email: *creatorg@sify.com*

1 Introduction

The hallmarks of modern economic development are open markets, competition and free flow of goods and services. The process of development coupled with increasing liberalisation and globalisation have resulted in rapid economic expansion of world trade that has exposed the consumers to a new lifestyle. Modern technological developments and proliferation of human needs have no doubt made a great impact on the quality, availability and safety of goods and services. Globalization and boom in the international trade and commerce has resulted in availability of large variety of goods and services to cater to the needs of the consumers. The rapid industrial development has not only brought new innovations and products into the market but has also changed the attitude and outlook of the consumers. Today the way consumers behave, think, eat and live have changed drastically. These developments have also resulted in the multiplication of the need of consumers and change in the tradition that guided our living in the past. The simple goods which once catered to needs of the consumers have now been replaced by complex and complicated products. The Gandhian concept of need appears to have been replaced by greed.

In the present scenario the consumer has become a victim of many unfair and unethical practices adopted by the industry and the business. The consumers are being cheated on the aspects of quality, quantity and prices of goods and services. They have become victims of exploitation at different fronts such as defective goods, deficient services, dubious hire purchase plans, high cost of products, spurious drugs, poor after sale services, high pressure selling, deceptive advertising, adulterated and substandard products etc. In addition, with the revolution in information technology the consumers are facing a new kind of challenges, such as cyber crimes, plastic money, unsustainable consumption, global warning etc., which affects the consumer in a number of ways. 'Consumer is sovereign' and 'customer is the king' are nothing more than myths in the present scenario particularly in the developing societies. The consumer who is referred to as 'king' is in actuality 'victim' of the market malpractices.

Consumer sovereignty in choice of goods and services has been greatly eroded by various forms of unfair, monopolistic and deceptive trade practices. The importance and utility of consumerism and the concern for consumer care has considerably increased, perhaps, due to the change in role of state as 'service state'. This demands that state and its sub-system must serve the people and that too with the best satisfaction. Satisfaction of the consumers generates confidence and in the confidence lays the credibility and respectability of the system.[1] Though people are consumers from time immemorial, it is only in the latter half of the twentieth century that consumer protection has gained importance. The contemporary era is marked as the era of consumers. Today the business is totally dependent on the consumers and hence no country can knowingly or unknowingly disregard the interest of the consumers. The doctrine of caveat emptor "let the buyer beware" has now been replaced by "let the seller beware".

Consumer protection, though as old as consumer exploitation, has assumed greater importance and relevance today. Consumerism is a recent and universal phenomenon and has been defined differently by different authors. Some authors have defined consumerism quite narrowly as an effort to increase the rights and powers of buyers to those of sellers.[2] While other definitions of consumerism allows one to view the consumer movement more broadly. *Buskirk and Rothe*[3] have defined consumerism as seeking of "redress, restitution, and remedy of dissatisfaction in acquiring the means to maintain their standard of living. *Maynes* defines consumerism as "the articulation of consumer discontent and the furtherance of corrective measures"[4]. *McGowan* defines consumerism as "a movement to inform consumers so that they can make knowledgeable judgments regarding purchases of private and public goods. It is a movement to further corrective action against misuse of both market and political power held by the suppliers of these goods. It is also a movement to make consumers aware of their responsibilities to deal openly and honorably with those from whom they purchase goods and services."[5] *Day and Aaker* write that the consumerism is "the widening range of activities of government, business and independent organizations that are designed to protect individuals from practices (of both business and government) that infringe upon their rights as consumers."[6]

Consumerism is a process through which the consumers seek redress, restitution and remedy for their dissatisfaction and frustration with the help of their all organized or unorganized efforts and activities.[7] It is, in fact, a social movement seeking to protect the rights of the consumers in relation to the producers of goods and providers of services. In its wider perspective, it seems as an item on the agenda of administrative reforms for accountability and responsiveness through the technique of decentralization, debureaucratisation and devolved planning process. In fact, consumerism is today an all pervasive term with meaning ranging from nothing more than people's search for getting better values for their money to challenging that goal of society that calls for an ever increasing amount of material goods through time. Consumerism has over the time developed into a sound force designed to aid and protect the consumer by exerting legal, moral and economic pressure on producers and providers in some of the developed countries. Today, protecting the interest of the consumers from unfair and deceptive trade practices is one of paramount concern to the society. *David Swankin* of Consumers' Union of United States has rightly stated, "The Consumer interest is not the interest of individuals as such, but of all citizens viewed from the point of view of consumption...it concerns itself with the question of both, the best use of productive resources from the point of view of consumers and also the matters of distribution of these resources".[8]

The global Consumer Movement received an impetus on April 9, 1985 when the General Assembly of United Nations by consensus adopted a set of General Guidelines for Consumer Protection.[9] The Guidelines represent an internationally recognized set of minimum objectives, potentially being of particular assistance to developing countries. The adoption of the Guidelines reinforced the increasing recognition that consumer policy issues can no longer be seen as being of purely local concern but must be seen in an international context.[10] The Guidelines as expanded in 1999 state that; Taking into account the interests and needs of consumers in all countries, particularly those in developing countries; recognizing that consumers often face imbalances in economic terms, educational levels and bargaining power; and bearing in mind that consumers should have the right of access to non-hazardous products, as well as the right to promote just, equitable and sustainable economic and social development and environmental protection, these guidelines for consumer protection have the following objectives:

(a) To assist countries in achieving or maintaining adequate protection for their population as consumers;
(b) To facilitate production and distribution patterns responsive to the needs and desires of consumers;
(c) To encourage high levels of ethical conduct for those engaged in the production and distribution of goods and services to consumers;
(d) To assist countries in curbing abusive business practices by all enterprises at the national and international levels which adversely affect consumers;
(e) To facilitate the development of independent consumer groups;
(f) To further international cooperation in the field of consumer protection;
(g) To encourage the development of market conditions which provide consumers with greater choice at lower prices; and
(h) To promote sustainable consumption.

Consumer Movement in India

India has an old historical tradition of consumer protection. The most famous work of Indian polity the *Arthashastra of Kautilya* dealt with consumer and his rights around 2,300 years ago. There are references of consumer protection against exploitation by the trade and industry, short weighs and measures, adulteration and punishment for these offences in Kautilya's *Arthashastra*. The text of the *Arthashastra* deals with many dos and don'ts dealing with consumer and his protection. Kautilya was very clear about different aspects of consumer activity and had dealt very well with regulating the trade and commerce so that the consumer cannot be taken for a ride either by the trader or by the government. The fourth *adhikarana* of the *Arthashastra* deals with consumer protection. In the first two chapters of this *adhikarana*, there are rules and regulations in connection with the craftsmen and traders. Kautilya says that they are always ready to make money at the cost of the consumer. He says that merchants, artisans, craftsmen, nomadic mendicants, entertainers and similar persons are all thieves, in effect, if not in name; they shall be prevented from harassing the people.[11] The *Arthshastra* had also ordained it the duty of superintendents to put the government products in the market under favourable conditions and supervise their sale at reasonable rates. Heavy punishment was to be meted to the merchants who cheated or interfered generally with the normal functioning of the markets.

In India, before independence government did not provide much for consumer welfare, its activities were mostly pro-producer though under the British regime some of the legislations enacted directly or indirectly protected the interests of consumers.[12] A few legislations were enacted which provided very specific but limited protection to the consumers. However, to protect the interests of the consumers a few consumer organizations came into being, but their activities were very limited and confined to specific goods, services and geographical area. It was only after independence that the Constitution of India laid responsibility on government for turning India into an egalitarian, secular and socialistic society. The fundamental law of the country is related directly or indirectly with the philosophy and mechanism for the protection of the interest, health and happiness of its citizens. The Constitution includes different provisions in the Fundamental Rights and Directive Principles of State Policy which lay emphasis on expansion of public enterprise, avoid undue concentration of economic power in few hands and restriction of private monopolies, safeguarding the interests of the consumers of manufactured goods and producers of raw materials etc. to further the concept of welfare state.[13] Thus, consumer justice is a part of social and economic justice enshrined in the Constitution. Following the Constitutional mandate, a number of laws were enacted and amended from time to time to deal comprehensively with consumer protection which related to food adulteration, standardisation, weights and measures, grading, packaging, branding etc.[14] But under these legislations the procedure is complex, cumbersome, time consuming and costly and the scope of remedies is limited. Except for the Monopolies and Restrictive Trade Practices (MRTP) Act, 1969, all the other Acts were mainly punitive and preventive in nature. Therefore, the effect of these legislations in protecting consumers' rights was very limited.

In spite of these Acts the consumers did not have any effective mechanism or institutional arrangements for the speedy redressal of their grievances and also the lack of effective popular movement isolated the consumer and his plight only increased. In 1986 the Government accorded high priority to the programme of consumer protection. Concern for Consumer Protection was included in Item 18 of the Twenty-Point Programme in 1986.[15] Seeing the pressure mounting from various consumer protection groups and the consumers themselves and to implement the UN Guidelines on Consumer Protection, the Parliament enacted the Consumer Protection Act in 1986. The enactment of Consumer Protection Act was a milestone in the history of social welfare legislations. The Act received the assent of the President on December 24, 1986. Thanks to the Consumer Protection Act, 1986 our country moved towards a vibrant consumer movement mainly due to the efforts of the government, consumer organisations and the establishments of the consumer courts.

The Consumer Protection Act is a weapon in the hands of consumers to fight against exploitation by traders, manufacturers and sellers on the one hand and providers of services on the other. The Act provides effective, people oriented, broad based and efficient remedy to consumers against unfair dealings and exploitation. It was enacted with an objective to provide better protection of the interests of the consumers. The Supreme Court in *Lucknow Development Authority* v. *M.K.Gupta*[16] highlighting the importance of the Consumer Protection Act, 1986 and observed that "In fact the law meets long felt necessity of protecting the common man from such wrongs for which the remedy under ordinary law for various reasons has become illusory." To provide redress to the grievances of the consumers the Act makes provision for the establishment of Consumer Councils and other quasi-judicial authorities for the settlement of consumer disputes. Now we can legitimately boast that we have in our country a statute, which provides more effective protection to the consumers than any corresponding legislation in force in countries, which are considered to be much more advanced and industrialised.

The Act applies to all goods and services whether by private, public or co-operative body. The remedy under CPA is in addition to and not in derogation of provisions of any other law for the time being in force. The Act guarantees six rights to the consumers which are right to safety, right to be informed, right to choose, right to be heard, right to seek redressal and right to consumer education. The consumer can file a complaint before the three tier redressal agencies for grievance relating to defect in product, deficiency in service, unfair trade practices and for excess price charged. Under the Act the Forums and Commissions can award suitable compensation besides other reliefs which is a distinct feature of the Act. The Act postulates establishment of advisory and adjudicatory bodies to safeguard the interests of consumers.

To provide for inexpensive, speedy and simple redressal to consumer disputes, three tier quasi-judicial machinery has been set up at each District, State and National level called District Forums, State Consumer Disputes Redressal Commission and National Consumer Disputes Redressal Commission respectively. At present, there are 621 District Forums, 35 State Commissions with apex body as a National Consumer Disputes Redressal Commission (NCDRC). These quasi-judicial bodies are required to follow summary procedure and principles of natural justice to provide quick and speedy justice to the consumers. As on 28.1.2011, 3528739 cases have been filed in the consumer courts of which 3166518 have been decided and 362221 are pending. The disposal rate for the quasi-judicial bodies is 89.74 per cent much higher than that of the civil courts.[17]

The Consumer Movement in India got an impetus when a separate Department of Consumer Affairs was established in 1991 as part of the Ministry of Civil Supplies, Consumer Affairs and Public Distribution. The Department was set up in response to the persistent demand of consumer activists and organizations. The Ministry has since been renamed as Consumer Affairs, Food and

Public Distribution. In 1991 the Central Government also set up a Consumer Welfare Fund in pursuance of the Customs and Central Excise Laws (Amendment) Act, 1991 that is not a part of the Consolidated Fund of India but is held in public account in trust by the Government. The Consumer Welfare Rules, 1992 provided for the utilization of the amount credited to the fund. The amount is being used for providing financial assistance to the voluntary consumer organizations and for the overall development of consumer movement.[18]

The Department of Consumer Affairs over the period has taken a number of initiatives to promote a responsible and responsive consumer movement in the country. These measures include strengthening the Consumer Forums and Commissions, the use of multi-media campaign for promoting consumer awareness and encouraging consumers' involvement through efforts of Government and Non-Governmental Organizations and others. The Department through its various programmes tries to involve and motivate various sections of the society, viz. women, youth, rural folk, and civil society organizations.

Though it is the responsibility of the State Government to establish and maintain consumer forums at the District levels, the Central Government has been implementing a number of schemes for improving the functioning of Consumer Forums/Commissions. The Central Government has been extending financial assistance to States/UTs for strengthening the infrastructure of the District Forums and State Commissions to enable them to function more effectively and efficiently. Under the CONFONET scheme all Consumer Forums and Commissions in the country are being computerized to allow consumers to access the status of their cases and information. This will also give a boost to the management of records and record-keeping.

One of the major hindrances in the consumer movement in the country is the lack of awareness among the consumers. The consumers apart from being largely unorganized do not have the mechanism to understand their rights and responsibilities. To generate awareness among the masses a number of schemes have been undertaken by the Department from the Consumer Welfare Fund. The Department is annually celebrating 24th December as 'National Consumer Day' and 15th March as 'World Consumer

Day' in which a number of awareness programmes are being organized in collaboration with other stakeholders.

Under one of the schemes consumer clubs have been set up in Schools and Colleges with an objective to involve the students in the consumer movement and also generate awareness among them, who are compulsive buyers and are often mislead by the advertisements. Structured study on consumer affairs has been introduced as a part of syllabus in high schools in a number of states. Besides this there is separate paper on the subject in the universities and colleges especially in the faculties of commerce, management, law, public administration, engineering, journalism etc. with a view to provide an insight into the subject to students who are the future of the country.

The Department has also launched the National Consumer Helpline in coordination with Delhi University and is also setting up State Consumer Helplines in the states where the consumers can seek telephonic counselling for problems they face relating to goods bought or services hired. Consumer Online Research and Empowerment (CORE) Centre set up by the Department is intended to provide the most scientific and effective system of collection and dissemination of consumer related information to generate consumer awareness and empowerment of all sections of the society.

With the objective of providing consumers with informed choice while making purchase of products and services, the Department has started Comparative Testing of the products and services through some VCOs. A number of products and services are tested every year and on the basis of the testing, the products/ services are ranked and evaluated. The test reports are published in consumer magazines and newspapers to educate consumers and help them take appropriate purchase decision.

The Department has set up a dedicated Centre for Consumer Studies at Indian Institute of Public Administration, New Delhi and has sponsored dedicated Chairs in Consumer Law and Practice in a number of Law Universities to promote research and documentation in consumer welfare and conduct awareness activities at various levels. IIPA is also implementing Scheme on "Promoting Involvement of Research Institutions/Universities/ Colleges in Consumer Protection and Consumer Welfare" under which research and evaluation studies in the field of consumer welfare are being sponsored to provide solution to the practical problems being faced by the consumers. Federation of Indian Chamber of Commerce and Industry (FICCI) has been sanctioned FICCI Alliance for Consumer Care (FACC) for setting up of a mechanism and providing platform for facilitating prompt redressal of consumer complaint through voluntary self-regulation and consumer education.

As empowering consumers through consumer education and awareness is the key for the success of consumer movement in the country, the Department has taken up a multi-media publicity campaign '*Jago Grahak Jago*' in order to ensure that the message of consumer protection reaches every citizen of the country. Under the campaign the Department has been releasing advertisements in National dailies/regional newspapers in local languages to educate the consumers about their rights and responsibilities. Video and audio spots of 30 seconds duration on various consumer related issues are being telecast through Doordarshan and Satellite channels and All India Radio and Private FM stations respectively. The Department in consultation with Department of Post has started disseminating consumer awareness messages through Meghdoot Post cards, posters and other postal stationary items to reach far-flung rural areas including North East States.

An effective, efficient and fair implementation of the Consumer Protection Act is one of the conditions precedent for promoting the culture of good governance and thereby ensuring the better promotion and protection of the rights of consumers. The Consumer Protection Act has succeeded to some extent in bringing about fair play in the supply of goods and services and the consumer courts have played an important role in this. Certain degree of success has been achieved in the last twenty-five years of the implementation of the Consumer Protection Act and lakhs of people have benefited from it. But with the opening of the economy in 1991, rapid changes in the consumption pattern of the modern day consumer have brought about new challenges to the consumer movement of the country, which calls for new approaches and strategies.

In an article way back in 1970, Day and Aaker[19] predicted that consumerism would eventually "subsume, or be subsumed by two other areas of social concern: distortion and inequalities in economic environment and the declining quality of the physical environment." The authors have cited Yohalem's view that the ultimate goal of consumerism is to end hunger and malnutrition, educate and train disadvantaged, alleviate pollution, in short to solve social problems.[20] The thing which was predicted by the authors in 1970s is an area of grave concern today as now sustainable consumption has become a burning issue of consumerism in the world we are live in. It is being fast realized that consumption cannot act as the engine that drives the economy but as a tool that delivers an improved quality of life. Over consumption now takes away large quantities of resources, many of which are being used far beyond their carrying capacity having adverse effect on the climate leading to global warming and environmental risks.

Technological changes have no doubt made our life easier and comfortable but at the same time have thrown new challenge for the consumers to deal with like e-commerce, plastic money, internet banking and related cyber crimes. Consumers everywhere enjoy greater choice in a global marketplace, especially online. However, there are issues like lack of assurances about quality of goods and services, non-application of the guarantee or warranty rules, absence of protection from hazardous goods and services, unfair trade practices etc. which are posing serious concerns for the governments world over. These and many such issues are there which are posing problems for the consumers today and they are getting deceived. There is thus a need to provide more teeth to the adjudicatory structure under CPA to make them capable to deal with these new age problems being faced by the consumers. There is also a need for the government to adopt appropriate policies and strategies to handle such problems in a more effective and efficient manner.

About the Book

The foundations of democracy lie in protecting the powerless consumers and holding the corporations accountable for their actions. In a complex market-place governments must remain open to different ways to address the problems of the consumers presented both by traditional marketing and also by the new mechanisms which are largely technology driven. It is in this context that policy makers need to equip consumers with enough knowledge and skills to make them capable of effective consumer decision-making. Consumer protection is a two-way process; it requires not just regulation and oversight of businesses but also ensuring consumers are adequately equipped to confront the array of choices available to them. Therefore, it is clear that government policies should seek to enable the consumers to obtain optimum benefit from their economic resources.

It's nearly twenty-five years that the Consumer Protection Act was enacted. With three amendments, the Act has achieved some measures of success in not only redressal of consumer complaints but also galvanizing the consumer movement in the country. However, there is much more to be achieved. We need to assess the impact of the legislation to move forward and it is in this context that the book assumes importance. The book is an outcome of a National Seminar on "Consumer Protection in India: Lessons Learnt and Future Challenges", organized by the Centre for Consumer Studies, Indian Institute of Public Administration, New Delhi.

The papers contributed by well known experts discuss some of the most important and critical issues pertaining to consumer protection in India. It evaluates the measures taken to strengthen the consumer movement in the country and through well researched case studies identifies the lacuna in the area of consumer protection and suggests future course of action.

Consumer Policy and Law

The paper on "Consumerism and Consumer Protection Act" by *Himadri Phukan,* discusses the concept of consumerism and emphasizes that consumerism is concerned with protecting consumers from all organizations with which there is a exchange relationship. She calls it a social movement of citizens and government to enhance the rights and powers of buyers in relation to sellers. According to her consumerism has over the time developed into a sound force designed to aid and protect the consumers by exerting legal, moral, and economic pressure on producers and providers in some of the developed countries. Enumerating the various components of consumerism the author opines that the first and foremost component is the self-protection by consumers as consumer's consciousness determines the effectiveness of consumerism. According to the author consumerism is likely to dominate the Indian market as the transition will be from a predominantly seller market to a buyers market. In the Indian context consumerism means the process of realizing the rights of the consumers as envisaged in the Consumer Protection Act, 1986. Highlighting the importance of the Consumer Protection Act she concludes by saying that in a competitive economic environment the consumer has to be educated to exercise his choice as well as his rights. There is a need for all the stakeholders to work together so that the consumer movement can move forward.

P.V.V. Satyanarayana Murthy in his paper "Working of Consumer Disputes Redressal Agencies" highlights the working of the Consumer Disputes Redressal Agencies which have brought the consumer justice delivery system close to the door steps of Indian consumers. He argues that through the Consumer Protection Act, 1986, the law makers intended to make an experiment to bring in a combination of experienced judicial officers and non-judicial persons as adjudicators in order to remove the shackles of lengthy judicial procedures and to create a consumer friendly ambience in the Redressal Agencies. But the strikingly seen setback for the functioning of these Redressal Agencies is that the non-judicial members are not trained extensively before they are put on the job. They are not so familiar with the judicial practices and procedures, and not quite conversant with writing orders.

Lack of appropriate judicial knowledge on the part of non-judicial members hinders the speedy justice. He opines that due to lack of proper infrastructure, some Fora are unable to render speedy justice. The three-tier judiciary is totally dependent on the Consumer Affairs Ministry for each and everything including appointment of members and the financial support. Under this backdrop the author suggests that it is necessary to change this situation and make these quasi-judicial bodies independent. The very idea of rendering simple, speedy and inexpensive justice is good but some of the provisions are not so congenial to provide better protection to consumers in order to achieve the legislative intention. It is necessary to empower the Fora to go beyond Section 14 in providing relief to the consumers, which are just and proper. The author suggests that the very definition of consumer should be broadened to include prospective buyer to remove ambiguity. It also needs to be review whether the time frame of three months, is practicable in the present circumstances.

The Consumer Protection Act empowers the State Government to establish a consumer disputes redressal agency known as District Forum in each district. The working of these redressal agencies has been a subject matter of debate. *Sapna Chadah* in her paper "A Study of the Perception of Presidents and Members of the District Forums in Jharkhand" highlights the operationalisation of the Consumer Protection Act in Jharkhand. Based on data from the fields she has brought into light the various merits and demerits of the working of the redressal agencies. The paper is based on the perception of the members of the district forum who constitute the backbone of the Forum as they play a major role in enhancing the faith of the consumers in the redressal mechanism. The author has made a number of important recommendations to reduce delay and strengthen the working of the forums and also the infrastructure. The need to build the capacity of the members is of paramount importance.

The Competition Act, 2002 is an important legislative instrument aimed to protect the consumer in India. It takes care of a number of issues that the Consumer Protection Act, 1986 did not address. *Madhav Sharma* in his paper "Emerging Issues in Consumer Protection: An Interface between Consumer Protection Act and The Competition Act" discusses the interface between Consumer Protection Act, 1986 and the Competition Act, 2002. The paper discusses the commonality between competition policy and law on the one hand and consumer protection policy and law on the other. The author is of the opinion that an effective competition policy lowers entry and exit barriers and makes the environment conducive to promoting entrepreneurship, which also provides space for the growth of small and medium enterprises consequently leading to employment expansion.

The paper brings to light that Competition Law concentrates on maintaining the process of competition between enterprises and tries to remedy behavioural or structural problems in order to re-establish effective competition in the market which leads to higher economic efficiency, greater innovation and enhancement of consumer welfare. Further on the other hand, the consumer protection policy and law are primarily concerned with the nature of consumer transactions, trying to improve market conditions for effective exercises of consumer choice. Thus, the two disciplines focus on different market failures and offer different remedies, but are both aimed at maintaining well functioning, competitive markets that promote consumer welfare.

Sharma opines that Mergers and Joint ventures can generate efficiencies as most of the mergers are either pro-competitive or competitively neutral. But, mergers that are anti-competitive, however, can lead to rise in consumer prices of magnitude at unpredictable intervals. Such questionable mergers might also significantly diminish product quality and output as compared consumer choice and innovation. The author concludes with an inference that the Corporate Law regime, which has introduced the Competition Law, would surely affect the Consumers' interest and is an emerging and the most important issue related to consumer protection.

One of the major criticisms against the working of the redressal agencies is that the pendency of complaints is increasing and the complaints are not disposed of as per the time stipulations as prescribed under the Consumer Protection Act. Therefore, there is a search for new ways and methods of redressal of consumer complaints. It is in this context that the paper "Alternative Disputes Resolution and Consumer Disputes Redressal Machinery" by *Ramesh Kumar* has to be viewed. The paper analyses and brings to light the drawbacks of the present redressal machinery under CPA and opines that though the Consumer Protection Act is a remarkable focused legislation with minimum legal and technical procedure and easily accessible redressal system yet the system is not able to provide relief to the consumer effectively.

Ramesh Kumar argues that it is a debatable question whether Consumer Courts are part of Alternative Disputes Resolution or not? He has tried to address the question as to why do we need ADR in Consumers' Disputes and what do we need in ADR for Consumers' Disputes? He highlights that ADR covers all methods of resolving disputes related to obligations resulting from contracts concluded between sellers of goods or service providers; this system includes Arbitration, Conciliation, Mediation and Negotiation. He opines that in the present open market economy with many international issues ADR should be accorded a priority to resolve consumer disputes. Advocating the concept of ADR the author opines that it can be more flexible and creative in finding solutions that satisfies both parties, while consumer protection agencies and courts may offer only limited remedies in resolving disputes, particularly where those remedies are prescribed by law or regulations.

There are very few studies which highlight the status of consumer movement in the North-East states of India. *G.P. Prasain* in his paper on "Consumerism in Manipur—An Overview", describes the status of consumerism in the state of Manipur. According to him till early 2001, Manipur was one of the leading States in North-East India regarding consumer movement and consumer education. In the initial stages a large number of cases were disposed of by the district forums. The largest number of cases were disposed by the District Forum of Imphal followed by Thoubal and Chandel Districts. A few cases were filed in Bishnupur, Ukhrul and Senapati Districts. No cases were filed in the remaining district forums. This was mainly because of non-appointment of the Presidents and Members of the State Commission and District Forums since 2001. Prasain opines that in the interest of the mass consumers there is an urgent need to strengthen the institutional mechanism in letter and spirit. Furthermore, imparting consumer education to the masses particularly to the pressmen or media persons is of paramount importance because media plays an important role in matters relating to consumer welfare. The author suggests that keeping in view the importance of consumer protection and welfare all stakeholders need to work together so that the consumer movement could gain momentum in the state. He further suggests that consumer rights education should, therefore, form an integral part of the academic curriculum so that the consumers do not become victims of poor quality, unsafe, under measurement, adulteration and false promises made by unfair trade practices.

G.C. Mathur and *Gauri Modwel* in their paper, "Strengthening Consumer Movement", have classified Consumer Protection into three elements, namely Protection, Awareness and Education and Consumer Protection is the amalgamation of consumer awareness and consumer education. The distinction between awareness and education is deliberate as both are linked and yet so distinct. The Consumer must first become "aware" of his basic rights. Once this awareness is imbibed, the process of structured and informal "education" must follow.

The authors opine that the community slogan *"Jago Grahak, Jago"* has done tremendous service in creating awareness of basic rights to the customers. But sustained consumer movements are essential for spreading awareness about the market trends and tactics. National Standards like ISI, AGMARK, etc. play a great role in the lives of consumers in identification of products of quality standards. The idea is, however, defeated unless publicized in the media on regular basis. Thus, for strengthening consumer protection the consumer clubs and voluntary consumer organizations should play a proactive role.

Awareness and education both are challenges which are to be met with vigour. Further it has been clearly pointed out that consumer protection is best served if government's policies, procedures and regulations are designed with consumer interests in mind. Implementation will be fast and effective if the procedures are uniform in federating States. All these and many more issues are very well depicted in the paper.

Megha Neelakshi Katheria and *Pragya Singh* in their paper "Food Standards in India—Need to Integrate with International Standards", concentrate on the problems faced by a domestic Indian consumer in a globalized economy. The paper deals with the issue of the failure of these goods to match up to the quality standards laid down by the FAO guidelines and the existing inadequacy in the Indian laws. The authors also deal with the issues of the lack of information provided to the consumers by the companies such as information about the ingredients of the product on the package. While explaining the loopholes in the Indian scenario, the Prevention of Food Adulteration Act, 1954 has specifically been examined in detail and illustrated with cases. The authors question whether the Food Safety and Standards Act, 2006 fills the gap that existed in the previous legislation and stands at par with the international standards set by the United Nations Food and Agricultural Organization.

The role of media in consumer welfare and generating awareness is very well documented. *D.S. Poornanada* in his paper "Expanding Media Market, Shrinking Consumer Choice" highlights how there has been an unprecedented increase in the media consumption in the last two decades. Expanding markets, advances in communication technologies and growth of literacy levels have made media accessible to millions of people. These radical changes have made global media empires feasible and lucrative in a manner unthinkable in the past.

Talking about the media corporation the author highlights that there are now only six media corporations that account for more than half of the media business. These six largest media firms are major producers of information, entertainment and media software and have global distribution network. The media industry had never witnessed such vertical integration. There have been cities where almost all Newspapers, Radio and TV channels are owned by the same company thereby completely eliminating the choices available to the consumers. The paper analyses whether the market for mass communication is exactly comparable to the market for detergents, analgesics of other consumer products in which the manufacturers either make what the public will buy or perish is a big question. In the expanded market, media have lost their diversity and their ability to present different points of view. This paper examines how the choices are shrinking for the media consumers and whether 'uses and gratifications' approach provides any answers.

Consumer Protection: Case Studies

Suresh Misra and *Sapna Chadah* in their paper, "Protecting the Rural Consumers: Need to Reorient Policies", highlight that the rural consumers are the most exploited and neglected consumers in the country. This is mainly due to ignorance and lack of awareness about consumer rights. According to them the rural markets, which were earlier ignored by most of the big international market players, have now become a land of great business opportunities. Rural markets are full of sub-standard goods and duplicity of branded goods is another major problem in rural areas. As there is no check on production and sale of such products in the rural markets, many consumers of these goods and products also sustain injuries. The expansion of service sector has added to the problem. The consumers lack information about basic services like banking, insurance and electricity and as a result fall prey to false promises made by the service providers. The vulnerable sections are generally women, children and farmers. It is common to find that farmers are supplied defective seeds, adulterated pesticides and other commodities. The expansion of mass media has further given impetus to consumerism in the rural areas. Spurious goods are very common in these markets.

The paper is based on an empirical research conducted in five states of India. The study reveals that the rural consumers lack awareness about various measures taken by the government. The multimedia campaign has not been able to educate the consumers to a large extent. The consumers in the rural areas lack awareness about various measures taken by the government. The multimedia campaign has not been able to educate the consumers to a large extent. Therefore, the authors recommend that the government should launch vigorous campaign to educate the consumers with the involvement of Panchayati Raj Institutions, local NGOs, schools and colleges. They also suggest that the redressal mechanism must be strengthened to dispense quick justice and justice should be made accessible to the rural consumers at their door step by providing for circuit benches of the district forums at the block level. They conclude by saying that the strategy should be to integrate the efforts of various stakeholders to take forward the consumer movement.

Savita Hanspal and *Sri Ram Khanna* in their paper, "Package Labelling in India: Impact on Consumer Welfare", discuss the impact of package labelling practices like permitting packaging in non-standard weights, MRP, absence of unit sale price, the nature and form of information and the like on the consumer choice and its influences on the price and quantity comparisons, highlighting the need to take a closer look at these issues as they adversely affect the consumer welfare. According to them package is the primary contact point between the manufacturer and the consumer after advertising as it not only attracts the consumers towards purchase but also provides information that is used in deciding about the purchase. The labels provide information on the quantity (weight, volume, etc.), price, ingredients, safety of use, date of manufacture and expiry, markings (related to their being of a specified quality or grade, their being environment friendly and so on).

With the expansion of the service sector a large number of complaints are being filed consumer redressal agencies. A majority of the complaints filed in the consumer forums relate to banking insurance, electricity and transport. *Sheetal Kapoor* in her paper on "Grievance Redressal Mechanism: A Study of Insurance Sector" discusses the grievance redressal mechanism available to the consumers in the Insurance sector which includes, CGC (Consumer Grievance Cell) at IRDA, Ombudsman (Quasi-Judicial forum), In-house-Internal Grievance Redressal Mechanism, Consumer Forums (District, State and National Commission) and Civil Courts. The author also discusses the merits of using the various grievance redressal tools for speedy redressal of consumer complaints and the remedies available to the consumers.

The author opines that the insured is always exposed to many kinds of risks such as, failure of the product to meet its forecast or perceived performance or the promises made by the agent about the product and its benefits, delay in services or not attending to the customer's request/queries/objections, etc. Further, there can be expectations based on the perception of the insured and rejection of the claims/delay in settlement of claims. The author clearly highlights that the individuals have considerably less knowledge about the product than the Agent/Financial Adviser and therefore, they heavily rely on the Insurer/Agent/Adviser or its intermediary for guidance and support. According to her in several cases the proposal papers are generally completed by Agents but the Insured/Claimant has to face its implications. Medical Reports/ Agents Reports are filed in a routine manner. This requires a regulated market with proper control to buy a product in a truly competitive market with the confidence that there is a regulatory system that will provide an environment of trust and even if something goes wrong, the grievances will be redressed.

Y.G. Muralidharan in his paper "Consumer Participation in Electricity Regulation" highlights as to how the regulatory commissions have not been able to create a conducive atmosphere where consumers can participate effectively as majority of the regulatory commissions have no mechanism for consumer involvement. Despite obstacles, a few resourceful consumer organizations and other Non-Governmental Organisations have been able to make their presence felt in raising matters of importance to electricity consumers. The author opines that the electricity sector reforms have taken place within the backdrop of a wider paradigm shift from state ownership and centralized organization of infrastructure industries to private ownership, public regulation, and market-oriented structures. The objectives of these reforms have been to achieve economic efficiency and lower prices for business and consumers.

Muralidharan says that the transformation of the electricity industry from a regulated monopoly to an industry where it is expected that the free play of market forces will play a greater regulatory role, has emphasized the need for consumer participation and involvement in the power sector. Therefore, in order that the transition of the sector to a competitive market be successful, it is important to ensure the participation of the consumers. Lack of enough consumer advocacy groups which can articulate issues related to electricity is the main reason for non-participation of consumers in this sector. Therefore, despite several structural changes in the power sector brought about by the Electricity Act like establishment of regulatory commissions, the consumer participation has not been given its due place. The author opines that Consumer participation in power sector reform process is a challenge that needs to be addressed seriously and advocates setting up of strong consumer groups with funding, technical and legal expertise so that consumers can play a meaningful role.

"Endangered Consumers: A Case Study of Bank Lok Adalat in Delhi" by *Som Raj Choudhury* and *Anu Sharma* explores and unravels the various diverse and entangled trajectories related to the bank lok adalats which are organized under the aegis of Delhi Legal Services Authority. It demonstrates how the discourse around consumers of the services related to banking sector is constructed in such adalats. The paper is a result of the ethnographic fieldwork done in Delhi wherein lok adalats are organized to "settle" cases related to personal loans and credit cards. Drawing upon the empirical data, it has been examined that there is a negation of consumer rights wherein the 'legal subjects' are coerced to "settle" the cases. It also highlights the documentary practices of such forums to boast about the higher number of cases "settled" thereby claiming their success in not only successfully settling but disposing of large number of cases which could have clogged the dockets of the regular courts.

It further, attempts to demonstrate the politics behind not choosing the site of consumer forums for settling such cases, as the consumers are not given the chance to avail the opportunity to go to such forums. The claims of speedy and economical justice seem faulty amidst such scenario. The authors have argued that the lok adalats are bypassing the consumer forums thereby denying the right to the consumers to seek redress under Consumer Protection Act. As a result of this various tactics is employed by the banks to harass and humiliate the consumers which goes unnoticed.

Ashok R. Patil in his paper, "Education as a Service under the Consumer Protection Act" feels that consumer protection is paramount due to the ever increasing population and the need for many goods and services for which there is no matching supply. The author opines that in India consumer exploitation is more due to lack of education, poverty, illiteracy, lack of information and the traditional outlook of Indians to suffer in silence.

The author in his paper describes the state of education sector in the present era which has lead to its commercialization. As a result, the educational service has become a costly affair and all the educational institutions are making unreasonable profit by collecting money for every function including conduct of examinations, evaluations, revaluations, re-totalling, infrastructural facilities and also collecting fund for institution's future developmental purpose. Based on a number of judgments of the Supreme Court the paper clarifies the present legal position of the educational institutions and the student community about, whether a student is a 'consumer' and educational institutions are providing service, as defined under the Consumer Protection Act.

The paper also discusses the observations of the Apex Court that Education used to be a charity or philanthropy in the good old times. Gradually, it became an "occupation". Some of the judicial dicta go on to hold it as an "industry". Whether to receive education is a fundamental right or not has been debated for quite sometime. But it, is settled that establishing and administering of an educational institution for imparting knowledge to students is an occupation, protected by Article 19(1)(g) and additionally by Article 26(a), if there is no element of profit generation. Supreme Court also observed that a government or semi-government body or a local authority is as much amenable to the COPRA as any other private body rendering similar service. In absence of any indication, express or implied, there is no reason to hold that authorities created by statute are beyond purview of the COPRA.

Based on the observations of the Apex Court he concludes by saying that a student is neither a 'consumer' nor education service rendered by university etc., a 'service' when the university/college is performing its "statutory duty" while holding examinations. But a student is a 'consumer' and education is also 'service' when educational institutions are performing administrative functions of issuing marks sheets, certificates, allotting exam seat number, etc., 'connected' with such 'statutory duty'.

Eqbal Hussain in his paper "Consumer Protection in Electricity Services: A Case Study of Delhi" discusses the concept of service under the Consumer Protection Act and highlights that deficiency in the services in supply of electricity and the issues related thereto are well covered under the Act. He has argued that the electricity problems in India and its solution can be studied from two angles. One is from the legislative aspect dealing with the electricity regulations and other from the consumer protection point of view, as its remedies are available in both Electricity Act as well in as the Consumer Protection Act. The paper describes the setting up of the Central Electricity Regulatory Commission or the CERC in 1998 under the Electricity Regulatory Commissions Act, 1998 to combat the electricity problems and improve the situation by the Indian Government. The main purpose of the CERC is to establish tariffs and related issues. It regulates electricity tariffs and transmission up to the boundaries of any of the states.

The paper indicates that the Department of Power, Government of NCT of Delhi has developed its own mechanism to redress the consumer grievances. Through this process around 21,000 cases settled under Amnesty Scheme, 3898 meters were replaced, 9718 new meters were installed in JJ cluster and 7429 cases of theft/DAE amounting to Rs. 21.45 crores were settled. The cases decided by the Delhi Consumer Courts cover a variety of problems and some of them are related to the disconnection of electricity, electrical Inspector, recovery of arrears and fluctuation of voltage, etc.

The Indian market is flooded with fake products. Rural markets are mostly affected by these products which have become a health hazard to the consumers. Due to ignorance and poor purchasing power the consumers are exploited. It s an important area as far as consumer protection is concerned. *D.Y. Chacharkar* in his paper "Fake Products Menace: A Case Study" discusses this aspect and highlights that like any other asset, brands are prone to various forms of attack. Counterfeiting, duplication, alteration, misuse, tampering or diversions are some of the various known and repeated forms of brand attacks prevalent all over the world. He opines that companies will never win the war against imitation on their own and at the best they will keep imitators on the run. In order to ebb the rising tide of imitation, the industry needs to work in tandem with the government and create consumer awareness.

The author has further stressed that both customers and retailers are equally responsible for promotion of the imitated brands. However, retailer's role in this is very prominent and he has a larger responsibility as simply for higher profit margin they put exchequer and the health of customers at stake. The paper is an outcome of a survey which focused on the presence of imitated brands and role of intermediaries in pushing imitated brands. The survey reveals very interesting results and to put a check on it the author has proposed some recommendations which includes that the marketers should think on increasing retailer's margin, reduction in the expenses on heavy advertisements and making the retailers to enjoy the share.

"Role of VCO in Consumer Protection: A Case Study of GOACAN" is authored by *Renji George Amballoor* and *Anu George*. The paper narrates as to how at times, the established formal government machinery characterized by bureaucratic and administrative hazards fails to reach out and empower the ordinary consumers. During the early 20th century the market economy propelled globalization along with the information economy which was considered as a panacea for all the socio-economic ills. People's participation through voluntary organizations emerged as the viable alternative for globalization. Voluntary organizations have been powerful bludgeons for coalescing the energies of different stakeholders and social capital for the benefit of citizens.

Discussing about the Goa Civic and Consumer Action Network (GOACAN), the author says that it was an initiative in activism launched in 2002 by the Goa Desc Resource Centre. GOACAN is a Voluntary Consumer Organisation (VCO) which is also working to strengthen the Civic and Consumer movement by networking with housing societies, Self-Help Groups (SHGs), Mahila Mandals among others. The paper analyses the success stories of the GOACAN and identifies its core competences for replication and model building in other regions of the country so that the consumer movement could reach the grassroots level.

Durga Surekha and *Swati Kulkarni* in their paper "Consumer Rights Awareness among Women: A Study of Navi Mumbai" discuss the insensitivity of women towards consumer rights. It presents an analysis of women from Navi Mumbai and exposes the level of awareness among women consumers. It is highlighted in the paper that well educated women on shopping trips in the city continue to be exploited by shopkeepers and many manufacturers. It was observed that they remain voiceless even when they get poor quality of goods and services mainly due to lack of awareness. They act ignorant, indifferent and inactive when it comes to utilization of consumer welfare services.

The paper is based on a general primary survey conducted to study the quantitative facts about the consumer awareness. It presents the findings of three hundred responses of women respondents drawn from the different shopping malls located in the residential areas of Vashi, Nerul, Belapur, Kharghar and Panvel. Covering the entire belt of Navi Mumbai, the findings reveal the general awareness towards consumer rights, consumer Acts, quality control and standardization measures in consumer markets, perception of consumers about protection mechanism, grievances, violation of rights and effectiveness of the laws.

"Media Literacy and the Consumers: A Critical Study", by *Mayuri Tiwari* and *Varun Thomas* describes how the idea of media education prompts an increasingly divisive debate among the educators who wish to protect the consumers from commercialization of the global markets and those who challenge media studies as critical, ineffective and outdated. There is a greater need to re-examine the theories of media literacy and consumer protection in the market society. The paper critically appraises the contemporary concerns for the consumer against an ever-expanding media influence in the global economy. New approaches are required in understanding marketing by multinational giants that encourage sedentary lifestyles, e.g. fast foods and the risk they pose to the public at large.

The paper initiates a debate with respect to the displacing effects that media causes on the consumers through advertisements and they are wooed to believe a large than life image. Through case studies as well as issues that have come before courts and consumer forums it dwells into the importance of media education programme and the importance of advertising literacy in scaffolding the ill-effects of commercialisation. It also brings forth the positive effects of media literacy on consumer protection and how the same can be the hot bed for future administrative and legal reforms in the consumer law on the one hand and provide effective consumer redressal on the other.

We are confident that the papers will add to the ongoing debate about the need to provide better protection to the consumers.

NOTES

1. S.S. Singh, *"Consumerism: Concept, Concern and Consumer Care"*, *Proceedings of Annual Journal Body 1991*, IIPA, pp. 118-135, at 118.
2. Furness, Betty, *"What is Consumerism"* cited in Laurence P. Feldman, *Consumer Protection: Problems and Prospects*, West Publishing Co., St. Paul, Minnesota, 1976; Kotler, Phillip "What Consumerism Means for Marketers", *Harvard Business Review*, 50, May-June 1972, pp. 48-57; see also Mayer, Robert N., "Consumerism in the 1970s:The Emergence of New Issues", *the Journal of Consumer Affairs*, Winter 1981, 15, 2, pp. 375-391 at p. 376.
3. Buskirk, Richard H. and James T. Rothe, "Consumerism—An Interpretation", *Journal of Marketing*, 34, October, 1970, pp. 61-65 at p. 62; see also Mayer, Robert N., "Consumerism in the 1970s:The Emergence of New Issues", *the Journal of Consumer Affairs*, Winter 1981, 15, 2, pp. 375-391 at p. 376.
4. Maynes, E. Scott, *Decision-Making for Consumers*, MacMillan Publishing Co., New York, 1976 at p. 306; see also Mayer, Robert N., "Consumerism in the 1970s: The Emergence of New Issues", *the Journal of Consumer Affairs*, Winter 1981, 15, 2, pp. 375-391 at p. 376.
5. McGowan, Daniel A., *Consumer Economics*, Rand McNally, Chicago, 1978, p. 6; see also Mayer, Robert N., "Consumerism in the 1970s: The Emergence of New Issues", *the Journal of Consumer Affairs*, Winter 1981, 15, 2, pp. 375-391 at p. 376.
6. Day, George S. and David A., Aarker, "A Guide to Consumerism", *Journal of Marketing*, 34, July, 1970, pp. 12-19 at p. 13; see also Mayer, Robert N., "Consumerism in the 1970s: The Emergence of New Issues", *the Journal of Consumer Affairs*, Winter 1981, 15, 2, pp. 375-391 at p. 376
7. N.C. Joshi, "Consolidating Consumerism in India", *Yojana*, April 16, 1980, p.10.

8. S.S. Singh, *"Consumerism: Concept, Concern and Consumer Care"*, *Proceedings of Annual Journal Body 1991*, IIPA, pp. 118-135, at 119,122.
9. Resolution No. 39/248, April 9, 1985.
10. David Harland, "The United Nations Guidelines for Consumer Protection", *Journal of Consumer Policy*, Volume 10, Number 3,(1987) pp. 245-266.
11. Mysore Nagaraja Sharma, *"Consumer Protection on the Kautilyan State"*, http://www.ourkarnataka.com/Articles/starofmysore/chanakya07_1.htm accessed on January 21, 2011.
12. Some of these legislations were the Indian Penal Code, 1860; the Indian Contract Act, 1872; the Sale of Goods Act, 1930; the Agriculture Produce (Grading and Marking) Act, 1937 and the Drug and Cosmetic Act, 1940.
13. Some of these provisions are Articles 14, 19 (1)& (6), 21, 38, 39, 42, 43, 46 and 47. Further there are some entries in the concurrent list that are relevant to consumer protection. These entries are Entry 7—Contracts, Entry 11A—Administration of justice, Entry 18—Adulteration of foodstuffs and other goods, Entry 33—Trade and commerce and production, supply and distribution of products of industry (where control is by Union), foodstuffs including oilseeds and oils etc., Entry 33A—Weights and measures, Entry 34—Price control.
14. Like Prevention of Food Adulteration Act, 1954; Drug and Magic Remedies (Objectionable Advertisements) Act, 1954; the Essential Commodities Act, 1955; the Export Quality Control and Inspection Act, 1963; the Monopolies and Restrictive Trade Practices Act, 1969: the Standard of Weights and Measures Act, 1976; the Prevention of Black-marketing and Maintenance of Supplies of Essential Commodities Act, 1980 were enacted.
15. S.S. Singh, "Consumerism: Concept, Concern and Consumer Care", *Proceedings of Annual Journal Body* 1991, IIPA, pp. 118-135, at 122.
16. III (1993) CPJ 7 (SC) 7.
17. NCDRC Statistics, http://ncdrc.nic.in/accessed on 26.02.2011
18. D.P.S. Verma, "Developments in Consumer Protection in India", *Journal of Consumer Policy*, 25, 2002, pp. 107-123 at pp. 115, 119.
19. Day George S. and David A., Aarker, "A Guide to Consumerism". *Journal of Marketing*, 34, July 1970, pp. 12-19.
20. Yohalem, Aaron S., *"Consumerism's Ultimate Challenge: Is Business Equal to the Task?"* cited in Day George S. and David A, Aarker, "A Guide to Consumerism", *Journal of Marketing*, 34, July 1970, pp. 12-19.

Section I

Consumer Policy and Law

2
Consumerism and Consumer Protection Act

Himadri Phukan

Introduction

Consumerism is a social movement of citizens and government to enhance the rights and powers of buyers in relation to sellers. Consumerism is concerned with protecting consumers from all organizations with which there is an exchange relationship. There are consumer problems associated with hospitals, banks, electricity, housing, and various other government agencies as well as with business firms. The consumer of the future will be increasingly demanding, skeptical and critical. Marketers who fail to understand the changes that are occurring in consumer behaviour in today's marketplace are bound to be less successful than they otherwise might be.

Consumerism is a recent and universal phenomenon. According to *McMillan Dictionary* (1985) "Consumerism is concerned with protecting consumers from all organisations with which there is exchange relationship. It encompasses the set of activities of government, business, independent organisations and concerned consumers that are designed to protect the rights of consumers." *The Chamber's Dictionary* (1993) defines Consumerism as the protection of the interests of the buyers of goods and services against defective or dangerous goods. Today consumerism is seen as a movement or policies aimed at regulating the products or services, methods or standards of manufacturers, sellers and advertisers in the interest of buyers, such regulation may be institutional, statutory or embodied in a voluntary code occupied by a particular industry or it may result more indirectly from the influence of consumer organisations.

Consumerism refers to wide range of activities of government business and independent organisations designed to protect rights of the consumers. Consumerism is a process through which the consumers seek redress, restitution and remedy for their dissatisfaction and frustration with the help of their all organised or unorganised efforts and activities. It is, in fact, a social movement seeking to protect the rights of consumers in relation to the producers of goods and providers of services. In fact consumerism today is an all-pervasive term meaning nothing more than people's search for getting better value for their money.

Consumer is the focal point of any business. Consumers' satisfaction will benefit not only business but government and society as well. So consumerism should not be considered as consumers' war against business. It is a collective consciousness on the part of consumers, business, government and civil society to enhance consumers' satisfaction and social welfare which will in turn benefit all of them, and finally, make the society a better place to live in.

Components of Consumerism

There are various components of consumerism. First and foremost is the self-protection by consumers. Consumer must be aware of his rights, raise voice against exploitation and seek redressal for his grievances. Consumers' consciousness determines the effectiveness of consumerism. It is the duty of the consumer to remain vigilant, identify his rights and also to protect them. Voluntary consumer organisations engaged in organising consumers and encouraging them to safeguard their interests is another important element of consumer movement. The success of consumerism lies in the realisation of the business that there is no substitute for voluntary self-regulations. Little attention from the business will not only serve consumers' interest but will also benefit them. Some businesses in India have come together to adopt a code of conduct for regulating their own activities. Regulation of business through legislation is one of the important means of protecting the consumers. Consumerism has over the time developed into a sound force designed to aid and protect the consumer by exerting, legal, moral and economic pressure on producers and providers in some of the developed countries.

A New Era in Consumerism

Consumerism is likely to dominate the Indian market in the next Millennium. The transition will be from a predominantly "sellers market" to a "buyers market", where the choice exercised by the consumer will be influenced by the level of consumer awareness achieved. 'Consumerism' means here the process of realising the rights of the consumer as envisaged in the Consumer Protection Act (1986) and ensuring right standards for the goods and services for which one makes a payment.[1] This objective can be achieved in a reasonable time frame only when all concerned act together and play their role. The players are the consumers represented by different voluntary non-government consumer organisations, the government, the regulatory authorities for goods and services in a competitive economy, the consumer courts, organisations representing trade, industry and service providers, the law-makers and those in charge of implementation of the laws and rules.

Over the time, however, the relationship between the two parties—consumers and businesses, has been changing significantly. As observed by *Vrontis and Thrassou*[2], the two components co-exist in a dynamic equilibrium of influence and interdependence, in which the balance of power in the relationship is in equilibrium. In developed countries, formal regulation and controls is simply a by-product of the co-existence of producers and consumers. Thus, it is likely that the future business-consumer relationship will be a form of co-existence. A classical model on the business-consumer relationship is shown in Figure 2.1. It illustrates two separate and distinct parallel entities, in harmonious co-existence. The relationship is seen relatively simple, in which a producer satisfies the needs of buyers who in turn reward it through profit. Figure 2.2, on the other hand, shows a macro-framework of the new business-consumer relationship. This model insists in minimising the independence of the two parties and incorporating the influence of the world beyond their respective walls. It encompasses the two entities in a system of co-existence and interdependence. The significance of the new relationship model is that each party will ensure the well-being of the other in the interests of its own existence.[3]

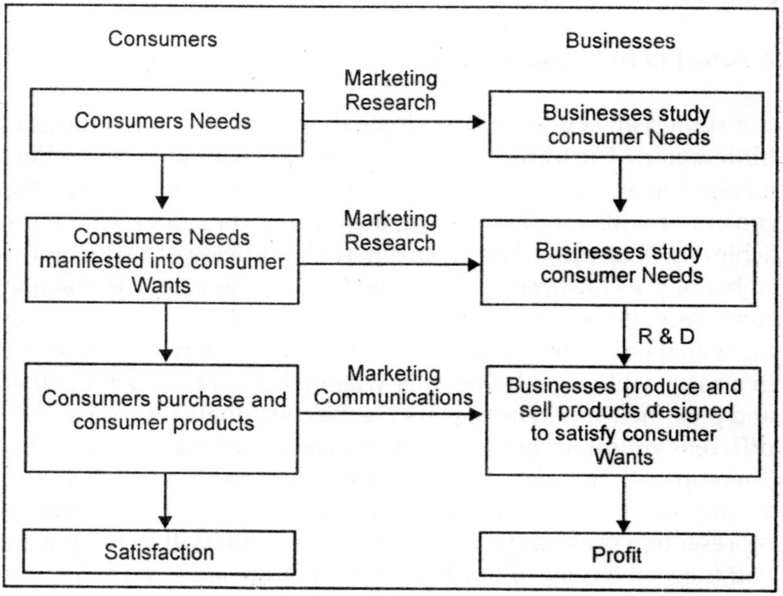

Figure 2.1: A business-consumer relationship model in developed countries[4]

The U.N. Guidelines for Consumer Protection

Consumer protection has become an important global issue. Taking into account the interests and needs of consumers in all countries, particularly those in developing countries; recognizing that consumers often face imbalances in economic terms, educational levels and bargaining power; and bearing in mind that consumers should have the right of access to non-hazardous products, as well as the right to promote just, equitable and sustainable economic and social development and environmental protection, the United Nations, through its guidelines for Consumer Protection has declared the following guidelines to protect the interests of the consumers.[6] These guidelines for consumer protection have the following objectives:

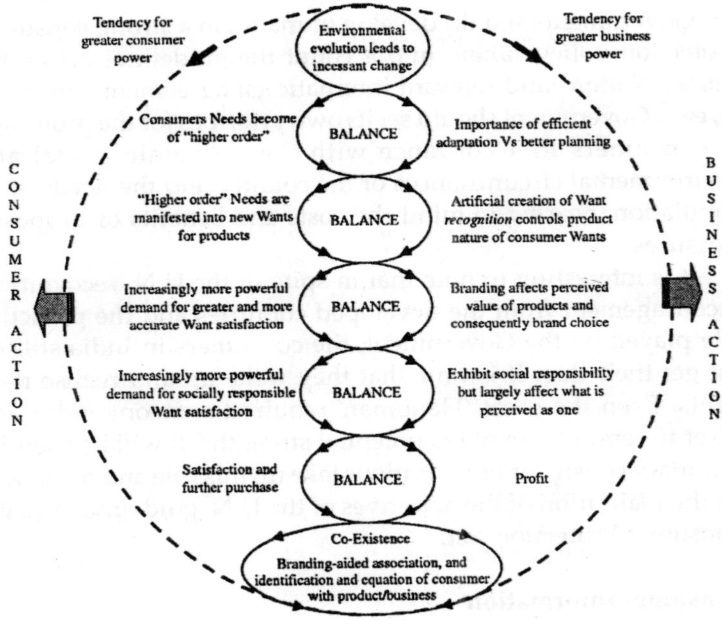

Figure 2.2: New framework for the business-consumer relationship in developed countries[5]

(a) To assist countries in achieving or maintaining adequate protection for their population as consumers;
(b) To facilitate production and distribution patterns responsive to the needs and desires of consumers;
(c) To encourage high levels of ethical conduct for those engaged in the production and distribution of goods and services to consumers;
(d) To assist countries in curbing abusive business practices by all enterprises at the national and international levels which adversely affect consumers;
(e) To facilitate the development of independent consumer groups;
(f) To further international cooperation in the field of consumer protection;
(g) To encourage the development of market conditions which provide consumers with greater choice at lower prices; and
(h) To promote sustainable consumption.

Governments should develop or maintain a strong consumer protection policy, taking into account the guidelines set by the United Nations and relevant international agreements. In doing so, each Government should set its own priorities for the protection of consumers in accordance with the economic, social and environmental circumstances of the country and the needs of its population, bearing in mind the costs and benefits of proposed measures.

It is interesting to note that in spite of the U.N. recognition, encouragement from the developed countries and the proactive role played by the Government, the consumers in India still do not get their due. It is time that they wake up and realise their rights. Even the great 'Hanuman' required someone older and wiser to remind him of his potential strength.[7] It will be useful if voluntary consumer organisations take up this role and make way for the realisation of the objectives of the U.N. guidelines and the Consumer Protection Act.

Consumer Information

Consumer rights with regard to information relate to the marketer's provision of adequate information which neither deceives nor misleads. Although numerous government agencies are involved in the area of preventing consumer deception, the Consumer Forum is probably the most active unit in the field. The consumer has the right to be heard in the marketplace. That is, consumer input as a means of setting government policies should be available and consumer complaints directed to businesses should be facilitated and, more importantly, responded to in an equitable way. The maxim relieved the seller of the obligation to make disclosure about the quality of the product. In addition, the personal relation between the buyer and the seller is one of the major factors in their relations, but with the growth of trade and its globalization the rule no more holds true. It is now impossible for the buyer to examine the goods before hand and most of the transactions are concluded by correspondence. Further, on account of complex structure of the modern goods, it is only the producer/seller who can assure the quality of goods. With manufacturing activity becoming more organised, the producers/sellers are becoming stronger and organised whereas the buyers are still weak and unorganised.

In the age of revolutionised information technology and with the emergence of e-commerce related innovations, the consumers are further deprived of information to a great extent. As a result, buyer is being misled, duped and deceived everyday. Mahatma Gandhi, the Father of Nation, attached great importance to what he described as the "poor consumer". According to him "A Consumer is the most important visitor on our premises. He is not dependent on us, we are on him. He is not an interruption to our work; he is the purpose of it. We are not doing a favour to a consumer by giving him an opportunity. He is doing us a favour by giving an opportunity to serve him".[8]

The role of consumer decision maker, as observed by *Marie J. Lachance and Frédéric Legault*, begins at a young age, and individuals are socialized in this role as they develop their knowledge, skills and values throughout their entire life. Consumption activities not only encompass the economic capacity to buy goods and services but also involve skills, attitudes and knowledge associated with a rational approach to consumption.[9] Consumer attitudes are an important and integral part of the marketing environment that managers need to be aware to understand potential forces that could curtail marketing activities. According to *Philip Kotler*, a leading researcher in the field of marketing management, failure to monitor the environment or misdiagnosis of environmental trends can lead to serious problems for marketers.[10] One way to gauge consumers' attitudes towards marketing is to examine their perceptions towards a wide range of marketing mix activities and issues pertaining to consumerism.

In spite of these views consumerism is still in its infancy. Consumer awareness is low due to the apathy and lack of education among the masses. No one has told them about their rights—to be informed about product quality, price, protection against unsafe products, access to variety of goods at competitive prices, consumer education etc. What consumerism lacks here is the education and information resources, testing facilities, competent leadership, price control mechanism and adequate quasi-judicial machinery.

Consumer Redress

There are numerous weapons at consumer's disposal which may be used to obtain redress. Such activities include complaint letters, boycotts, class action suits and other means. The remedies sought by these means include restitution, which means that the offender may have to engage in affirmative disclosure, corrective advertising, arbitration, or make refunds and the other kind is punishment. But the best way the marketer can be protected from consumer redress is to prevent problems before they happen.

In present situation, consumer protection, though as old as consumer exploitation, has assumed greater importance and relevance. Still, the present scenario is not very encouraging. Unfortunately the consumer courts have become replica of legal courts, as the procedure is no longer simple and quick. The consumer redressal process is relatively cumbersome and more expensive and time-consuming than desired. The process involves engaging professional personnel, requires time for filing the case and attending the court proceedings and certain other formalities like producing the bill, warranty cards etc. These procedures need to be made simpler and quicker for making the process more meaningful and realistic.[11]

Consumer Protection in India

The issues relating to consumer welfare affects the entire population of a country since everyone is a consumer in one way or the other. Ensuring consumer welfare is the responsibility of the government. The Government has to play an important role, by enacting suitable laws and enforcing them effectively. India has been observing 15th March, since 1989, as the World Consumers' Day. This day has a historic importance as it was on this day in 1962, that the Bill for Consumer Rights was moved in the US Congress. The consumer movement in India is as old as trade and commerce. In *Kautilya's Arthashastra*, there are references to the concept of consumer protection against exploitation by the trade and industry, short weight and measures, adulteration and punishment for these offences. However, there was no organised and systematic movement actually safeguarding the interests of the consumers. Prior to independence, the main laws under which the consumer interests were considered were the Indian Penal Code, Agricultural Production, Grading and Marketing Act, 1937 and Drugs and Cosmetics Act, 1940. Even though different parts of India exhibited different levels of awareness, in general, the level of awareness was pretty low, far from being vigilant.

However, a major breakthrough came in 1986 when Parliament passed the Consumer Protection Act. This Act has been regarded as the most progressive, comprehensive and unique piece of legislation. The special feature of this Act is that it provides a speedy and inexpensive redressal to the grievances of the consumers and provides him relief of a specific nature and awards compensation wherever appropriate. The Act also ensures the rights of the consumer, viz. the right of choice, safety, information, redressal, public hearing and consumer education. The Act applies to all goods and services unless specially exempted by the Central Government. It covers all the sectors whether private, public or cooperative. The provisions of the Act are in addition to and not in derogation of the provision of any other law for the time being in force. The Act provides a three tier system of redressal agencies: one at district level known as 'District Forum', second at state level known as 'State Commission', and the third at national level known as 'National Commission'.

The Act defines the consumer as one who purchases goods and services for consideration. The user of such goods and service with the permission of the buyer is also a consumer. However, a person is not a consumer if he purchases goods and services for resale purpose. In the Act complaint can be filed for defective goods and deficiency in services.

An average Indian consumer is noted for his patience and tolerance. Perhaps because of these two traditional traits and due to the influence of the *Mahabharata*, the *Ramayana* and the *Bhagavad Gita*, he considers the receipt of defective goods and services as an act of fate or unfavourable planetary position in his horoscope. When a new television or refrigerator purchased by him turns out to be defective from day one, he takes it recently, blaming it on his fate or as the consequence of the wrongs committed by him in his previous birth. Very often he is exploited, put to avoidable inconveniences and suffers financial loss. It is rather paradoxical that the customer is advertised as the "king" by the seller and service provider; but in actual practice treated as a slave or servant. Goods are purchased by him along with the label "Items once sold by us will never be received back under any circumstances whatsoever"—a mere exhibition of sellers' dominance.

There are a number of areas where the procedure has to be made simple and consumer friendly. In the area of "investor protection" in spite of several steps taken by the regulatory authorities such as the 'Reserve Bank of India' and the 'Securities and Exchange Board of India', exploitation of consumers is increasing. This is an area of grave concern and requires concerted action by the regulators, government and the consumer organisations. Different ways are to be found out to save the consumers from the unscrupulous functioning of non-banking finance companies.

Another category is the protection of consumers from the private sector dealing with goods and services. It is not to be construed that the entire business sector is keen on exploiting the consumers. These are established business firms which really care for consumer satisfaction, their own reputation and goodwill. Voluntary bodies like the Fair Business Practices Forum are functioning effectively and are quick in removing the grievances of the consumers. These can go a long way in reducing the number of cases in the consumer courts.

The Government is to take a proactive role in increasing consumer awareness, encourage consumer education, training and research and administer the infrastructural need of the consumer courts for which it should have enough funds. For budget allocations for various objectives the Central Consumer Welfare Fund is to be approached even at the State level also. The consumer has to be aware of his rights and play a key role.

Conclusion

In this millennium, every consumer has to realise his role and importance in consumer welfare. In a competitive economic environment the consumer has to exercise his choice either in favour of or against the goods and services. His choice is going to be vital and final. He should realise his importance and prepare himself to exercise his rights with responsibility. Similarly, the consumers' position in the market depends upon what they do or do not do. It is a known fact that 'consumer empowerment' in India has a long way to go. The topic of consumerism is of prime importance for the marketer because it holds an important key to the present as well as the future. Understanding consumers are being able to adapt to their changing demands rewards the innovative marketer. The consumer movement can be successful only with the active involvement of the consumers. It requires a voluntary effort involving the participation of one and all. If the consumers remain passive, they will continue to be exploited. It is necessary that consumers take action with solidarity to get a fair deal and timely redressal. A vigilant consumer is a safe consumer. There is a need for all stakeholders to work together so as to take the consumer movement forward.

NOTES

1. An Era in Consumerism, *The Hindu*, October 31, 1999.
2. Demetris Vrontis and Alkis Thrassou, *A New Conceptual Framework for Business-Consumer Relationships*, Marketing Intelligence & Planning, 25 (7), pp. 789-806, 2007.
3. *Ibid.*
4. *Ibid.*
5. *Ibid.*
6. Department of Economics and Social Welfare, *United Nations Guidelines for Consumer Protection*. (as expanded in 1999). United Nations, New York 2003. (URL: www.un.org/esa/sustdev/publications/consumption_en.pdf [accessed on 31.07.08])
7. Demetris Vrontis and Alkis Thrassou, "A New Conceptual Framework for Business-Consumer Relationships", *Marketing Intelligence & Planning*, 25 (7), pp. 789-806, 2007.
8. Gomathi Viswanathan, *Consumer Protection in India*, in URL: http://www.corecentre. org/Article1_16july08 (accessed on 31.07.2008).
9. Marie J. Lachance and Frédéric Legault, College Students' Consumer Competence: Identifying the Socialization Sources, *Journal of Research for Consumers*, Issue: 13, pp. 1-21, 2007.
10. Kotler Philip, *"Marketing Management – The Millennium Edition"*, Pretince Hall of India Private Limited, New Delhi, 2001.
11. Neeraja Rashmi, *Consumer Awareness: Rights & Responsibilities in URL*: http://www. corecentre.org/Article3_july08 (accessed on 31.07.2008).

3
Working of Consumer Disputes Redressal Agencies

P.V.V. Satyanarayana Murthy

Introduction

Consumer Protection Bill was drafted in consonance with the spirit of United Nations Guidelines, 1985. The said Act has come into force from 1987. While some of the states in India were not so enthusiastic in establishing Consumer Fora, Andhra Pradesh established Consumer Fora in every district and made them functional. Since 1988 some of these special courts/tribunals, have become operational bringing justice to the door steps of consumers. But unfortunately many of the State Governments failed to establish consumer disputes redressal agencies even after a long lapse of time. Five years of constant goading by the Supreme Court to get the States establish the District Fora as required by the law is in itself an eloquent testimony to the apathy of the Governments.[1] In states like Bihar, the governments did not evince interest for the establishment of Consumer Disputes Redressal Forums. Frustrated by the apathy of various state governments in establishing these Fora, a voluntary organization from Delhi by name 'Common Cause', lead by H.D. Shourie, moved the Supreme Court by way of public interest litigation in 1989.

In this case, *Common Cause* v. *Union of India,* the Supreme Court gave directions to all States and Union Territories to constitute District Forums and State Commissions within six weeks[2]. Again in 1992, in the same case, the Supreme Court observed as follows:

"to say the least the emerging scenario is far too depressing betraying a total lack of willingness on the part of the most of the states to implement seriously one of the most benevolent legislation. It is such indifference, which renders a well-meaning legislation intended to protect a large body of consumers from exploitation ineffective"[3]. However, with persistent follow up from the Central Government and by the directions of the Supreme Court the pace was quickened and the road blocks obstructing the implementation were cleared. But for the intervention of the Supreme Court, establishment of these agencies would have taken much more time. The establishment of Redressal Forums has instilled tremendous confidence in large sections of consumers and the wide range of decisions handed down by some of the Forums have convinced the consumers that these courts can become effective instruments of consumer justice[4].

Through this Act an effort has been made to cut down procedural delay. Constitution of an adjudicatory panel with a majority of non-judicial personnel and the encouragement given to consumers to use these user friendly Forums made this Act unique. As observed by the Supreme Court, in *Lucknow Development Authority* v. *M.K.Gupta*[5] "C.P. Act meets the long felt need of protecting the common man from such wrongs for which the remedy under ordinary law for various reasons has become illusory... We can legitimately be proud that we now have in our country a statute, which provides more effective protection to the consumers than the corresponding legislations in force in many countries, which are considered to be more developed and advanced." Consumer Protection Act, 1986 envisages simple, speedy and inexpensive justice.

Speedy Dispensation of Justice

The avowed objectives of this legislation can be fulfilled only by the three-tier judiciary established for this purpose under the provisions of the Act. The effectiveness of these Fora can be seen only in quick dispensation of justice. 621 District Fora, 35 State/ Union Territory Commissions and The National Commission, put together, settled over 28,49,935 consumer disputes and achieved 88.67 per cent of disposals as on 11.6.2009. The total number of cases filed so far in various Redressal Agencies since inception is

32,13,949[6]. From these figures it is evident that number of consumers (evidently from urban and semi-urban areas) are approaching these Redressal Agencies to resolve their consumer disputes. Realising the problems in providing quick disposal of cases and in order to make these Fora more effective, Indian Parliament amended the Consumer Protection Act, 1986, for the third time, and included sub-section 3A to Section 13 which reads as under:

> "**Section 13(3A):** Every complaint shall be heard as expeditiously as possible and endeavour shall be made to decide the complaint within a period of three months from the date of receipt of notice by the opposite party where the complaint does not require analysis or testing of commodities and within five months if it requires analysis testing of commodities. Provided that no adjournment shall be ordinarily granted by the District Forums unless sufficient cause is shown and the reasons for grant of adjournment have been recorded in writing by the Forum. Provided further that the District Forum shall make such orders as to the costs occasioned by the adjournment as may be provided in the regulation made under this Act. Provided also that in the event of a complaint being disposed of after the period so specified, the District Forum shall record in writing, the reasons for the same at the time of disposing of the said complaint."

The legislative intent is very clear from the above provisions that these Consumer Disputes Redressal Agencies shall deliver speedy justice without giving more adjournments. But in practice it is becoming necessary to grant adjournments. With due respect to the advocates, it is observed that majority of them are keen on obtaining grant of adjournments than the final disposal of the complaint. In this process there is a clash of interests between the legal professionals and the spirit of the legislation. On many occasions, both the counsels for complainant and opposite party are absent on the day of advancing arguments, leaving no choice to the Fora even to order costs. If the parties are absent, against whom the costs can be ordered and to whom they are payable? Some may say that costs can be imposed on both the absenting parties and direct them to deposit the costs in Legal Services Authority account. But such order as to costs can be given occasionally but it is not proper to make it a regular practice. Under such circumstances the matter is simply adjourned as both parties are not ready.

Further, it is observed that majority of the Fora are not writing the reasons for granting the adjournments. Granting frequent adjournments is undoubtedly an act that goes against the spirit of the legislation. Prior to 2000 the situation was more precarious and in the case of some disputes even more than 100 adjournments were given. Some disputes took even 10 years for disposal. If these Fora cannot provide speedy, simple and less expensive justice, the very purpose of the Act gets defeated. Quick dispensation of justice is only 'mantra' for gaining confidence of consumers, for whose benefit these Fora are established.

In order to strengthen the hands of Consumer Fora to prevent unnecessary adjournments Regulation No. 11 has been inserted to the Consumer Protection Regulations made by the National Commission on 31st May, 2005, which is usefully extracted hereunder:

11. Adjournment:

(1) Every proceeding before a Consumer Forum shall be conducted as expeditiously as possible and as per the requirement of the Act.

(2) The Consumer Forum shall record the reasons for any adjournment made by it.

(3) The cost of adjournment, if asked by the opposite party or parties, shall not be less than five hundred rupees per adjournment and could be more depending upon the value and nature of the complaint as may be decided by the Consumer Forum.

(4) The complainant, appellant or petitioner, as the case may be, may also be burdened with cost unless sufficient cause is shown for seeking adjournment. Provided that in the circumstances of a particular case, the amount of cost imposed may be less than five hundred rupees but in no case less than one hundred rupees.

(5) The cost imposed may be given to the other party or parties to defray his or their expenses or be deposited in the

Consumer Legal Aid Account to be maintained by the respective Consumer Forum, as the Consumer Forum may order.

(6) If any adjournment is granted without awarding cost, the order sheet shall mention the reasons thereof.

(7) All orders adjourning the matter shall be signed by the president and members constituting the bench and not by the court master or bench clerk.

(8) Non-availability of a lawyer who is representing the party shall not be a ground for seeking adjournment of the matter unless absence is beyond the control of the lawyer such as his sudden illness or bereavement in the family.

But in many of the Fora, these regulations are found often disregarded than followed. The National Commission through its D.O. letter[7] motivated Fora to dispose of as many number of cases as possible every month. Some of the important points mentioned in the letter are reproduced as follows:

> "Regulation No.19(1) of the Consumer Protection Regulations, 2005 provides that a Consumer Forum should at least dispose of 75-100 matters every month. However, it has been observed that some of the District Forums are not adhering to the norms. As the consumer awareness is gaining momentum, more and more cases are likely to be filed in the Consumer Fora, therefore, the following should be the 'Benchmarking' for evaluation/grading:

Number of cases disposed of	*Grading*
100	Very Good
75	Good
50	Average
30	Poor

> In view of the aforesaid norms, it is directed that the District Forums, which dispose of less than 30 matters should be considered 'Poor' and after seeking explanation, proper action can be taken against them, including removal."

But in majority of District Fora, particularly in North Eastern region the filing is too low and as such question of disposing of 75 to 100 cases does not arise in any case. Even in a state like Andhra Pradesh where consumer movement is said to be stronger, filing of complaints before the Fora is not satisfactory. The reason apparently is that the rural consumers are not enthusiastic to approach Consumer Fora for several reasons. Even in cities like Vijayawada and Guntur where the business activity is hectic, filing is not in proportion to the expectations. It is observed that there is no consistency in the number of cases filed in each Forum every year/month. Whenever there is a failure on the part of the service providers, like non-banking financial institutions, chit funds, cold storage etc., where large number of consumers are put to loss, then the complaints would increase suddenly. For instance, an increased number of filing of cases is found in Guntur Forum when a cold storage failed to maintain proper cooling, resulting in damage to commodities stored in the warehouse. Similarly, when a chit fund company was closed depriving the subscribers of their money, hundreds of cases were filed in Krishna District Forum-I.

However, the present performance of Consumer Fora is not satisfactory in the sense that they are not able to decide the complaints within the time frame of three months. Though some Fora are disposing of 98 per cent of the cases per annum, majority of these cases are being disposed beyond the time frame. Some of the reasons for the delay in quick delivery of justice are interlocutory applications, the mind set of the legal professionals and non-filling of vacancies of presidents and members promptly. Author of this paper visited Maharashtra State Commission and found to his dismay that the employees working for the State Commission are on deputation from department of Legal Metrology. Virtually the State Commission has no control over these employees in the sense that their leaves and other issues are being looked after by Legal Metrology Department and not by the State Commission. The employees simply apply for leave of absence to the parent department and even without intimation to the State Commission they go on leave. Thus, the State Commission of Maharashtra is finding it difficult to work with the employees of some other department.

In order to understand the realities and to arrive at right conclusions it is desirable to conduct a survey on different aspects and procedures being adopted by these Fora. It is necessary to evaluate the reasons for the failure of these Fora in providing speedy dispensation of justice. Though the superior courts held that only sound principles of Civil Procedure Code would apply to the proceedings before the Fora, in order to minimize the delays, still procedural laws are finding their place through interlocutory applications. It is also necessary to formulate uniform procedures to avoid delays. A system to appraise the performance of various Fora *vis-à-vis* the members, on a regular basis, may provide many answers. It is also a fact that the staff of the Consumer Forums is not properly trained on the judicial procedures. The staff members initially were on deputation from revenue/other departments. Later in some states these employees are replaced by recruiting employees by State Commissions. Except short-time training on computers, adequate training is not given to the staff on the procedures and court functioning.

If we look at the percentage of disposals of National Commission, State Commissions and District Forums, the figures are far from satisfaction which are as follows: "National Commission 77.44 per cent, State Commissions 69.29 per cent and District Forums 89.10 per cent."[8]

Ex parte Orders

Passing an order *ex parte* (in absence of a party) and making a person *ex parte* are two different aspects, which cannot be equated. If any opposite party in the complaint does not attend the Forum on the date of adjournment or does not take steps as directed by the Forum, it is likely that the Forum may make the opposite party *ex parte* and proceed further on the dispute. In such a case, the party who was made *ex parte* may approach the Forum with a petition to set aside *ex parte* order under the provisions of CPC. As all provisions of CPC are not applicable before the Fora, the Fora may reject such petition or may ask the petitioner to file judicial references. Whether he is able to produce such references are not, the principles of natural justice clearly say that no person should be condemned unheard. This principle makes it obligatory on the part of the adjudicating authority to allow the petition to set aside the *ex parte* order and allow the version of the opposite party. The decision of the National Commission that only sound principles of CPC would apply may be reviewed because every principle in CPC is a sound principle depending on the facts and circumstances of each case.

Findings of the District Forum (Section 14)

Section 14 provides twelve remedies basing on which the District Forum shall issue an order to the opposite party directing him to do one or more of the remedies shown. The point for discussion is whether the Redressal Agencies should strictly confine to the provisions of Section 14 or can go beyond the provisions of this section. If they have to go strictly according to Section 14 they may not be able to give just and proper relief. Section 13(3B) provides authority to District Forum to pass such interim order as is just and proper in the facts and circumstances of the case. Prior to this amendment the decisions of the courts are as follows: In *Gujarat Electricity Board* v. *M.B. Anthony*[9] it was held by Gujarat State Commission that the Consumer Forums have no inherent powers as provided under Section 151 of Civil Procedure Code, 1908. Thus, these decisions make it clear that the Forums can pass orders only as enumerated under Section 14 of the Act. In *Rajasthan State Industrial Corporation* v. *Premier Paints*[10] decided by National Commission it was held that the redressal agencies may grant only such reliefs as are enumerated in Section 14(1) of the Act and not beyond.

According to this decision Forums cannot go beyond Section 14. However, as Sub-section 3B has been inserted by 2002 amendments much later than the above decisions, there is a presumption that the Forums are empowered now to go beyond Section 14 and can pass orders as is just and proper in the facts and circumstances of the case only with reference to interim order. If the Fora have such powers in interim order obviously the same powers may continue even for the final order. As the Fora, sometimes may have to pass order over and above the remedies enumerated under Section 14, this matter requires clarification in the proposed 4th amendments. For instance, if a builder fails to register the flat in the name of the complainant the Forum has to be necessarily give an order directing the builder to register the flat in his name. But such remedy has no sanction of Section 14.

Shrinking Jurisdiction of Consumer Courts

The public utilities established under respective legislations are providing most important services to the consumers. In fact, for most of the services rendered by the public utilities there is no competition. For instance, services like Railways, Postal Department, Electricity supply, Water supply etc. have no alternatives. Though services like telecommunications, road transport, airlines, insurance etc., are being provided by other private players but majority of the consumers are still availing services of public sector undertaking and hence these public utilities still remain in a state of monopoly. These public utilities which are constituted under various legislations are very well protected by the respective legislations. In other words, these legislations protect the interest of these public sector organisations more than consumers. For instance, Indian Posts and Telegraphs Act states that no employee of the postal department shall be made liable unless fraud or mischief is proved against such employee. It is very difficult for the user of postal services to establish a case against the employees. At the most he can prove that some injury is caused to him by the department. He may not even know which employee of the postal department is responsible for the loss.

In a recent decision the Hon'ble Supreme Court, held that Consumer Fora had no jurisdiction to adjudicate complaints against Postal Department. Section 3 of the Consumer Protection Act envisages that the Act is an additional remedy and the provisions of the Act shall not be applied in derogation to other laws, for the time being in force. It is likely that other departments also may approach Parliament to oust the jurisdiction of civil courts as they are constituted under a separate legislation. For that matter Electricity services, Telephone services, Railways, Insurance, Banks, Medical profession etc., have separate legislations. Following example suffice to say how the jurisdiction of these Fora is narrowed. Earlier, all the States had Chit Funds Acts and subsequently a Central Act come into force which ousted the jurisdiction of the civil courts and as such the chit subscribers cannot avail the provisions of Consumer Protection Act. The Chit Registrar is the only competent person to adjudicate the disputes arising between the chit fund company and its subscribers. Certainly, these developments may prejudice the interests of consumers.

Enforcement of Orders by the District Forum (Section 25)

In 2002 amendments to the construction of this section has been thoroughly changed with a good intention to provide effective execution of the Forum orders. But this change proved to be more troublesome affair to the complainants than before, because the amended Act removed the power of the Redressal Agencies to enforce the orders under civil process. At present the Redressal Agencies have power only to issue a certificate to the District Collector for recovery of the amount as per the provisions of the Revenue Recovery Act in case of final order. When these decree holders approach the District Collector, they are not even in a position to get the audience of the collector. There is abnormal delay in the recovery of the amount and in many cases the decree holders are coming back to the Fora for cancellation of the certificate issued to the collector. As the collectors are overburdened with their regular routine they are not able to devote their time on such issues. Interestingly, in case of an interim order, the same Section 25 provides powers to attach the property of the judgment debtor for non-compliance and if the non-compliance continues for more than 3 months from the date of such attachment the property can be sold and the amount be paid to the petitioner. Because of these practical problems in recovery of the amount by the District Collector, there is need to review the present situation and accordingly amend this section once again to make it more consumer friendly.

Further under Section 25 the petitioner has to proceed against the properties of the Judgment debtor and for that he has to get the information regarding the properties of the Judgment debtor, which is impossible to collect, more so, in the case of a person who lives in other states. The petitioner may have to appoint an investigating agency for collection of such information, which costs him very heavily. Considering all these problems the petitioners are choosing to file a petition under Section 27 instead of under Section 25. In *Deepthi Coaching Centre* v. *Itta Krishnaiah*[11] the A.P. State Commission held as follows: "It is well established that proceedings under Section 25 of the Act are of civil nature and that they are independent and different from proceedings initiated under Section 27 of the Act, which are of criminal or quasi-criminal nature. If action is sought to be taken under Section 27 and after reasonable opportunity to him only, appropriate orders imposing punishment under that section can be made."

Section 27

After 2002 amendments Section 27 has been subjected to thorough change and the Consumer Forums are conferred with the powers of first class judicial magistrate, and the order passed under this section is now appealable. There are no guidelines provided in the Act as to when a decree holder can invoke Section 25 and when shall he proceed under Section 27. It is not clear whether decree holder should invoke section 27 only after exhausting the remedy provided under Section 25. Delhi State Commission held in *Batia v. Deepu Chits Pvt. Ltd. & Ors.*, that an application under Section 27 of the Consumer Protection Act is maintainable by the decree holder against the judgment debtor, in spite of the fact that a remedy by way of execution is available to him under Section 25 of the Act.[12] But Maharashtra State Commission held a different view in *Nirmala Sundar Jaipuria* v. *Canbank Mutual Fund*[13], which is as follows: "The exceptional remedy available under Section 27 of the Consumer Protection Act should not be permitted to be resorted as a handle of vengeance. It is only when normal attempts of recovery of the awarded compensation fail, then the same should be resorted to."

It is in this context necessity arises to review the provisions of the Act to suitably amend the Act to provide more clarity. If the petitioner is asked to first exhaust the provisions under Section 25 and then only to invoke the provisions of Section 27 it takes long time for the petitioner to pursue his remedy under Section 27. In view of this, both the sections need a thorough reconstruction. It is suggested that the Consumer Courts should be empowered to execute the order on its own instead of depending on the District Collector. Similarly, to make Section 27 more effective, necessary mechanism should be provided to the Fora to produce the person, who is not complying with the order, before the Fora for initiating necessary action. For this purpose, police personnel are required to provide teeth to the Forum. At present the warrants sent to police department are not executed promptly. In many cases the police department is sending a reply stating that the person against whom the warrant is issued is not traceable. Unless the order of the Forum is implemented at the earliest, consumers may lose faith in this three-tier judiciary, specially constituted for their protection.

Are Redressal Agencies Dependent on Consumer Affairs Department?

The State Governments are not allotting money promptly to these redresssal agencies and the Registrars are made to go around the Civil Supplies and Consumer Affairs Department for allotment of funds. If the allocation of financial requirements of the Redressal Agencies is included in the planned expenditure and if the funds flow directly to the State Commissions without any effort, the redressal agencies need not depend on the Government departments, which in fact is not proper. It may even adversely affect the quasi-judicial freedom of the redressal agencies. There are instances of Consumer Affairs Ministry giving directions regarding disposal of some disputes pending before the Fora.

Functioning of Circuit Benches

Circuit benches are created with a sole aim to bring justice delivery mechanism more close to consumers. The purpose of creating circuit benches is to provide an opportunity to the parties to represent their matters close to their places instead of going to the usual place of sitting of State Commission. Accordingly, these circuit benches are conducting proceedings at some identified places in various parts of the State. In case of National Commission, the circuit bench is sitting at various important cities in India. The practical difficulty for the parties in this regard is that they would engage lawyers at the place of sitting of State Commission or the National Commission and if the hearing is posted at some other place, the advocates travel from state/national capital to the place where the circuit bench is sitting, at the cost of the parties. There is not even an iota of evidence that the disputes are resolved faster by these circuit benches. Many a times, it is felt that the cause list is not made available to the lawyers well in advance or the parties are communicated prior to the holding of such circuit bench at such place. If advance intimation is not given, parties simply ask for adjournments defeating the very purpose of establishment of circuit benches. If these circuit benches conduct proceedings regularly on set days at the designated places and the appeals relating to various Fora are grouped and assigned to that particular place, then it would be convenient for the parties to appoint advocates accordingly. Parties should be assured that such matters taken up by circuit benches would be handled by the circuit bench only and not by the State Commissions/National Commission at their usual place of sitting.

Cases on Medical Negligence

A few years ago the Presidents of State Commissions at a meeting held at Delhi proposed that complaints against medical professionals should be first referred to a medical body or local branch of Indian Medical Association to find out if there is a *prima facie* case on the medical negligence. Referring a dispute to a private body to find out whether there is any negligence on the part of the medical professional is basically wrong when the matter is filed before an adjudicating authority, legally constituted. Such reference would have adverse impact on the further proceedings of the matter. How these legally constituted tribunals can depend on a private body of persons to decide primarily the negligence of medical professionals? It gives wrong feeling to the complainants as if these Fora are adjudicating the matters in consultation with the peers of opposite parties.

Capacity Building of Staff of Fora

At the time of inception of Consumer Forums the respective Governments did not make proper exercise on recruitment of the staff and for their training. Surplus personnel belonging to other departments having no knowledge of the judicial procedures are sent to these Consumer Forums. Only the office superintendents/ *sheristadars*/chief ministerial officers by whatever name they are called, are only experienced persons in judicial procedures. It goes without saying that the untrained staff would be a greater hindrance for quick dispensation of justice. All the staff members concerned are to be specially trained in judicial procedures before they handle the Forum matters. Sometimes the attenders (substaff) are promoted as junior assistants and entrusted with important work without providing them required training.

Training of Non-Judicial Members

Members are appointed according to the provisions of Consumer Protection Act, 1986 by the respective Governments. Any employee selected to Government service should first undergo training before he/she is entrusted with any work of the department. But in case of members of District Forums, State Commissions this most essential rule is ignored and the selected members are allowed to function without any training whatsoever. After sometimes they may be sent for some orientation, which cannot be described as training. An untrained member cannot understand the implications in implementation of legal provisions and the advocates may raise their eyebrows on the capacity of these untrained members. Even after the training some of these members are not in a position to decide the step that follows in the next adjournment. In absence of the president a senior member can officiate as the president of the Forum. Under such circumstances, if he/she is unable to decide the next step it becomes embarrassing to him/her. Particularly these non-judicial members should be given extensive training on how to write the orders. Till such time they should not be entrusted with writing the orders.

Co-ordination Meetings

Constituting an adjudicatory body of three persons out of which two are lay persons is an experiment made by the law makers to make the Consumer Fora user friendly. When two lay members who are in majority makes the decision it becomes the order, and hence, the adjudication of matters should be done with utmost care and caution. In order to make this experiment successful there should be proper understanding between the Presidents and other members. The Presidents should act as mentors and become friends, philosophers and guides to these members giving them quasi-judicial freedom. Presidents should discuss issues but should not dictate. In reality, these Presidents, per force of habit, are confining themselves to the four walls and are not able to freely discuss the matters with other members. In order to bring a change in their mind set, National Commission has to give guidelines and also there should be co-ordination meetings between Presidents and members. Holding annual meetings by the State Commission to discuss co-ordination problems and other issues jointly with all the Presidents and members would improve the situation to a greater extent. One should not forget that this Act is designed to provide simple, speedy and less expensive justice to consumers. In order to achieve the spirit of this legislation there need to be a change in the mindset of the Presidents who lived for a long time in isolation giving importance to the procedural aspects, which appear to be totally irrelevant to the lay members.

Discriminatory Treatment to Non-Judicial Members

Non-Judicial members are not involved at any stage, in some Forums, in the admission of complaints unless it is posted for hearing on the bench. Majority of the complaints are registered without the knowledge of Non-Judicial members. As these members are full-time members and are available at the Forums all the time, there is nothing wrong in consulting them or at least informing them about the cases filed and admitted. Further, the matters coming up on the bench are not furnished to these members in advance. In majority of the cases these members are blindfolded. They would come to know about the details of a particular case only when they are asked to write the order. Even at the time of recording the deposition of the parties, no details are supplied to the Non-Judicial members at least on the bench. Further, some Governments are not treating the members and the President equally in providing travelling expenses and other allowances. According to the provisions of Consumer Protection Act, 1986 there is no such discrimination. Section 2(1)(jj) categorically states that 'member' includes president and member of the National Commission or a State Commission or a District Forum, as the case may be. According to Consumer Protection rules these members should be treated as Grade-I officers of the Government and accordingly they are entitled for reimbursement of expenses. Presidents are paid Two-tier A/c class by railways whereas other members are being paid second class sleeper fare. There is no justification in this kind of discriminatory treatment by the Government violating the provisions of the Act. In view of this, the Hon'ble National Commission should take up this issue with the respective State Governments to put an end to such discriminations. Necessary instruction may be given to all the State

Commissions to treat all the members including Presidents equally.

No Complaints on Violation of Rights

It is a matter to be seen whether the Consumer Fora can effectively adjudicate a complaint on violation of any of the consumer rights as envisaged under Section 6. Promotion and protection of consumer rights is entrusted to Consumer Protection Councils at National, State and District level, which do not have any powers to achieve the assigned responsibility. Suppose, if any consumer files a complaint before the District Forum that his right to information is violated or he is not provided with consumer education what the Forum can do? So far, it has not come to light whether such complaints are filed before any Forum. Are there any effective remedies for complaints regarding violation of rights? There are some limited remedies regarding right to safety, right to redressal. For the rest of the four rights there are no effective remedies. Similarly, if the provisions under Chapter II are violated by the officers concerned where the remedy lies? If the Government fails to establish consumer protection councils or if the mandatory meetings are not convened the remedy is available only in the constitutional courts. Instead, the Consumer Fora should be empowered to take up failures in implementing the provisions of Chapter II of Consumer Protection Act, 1986 dealing with Consumer Protection Councils and corresponding consumer rights envisaged therein.

In conclusion, it is emphasized that the Consumer Courts can provide better protection to consumer, as envisaged in the preamble, if they adopt a pragmatic approach in quick dispensation of justice and make orders as is just and proper in the facts and circumstances of the case, instead of following a thumb rule.

NOTES

1. Editorial, *The Hindu*, 24.6.93, p. 8
2. P.V.V. Satyanarayana Murthy, *Consumer Justice*, Indian Institute of Public Administration, p. 37, New Delhi, 2006.
3. *Common Cause* v. *Union of India*, (1993) CPJ 1 (SC).

4. Sathi Nair, *Proceedings of the National Seminar on Consumer Redress*, CAG & IOCU Consumer Action Group, Madras, p. 15, 1992.
5. 1993 III CPJ 7 (SC).
6. *Source*: Records of National Commission, New Delhi and www.ncdrc.nic.in.
7. Letter no. D.O.No. A-104/NCDRC/2007 dated 5th December, 2007.
8. S.S. Singh and Sapna Chadah, 'Consumer Protection in India—Some Reflections', p. 16, Indian Institute of Public Administration, New Delhi, 2005.
9. II (1993) CPJ 1013, Gujarat State Commission.
10. II (1991) CPJ 599.
11. I (1999) CPJ 208.
12. P.V.V. Satyanarayana Murthy, *Consumer Justice*, Indian Institute of Public Administration, p. 255, New Delhi, 2006.
13. 2004 CTJ 1092.

4
Perception of Presidents and Members of the District Forums in Jharkhand

Sapna Chadah

Introduction

The growing interdependence of the world economy and international character of many business practices have contributed to the development of universal emphasis on consumer rights protection and promotion. Consumers, clients and customers' world over, are demanding value for money in the form of quality goods and better services. Modern technological developments have no doubt made a great impact on the quality, availability and safety of goods and services. But the fact of life is that the consumers are still victims of unscrupulous and exploitative practices. Exploitation of consumers assumes numerous forms such as adulteration of food, spurious drugs, dubious hire purchase plans, high prices, poor quality, deficient services, deceptive advertisements, hazardous products, black marketing and many more. In addition, with revolution in information technology newer kinds of challenges are thrown on the consumer like cybre crimes, plastic money etc., which affect the consumer in even bigger way. 'Consumer is sovereign' and 'customer is the king' are nothing more than myths in the present scenario particularly in the developing societies. Now it has been realized and rightly so that the consumer protection is a socio-economic programme to be pursued by the government as well as the business as the satisfaction of the consumers is in the interest of both. In this context, the government, however, has a primary responsibility to protect the consumers' interests and rights through appropriate policy measures, legal structure and administrative framework.

In present situation, consumer protection, though as old as consumer exploitation, has assumed greater importance and relevance. Now there exists laws and policies which focus on consumer protection and welfare. In India various Acts intended to protect the consumers directly or indirectly against different forms of exploitation were enacted from time to time. However, except for the Monopolies and Restrictive Trade Practices (MRTP) Act, 1969, all the other Acts were mainly punitive and preventive in nature. In spite of these Acts the consumers did not have any effective mechanism or institutional arrangements for the speedy redressal of their grievances and also the lack of effective popular movement isolated the consumer and his plight only increased. Seeing the pressure mounting from various consumer protection groups and the consumers themselves the Parliament enacted the Consumer Protection Act in 1986.

Enactment of CPA: A Milestone

The enactment of the Consumer Protection Act in 1986 was a milestone in the history of consumer movement in the country. Before this most of the legislations to protect the consumers were punitive in nature and did not provide for a holistic protection to the consumers in a cost effective and time bound manner. There were no institutional mechanisms available to the consumers which would redress their grievances in a simple and expeditious manner unlike the civil courts which took a lot of time and money to decide a case. The Consumer Protection Act, 1986 is a benevolent piece of social welfare legislation. The Act seeks to provide for better protection of the consumers and stipulates the establishment of authorities for the settlement of consumer disputes. The Act applies to all products and services whether provided by public, private or cooperative body. The remedy provided under the Consumer Protection Act to the consumer is in addition to and not in derogation of the provisions of any other law for the time being in force.

The Act enumerates the six rights of the consumers and provides for speedy and simple redress to consumer disputes for which quasi-judicial machinery is sought to be set up at the district, state and the national level. The quasi-judicial bodies are to observe the principles of natural justice and have been empowered to give relief of a specific nature and to award, wherever appropriate, compensation to consumers. Penalties for non-compliance of the orders given by the quasi-judicial bodies have also been provided.

Establishment of District Forums

The Act empowers the State Government to establish a consumer disputes redressal agency known as District Forum in each district. The State Government, if it deems fit can establish more than one District Forum in a district. The Consumer Forum is an alternative forum, less formal and more consumer friendly for providing, speedy and inexpensive justice. Cases are decided on the basis of justice, equity and good conscience, and Principles of Natural Justice are required to be adhered to. The rigours of the technicalities of civil law have no place. Some provisions of the civil law have been incorporated in the Consumer Protection Act which provides guidelines for conducting the proceedings and to receive evidence on affidavits. Strict rules of evidence and procedure do not come in the way of the working of the Consumer Forums. Material which has probative value and can pass the test of a reasonable man is accepted.

Each District Forum shall consist of a President, who is, or has been, or is qualified to be a District Judge and two other members, one of whom shall be a woman. The person to be a member should not be less than thirty-five years of age, possess a bachelor's degree from a recognised university and be a person of ability, integrity and standing, and have adequate knowledge and experience of at least ten years in dealing with problems relating to economics, law, commerce, accountancy, industry, public affairs or administration. Every appointment to the District Forum shall be made by the State Government on the recommendation of a Selection Committee consisting of the President of the State Commission as Chairman, Secretary, Law Department of the State as Member and Secretary in-charge of the Department dealing with Consumer Affairs in the State as Member. Every member at the District Forum shall hold office for a term of five years or up to the age of sixty-five whichever is earlier.

The District Forum has the jurisdiction to entertain complaints where the value of the goods or services and the compensation, if any, claimed does not exceed rupees twenty lakhs. A complaint shall be instituted in a District Forum within the local limits of whose jurisdiction (a) the opposite party or each of the opposite parties, where there are more than one, at the time of the institution of the complaint, actually and voluntarily resides or carries on business or has a branch office or personally works for a gain, or (b) any of the opposite parties, where there are more than one, at the time of the institution of the complaint, actually and voluntarily resides or carries on business or has a branch office or personally works for gain, provided that in such case either the permission of the District Forum is given, or the opposite parties who do not reside or carry on business or have a branch office or personally work for gain, as the case may be, acquiesce in such institution, or (c) the cause of action, wholly or in part arises.

Every complaint shall be heard as expeditiously as possible and endeavour shall be made to decide the complaint within a period of three months from the date of receipt of notice by opposite party where the complaint does not require analysis or testing of commodities and within five months, if it requires analysis or testing of commodities. No adjournment shall be ordinarily granted by the District Forum unless sufficient cause is shown and the reasons for grant of adjournment have been recorded in writing by the Forum. Further, the District Forum shall make such orders as to the costs occasioned by the adjournment as may be provided in the regulations under the Act.

If after conducting the proceedings, the District Forum is satisfied that the goods complained against suffer from any of the defects specified in the complaint or that any of the allegations contained in the complaint about the services are proved, it shall issue an order to the opposite party directing him to do one or more of the following things: (i) to remove the defects, (ii) to replace the goods with new goods of similar description, (iii) to return to the complainant the price or the charges paid by the complainant, (iv) to pay such amount as may be awarded as compensation to the consumer, (v) to remove the defects or deficiencies in the services in question, (vi) to discontinue the unfair trade practice or restrictive trade practice, (vii) not to offer the hazardous goods for sale, (viii) to withdraw the hazardous goods from being offered for sale, (ix) to cease manufacture of hazardous goods, (x) to pay such sum as may be determined by it, if it is of the opinion that loss or injury has been suffered by a large number of consumers who are not identifiable conveniently. Provided that the minimum amount of sum so payable shall not is less than five per cent of the value of such defective goods sold or services provided to such consumers. The Forum can also direct to issue corrective advertisement to neutralise the effect of misleading advertisements at the cost of the opposite party responsible for issuing such misleading advertisements. It can also impose adequate costs to the parties.

The Act provides that every proceeding of the District Forum shall be carried out by the President and at least one Member sitting together. Every order made by the District Forum shall be signed by its President and a Member or Members who conducted the proceedings. It is further provided that where the proceeding is conducted by the President and one Member and they differ on any point or points, they shall state the point or points on which they differ and refer the same to the other Member for hearing on such point or points and the opinion of the majority shall be the order of the District Forum. The State Commission shall have administrative control over all the District Forums within its jurisdiction.

Section 25 of the Act provides that, where an interim order made under this Act is not complied with the District Forum may order the property of the person, not complying with such order to be attached. In case any amount is due from any person under an order made by the District Forum the person entitled to the amount may make an application to the District Forum and the District Forum may issue a certificate for the said amount to the Collector of the district and the Collector shall proceed to recover the amount in the same manner as arrears of land revenue. As per Section 27 of the Act, in case a trader or a person against whom a complaint is made or the complainant fails or omits to comply with any order made by the District Forum, such a trader or person shall be punishable with imprisonment for a term which shall not be less than one month but may extend to three years, or with fine which shall not be less than two thousand rupees but which may extend to ten thousand rupees or with both. Thus, in the legislative scheme of consumer protection, the District Forum is the most important redressal mechanism as the faith and confidence of the consumers in these adjudicatory bodies will depend to a large extent on the functioning of these forums. They are the first contact point for the consumers, where they seek redress to their grievances. The consumer forum provides the way to the consumers to get speedy and inexpensive justice against the producers and the service providers.

However, the working of the District Forums has come into sharp criticism by various stakeholders. The delay in disposal of the cases, being the most important criticism. There have also been allegations that the lawyers have taken over the consumer courts and as the consumer is unaware of the legal procedures and processes he hesitates to file a complaint in the consumer court. During various interactions the point is stressed that the consumer courts are people's court and the interest of the consumers is supreme.

The Research Study

The Consumer Protection Act was enacted by the Parliament in 1986 for better protection of the consumers. The state of Jharkhand came into existence in 2000 and the State Consumer Disputes Redressal Commission came into existence in December 2001. Up to March 2002 for periods ranging between sixteen months and thirty-six months the posts of the Presidents and the Members remained vacant. During the period no Consumer Protection Councils were established at the state level and the district level. However, in Jharkhand since inception up to 31.1.2009, 29544 cases were filed in the District Forums out of which 27283 cases have been disposed of and 2261 cases are pending. The disposal of cases stands to 92.35 per cent.

The Presidents and Members of the District Forum play a major role in enhancing the faith of the consumers in the redressal mechanism. There have been various studies highlighting the reasons for non-disposal of cases, the lack of manpower and infrastructural facilities. However, there is no study which focuses on the perception of the Presidents and the Members of the District Forums towards the Consumer Protection Act and the working of the Forums. This study essentially fills that gap.

It looks at various aspects with which the Presidents and Members of the Forum have to deal with. The study is an attempt to examine the implementation of the Consumer Protection Act in the state of Jharkhand and also to assess the effectiveness of the District Forums in disposal of the cases and the problems faced by them.

The Broad Objectives of the Study are

1. To evaluate the implementation of the Consumer Protection Act in the state of Jharkhand.
2. To critically examine the perception of the Presidents and Members of the District Forums towards the Consumer Protection Act.
3. To identify the nature of problems being faced by the Presidents and Members of the District Forums in discharging their functions.
4. To recommend suggestions for improving the working of the District Forums.

Methodology and Data Collection

Jharkhand is divided into twenty-two districts and each district has a District Forum for redressal of consumer's grievances. Out of these only twenty-one District Forums are functioning as per data available up to March 2009. In these twenty-one Forums there are six vacancies, two of Presidents and four of Members of the District Forums. In the State there are a total of fifty-seven Presidents and Members of the District Forums. The Data was collected through a structured questionnaire, which was administered to a sample size of 35 persons which included seven Presidents and twenty-eight Members. Apart from the questionnaire discussions were also held with them regarding the working of the District Forums and the problems faced by them. Discussions were also held with the President of the SCDRC to ascertain his views on the working of the District Forums. Various reports and other published materials were also scanned. The data so collected was tabulated and is presented in a report form. Table 4.1 indicates the number of Presidents and the Members of the sample size and the coverage of the District Forums.

Table 4.1: Sample Size, Position and Coverage of the Respondents

District	*President*	*Members*	*Total*
Ranchi	0	2	2
Lohardagga	0	1	1
Gumla	1	1	2
Simdega	1	1	2
Palamu	0	1	1
Latehar	0	1	1
Garhwa	0	1	1
West Singhbhum	0	1	1
Saraikela	0	1	1
East Singhbhum	1	1	2
Dumka	1	1	2
Jamtara	0	2	2
Sahebganj	0	2	2
Godda	0	2	2
Hazaribagh	0	1	1
Chatra	1	2	3
Koderma	1	0	1
Giridih	1	2	3
Dhanbad	0	2	2
Bokaro	0	1	1
Deoghar	0	2	2
Total	**7**	**28**	**35**

Perception of the Presidents and Members of the District Forums

1. *Profile of the Respondents* — The sample size consists of 35 respondents, which includes 7 Presidents and 28 Members. Out of the total respondents 34 per cent of the respondents are women and 66 per cent are males. As far as the age of the respondents is concerned 49 per cent are above 60 years of age because of the appointment of retired District Judges as Presidents of the Forums. 20 per cent of the respondents are less than 40 years of age. 20 per cent are between the age group of 40-50 years and 11 per cent belong to the age category of 50-60 years.
2. *Educational Qualification of the Respondents* — 57.14 per cent of them are law graduates, 22.86 are graduates, 5.71 per cent have done LL.M., 5.71 have B.Sc. degree, 5.71 possess M.A. and 2.86 M.Com. degrees respectively. An overall look at the educational qualification reveals that most of the respondents are well qualified.

3. *Previous Occupation of the Respondents* — 25 per cent of the respondents are from the judicial services, 20 per cent are from government service, 11 per cent are lawyers, 17 per cent belong to the private sector, 9 per cent are social workers and 6 per cent are housewives. The District Forums have a mix of people from various professional backgrounds. This has brought in people with varied experience and backgrounds thereby enlarging the scope of the consumer movement.
4. *Understanding of Law* — Of the total respondents 62.86 per cent are law graduates and 37.14 do not possess law degree but have degrees from other disciplines. Only 5.71 per cent of the respondents who do not possess law degree agreed that they experienced problems in discharging their functions. 51.43 per cent said that they do not experience any difficulty in discharging their duties due to lack of a law degree. What is more interesting is that 42.86 per cent of the respondents did not answer this question. 95.45 per cent of the respondents with a law degree do not have any difficulty in passing a legal order, while on the other hand 30.77 per cent of those not having a law degree have difficulties in passing a legal order.
5. *Knowledge of Consumer Protection Legislations and other Procedures* — Only 11.40 per cent of the respondents felt that to discharge their functions effectively it was not essential to know all the consumer protection legislations and the procedures. But they agreed that one should have a thorough understanding of the Consumer Protection Act. Majority of them (88.60%) accepted that to effectively discharge their functions it is imperative that one should have a thorough knowledge and understanding of the provisions of various laws and the procedures to be followed. 14 per cent agreed that not knowing other consumer protection laws created difficulty in passing an order, while 86 per cent said that it did not create any such difficulty.
6. *Functioning of the District Forum* — 91.43 per cent of the respondents agreed that the functioning of the District Forums was good and only 8.57 per cent said it was satisfactory. 94.29 per cent agreed that the sittings of the District Forums were held regularly and the Members

were punctual. As regards the working relationship between the Members of the District Forums, 77.14 said that the relationship was very cordial and they functioned like a team. However, 22.85 felt that the relationship was cordial but there were problems especially between the President and the Members.

7. *Major Hindrance faced by the District Forums* — 72 per cent of them said that they lacked the required manpower and as such they were not able to function effectively. 58 per cent felt that the problem was due to lack of laboratory testing facilities. It took a long period to get the report after the tests are done. Lack of funds was another major problem faced by 48 per cent of the respondents. 45 per cent felt that in spite of Central Government providing the fund, infrastructure remains a problem. Nearly 40 per cent of the respondents felt that after filing the complaint the parties do not take the required interest which creates a lot of problem. 22 per cent said that when a member retires his position is not filled up in time and due to the vacancy delay in disposal of complaints takes place.
8. *Need to Amend the Consumer Protection Act* — 37.14 per cent of the respondents agreed that there was a need to amend the Act to provide more teeth to the Consumer Redressal Agencies.
9. *Fee Structure for Filing a Complaint* — 65.71 per cent of the respondents are of the view that the prescribed fee is reasonable and any hike in fee will deter the consumer from coming to the consumer forums to file a complaint. 34.29 per cent of them felt that it is unreasonable. Most of them felt that no fee should be prescribed for value of goods or services and the compensation claimed up to one lakh rupees.
10. *Level of Awareness among Consumers about Consumer Rights* — According to the respondents only 20 per cent of the consumers are aware about their rights and 28.57 per cent are aware to some extent. 51.42 per cent of the consumers are not at all aware about their rights and the Consumer Protection Act. 68.6 per cent of the respondents felt that the consumers do not approach the District

Forums as they are ignorant about their rights and the existence of any redressal mechanism. 54.72 per cent don't have much idea about the Consumer Protection Act. 22.9 per cent are afraid of the technicalities involved in approaching a consumer court, 17.1 per cent don't want to assert their rights, 17.1 per cent don't have much faith in the long procedures and only 8.6 per cent believe in mutual settlement than filing a complaint in the consumer forums.

11. *Involvement of NGOs in filing of Complaints* — 68.57 per cent of the respondents are of the view that the NGOs must be involved in filing a complaint while 22.86 per cent did not favour the involvement of the NGOs in filing a complaint.
12. *Representation by Advocates in the District Forums* — Nearly 66 per cent of the respondents agree that the advocates should represent the parties in the District Forums, while 31.43 felt that the advocates should be kept away from the consumer courts. The Members felt that there are a number of legal issues that the consumers are unable to understand and hence the cases are taking longer time to settle.
13. *Difficulty in Execution of the Orders of the District Forum* — 37.12 per cent agreed that there is a problem of non-execution of the orders of the Consumer Forums.
14. *Efforts to Settle Cases through Mediation or Mutual Consent* — Majority of the respondents 91.42 per cent are of the view that large number of complaints being filed in the District Forums could be solved through mediation or mutual understanding if there is a structured system available to the consumers before coming to the District Forums.
15. *Capacity Building Programmes* — 71 per cent of the respondents have attended a training programme and 29 per cent have not attended any training programme. However, among those who have attended a training programme 74.29 per cent found the programme to be very useful and 22.86 benefited to some extent.
16. *Computer Literacy* — Nearly 74 per cent of the respondents are not computer literate. Only 2.65 per cent of the respondents are computer literate and 24 per cent are computer literate to some extent.

17. *Consumer Awareness Programmes* – Nearly 70 per cent of the respondents agreed that the responsibility for organising consumer awareness programmes should be with the District Forums for which the Central/State Government should give adequate funds. 18 per cent preferred the District Administration and 15.60 per cent felt that it should be the responsibility of the State Government.

Findings and Suggestions

- The District Forums are functioning well, the sittings of the Forums are held regularly and the members are punctual. The delay in the disposal of the cases is because of other reasons and not due to the absence of the members. Most of them agreed that the work environment was very cordial and they functioned as a team.
- The District Forums have been facing a number of problems, like lack of manpower, funds, infrastructure, laboratory testing of products, non-cooperation by the parties, etc. The computers have been acquired and installed but due to lack of manpower it is not of much help. The record rooms are not up to the mark and there is not much space to store the records. Computerisation of the records is the need of the hour. The members do not have any financial power which is creating a lot of delay. Even adequate stationary is not available in some of the District Forums. Moreover, the working condition of the employees also needs to be improved.
- Most of them are satisfied with the major provisions of the Consumer Protection Act. However, some feel that there is a need to amend the Act to give more teeth to the consumer courts. As far as the fee structure is concerned the majority of the respondents felt that it is reasonable.
- Major impediment in the implementation of the Act is lack of awareness among the consumers. Due to this the consumers do not approach the consumer courts for redressal of their grievances. Efforts must be made to educate the consumers about their rights and also create awareness about the benefits of the Consumer Protection Act. The District Forums can play a major role at the

District level in organising suitable awareness programmes for the consumers. At present, the funds for awareness programmes are at the disposal of the District Administration and not the District Forum. Due to the lack of awareness about their rights and also the procedures under the Act, the consumers hesitate to approach the consumer forums in case of a complaint.

- Majority of the respondents felt that the NGOs should play a proactive role and help the consumers in filing of the complaints. Involvement of NGOs in filing of the complaints will streamline the process and help in quick disposal of complaints. The consumers are not aware of the procedures of filing a complaint and the documents they are required to submit, the NGOs could themselves file the complaint on behalf of the consumers. This will avoid delay in disposal of cases.
- The procedures to be followed by the consumer courts are very simple but with the involvement of the advocates the process has become very technical and legal. Even though the Act does not envisage the involvement of an advocate yet based on their experience majority of the respondents are of the view that the advocates should represent the cases. As the manufacturers and service providers are hiring the services of advocates the consumer is at a loss as he lacks the required knowledge of the legal procedures. Moreover there are a number of technical issues involved, which only the advocates know.
- Execution of the orders of the District Forums is a major problem. The District Administration and particularly the police do not cooperate. No policeman is attached to the District Forums for execution of the orders of the forum. As a result, large number of execution cases is pending mainly due to non-execution of warrant of arrest or attachment order by the police authorities. This is sending a wrong signal among the consumers. The Act needs to be amended and appropriate measures are required to be taken to ensure that execution of the orders of the forum is done in a time bound manner, otherwise the consumer will loose faith in the consumer courts.

- The members are in favour of ADR before the complaint is filed in the District Forum. There should be some mechanism, at the level of the producer/service provider so that the grievances of the consumers can be addressed by mutual settlement failing which the consumer can file a complaint in the District Forum. Majority of them agreed that they do give an opportunity to the parties to settle their dispute through mediation or mutual consent. The Government of West Bengal has appointed District Consumer Welfare Officer who plays the role of a mediator. This system can also be introduced in other states provided a separate Department of Consumer Affairs is created as in the case of West Bengal.
- As the scope of the consumer courts and the nature of complaints being filed are increasing, it is important that efforts are made to build the capacity of the members. Training has to be more systematic. Users' manuals in the local languages should be prepared for the use of the members of the District Forums. It would be better if induction training programmes are organised for the members of the District Forums. The recommendation of the Shenoy Committee set up by the NCDRC should be accepted by the State Governments and funds be made available to organise such induction training programmes.
- Though the scheme of computerisation and computer networking of consumer forums was launched, but the working of the District Forums has not improved to a large extent. The District Forums are not able to take the full benefit of computerisation and computer networking. Adequate staff needs to be sanctioned for manning the computers. The members and other staff of the Forums should be imparted training in computer literacy and the operation of the software.

5

Emerging Issues in Consumer Protection: An Interface between Consumer Protection Act and the Competition Act

Madhav Sharma

Introduction

Interface between the Consumer Laws and the Competition Laws can be explained as the common goal which both consumer protection laws and the competition laws share, that is, the protection of the consumer.[1] Consumer Protection Law in India in the form of the Consumer Protection Act, 1986 is termed as the saviour of the consumers in India. On the other hand, Competition Act, 2002 is an extension to the Consumer Protection which serves the policy of consumer protection by regulating the *economic entities* of the market and by creating a smooth and fair competition in the Indian market that can prohibit the economic entities to indulge into such activities that can harm the very base of the *Law* itself, that is, *salus populi suprema lex*, meaning, welfare of the people is the supreme aim of law. Competition Act, 2002 came to hold the hands of Consumer Protection Act, 1986 saying it will serve the very aim of the latter where the latter hasn't expanded its protective arms to save the consumer population.

An effective competition policy lowers entry and exit barriers and makes the environment conducive to promoting entrepreneurship, which also provides space for the growth of small and medium enterprises and consequent employment expansion. Competition law concentrates in maintaining the process of competition between enterprises and tries to remedy behavioural or structural problems in order to re-establish effective competition in the market. The consequence of this is higher economic efficiency, greater innovation and enhancement of consumer welfare. On the other hand, the consumer protection policy and law are primarily concerned with the nature of consumer transactions, trying to improve market conditions for effective exercises of consumer choice. Thus, the two disciplines focus on different market failures and offer different remedies, but are both aimed at maintaining well functioning, competitive markets that promote consumer welfare. The two disciplines are mutually re-enforcing. Although most of the principles of unfair competition law are based on the interests of competing business concerns, it appears that as a result of the consumer movement which started in the early 1960s, the ever-increasing call for more extensive consumer protection has led to closer and more effective blending of unfair competition law with consumer protection. Paying respect to the role of consumer interests is a worldwide tendency in the development of unfair competition laws.[2] The development of the idea of consumer protection as an integral part of unfair competition law took quite different avenues in different countries.

In USA, the unfair competition rules and consumer protection rules developed concurrently, but independently. Although in theory unfair competition rules do incorporate some key aspects of consumer protection—Section 43(a) of the Lanham Act gives any person (including consumers) who believes he is likely to be damaged by the use of unfair trade conduct a form of action, albeit in practice, these provisions are not enforceable, and are largely ignored by the courts. In United Kingdom, although customer or consumer confusion is an indispensable factor to establish a passing-off action, passing-off does not protect consumers directly, because only competitors, or potential competitors, of the defendant can sue to obtain a remedy. Consumer protection was merely a device for applying the misrepresentation test for infringement and ensuring a competitor's rights. Consumers themselves cannot obtain complete protection because they are not able to participate directly in the rules that govern unfair competition.

The integration of consumer protection and unfair competition law presents a different story in Germany. Germany started (cautiously) to integrate consumer protection with unfair competition law quite early in its development. This is no more than a logical consequence of the idea that unfair competition law not only serves to protect the interests of competitors, but is also designed to protect the public interest at large. The introduction of statutory provisions give consumers their own legal standing in court to fight unfair trade practices directly and independently. Consumers everywhere, including the purchasers even in the most developed countries, have poor information of the necessary particulars of any product, including the current market price, the price range or the qualities of the suppliers, and comparable products or services.[3] Competition law is just one tool used by governments to try to achieve maximum sustainable growth in their economies. Anti-dumping, consumer protection, corporate governance, deregulation, industrial (i.e., promoting national industries), intellectual property ("IP") liberalization, privatization, and trade policies are generally pursued simultaneously and may at times conflict or concur with the aims of competition policy.[4] Consumer Protection is most crucial aim that Competition Law in any country has to fulfil. Thus, there lies an interface between the Consumer Protection and Consumer Welfare which has been recognized everywhere in the world.

The Preamble to the Competition Act, 2002 itself states that it has been enacted to save the interests of the consumers.[5] Thus, it can be asserted that Consumer Protection and the Competition Law, both are the *two wings of the same house*.[6] The purpose of this paper is to show the interface between the Consumer Protection Act and the Competition Act. Consumer Protection Act, 1986 defines the Restrictive Trade Practices[7] and Unfair Trade Practices.[8] Competition Act, 2002 provides a wider description and a broader view to such activities like Price Ridging, Cartel Formations, and Abuse of the Dominant Position etc. Earlier MRTP Act existed in India, but its failure in restricting such activities affecting the consumer welfare directly gave birth to Competition Act, 2002. Both competition law and consumer protection law deal with distortions in the marketplace, which is supposed to be driven by the interaction between supply and demand. Antitrust offenses, like price fixing or exclusionary practices, distort the supply side because they restrict supply and elevate prices. Consumer protection offenses, like deceptive advertising, distort the demand side because they create the impression that a product or service is worth more than it really is. In other words, both sets of offenses can be analyzed in economic terms, and appreciation of this nexus will help to resolve some apparent tensions.[9]

There is another interesting parallel between competition law and consumer protection law. In competition law, there is the traditional distinction between *"per se"* cases and *"rule of reason"* cases. In a *per se* case, the only issue is whether the conduct occurred; in a rule of reason case, it is necessary to prove adverse market effects, and conduct may be defended on the ground that adverse effects are outweighed by beneficial ones. Agreements that are illegal *per se* could also be condemned under a rule of reason, of course, but it is unnecessary to plead them that way when adverse effects can be conclusively presumed. Rule of reason.[10] In the Competition Act, 2002, most agreements are subject to the rule of reason, and it is up to the Competition Commission of India (hereinafter CCI) to establish that the agreement has an "appreciable adverse effect on competition" based on an effects analysis.[11]

Anti-Competitive Activities under Competition Act

The major aim of the Act is to prevent the anti-competitive activities, which may be broadly discussed as the Anti-Competitive Agreements and the Abuse of Dominant Position. These activities put adverse effect on the competition in the market hence, prohibited. The provisions regarding it are very much similar to the EC Competition Laws.[12]

Rationale behind Prohibiting Anti-Competitive Agreements

Competition among the suppliers of the goods and services will, in a market whose operation is unhindered, stabilize the prices at a reasonable level. The principle objective of suppliers of goods and services who are in a position to manipulate the market is to maintain their profits at pre-determined levels. They seek to achieve this through various means. Agreements for price-fixing, limiting the supply of goods or services, dividing the market, etc., are the usual modes of interfering with the process of competition and ultimately reducing or eliminating competition. Where competition is adversely affected to an appreciable extent, such agreements would be anti-competitive.[13]

Types of Anti-Competitive Agreements

Horizontal Agreements

Section 3 of the Competition Act, 2002, deals with such anti-competitive agreements. Section 3(1) puts a general prohibition on an agreement in the supply of goods or services that causes or is likely to cause an appreciable harm to the competition within India.[14] Agreements between two or more enterprises that are at the same stage of the production chain and in the same market constitute the horizontal variety.[15] The parties to such arrangements can be the parties including the enterprises, associations of enterprises,[16] persons or association of persons or any combination of these entities. Types of agreement may include agreements for the exchange of information. The agreement based on the exchange of information depends on the type of information that is being exchanged. The competition must be enhanced by the exchange of information not adversely affected by it. *The UK Agricultural Tractor Registration Exchange Case*[17] was one of the landmark cases where the agreement for the exchange of Information was considered to be the anti-competitive by the European Competition Commission. Point to be noted here is that the definition of the 'activity' stated in the explanation, the law relating to competition will apply to the professions such as medical, legal, accountancy and such other professions.[18] Some forms of Horizontal Agreements:

1. Agreements Regarding Prices.
2. Agreements Regarding Bids.
3. Agreements Regarding Market Sharing.
4. Agreements Regarding Quantities.

Cartels and Similar Groups

Section 3(3) deals with the enterprises which are engaged in the supply of the identical or similar goods or services or constitute a cartel and which engage in certain anti-competitive agreements, practices or take certain decisions set out therein.[19] A cartel includes an association of the producers, sellers, distributors, traders or the service providers who, by agreement amongst themselves limit, control, or attempt to control the production, distribution, sale or price of, or, trade in goods or provision of services. The word 'includes' is intended to provide that a cartel may be an association or any other form of organisation. A cartel is always with reference to a sector. There could be sugar cartels, tobacco cartels, cement cartels etc.[20] It is a horizontal agreement to fix the prices, allocate customers or territories, restrict bids or rig bids. A cartel is regarded as the most pernicious form of violation of competition law since it unequivocally damages the competition and causes loss to the economy and the consumers.[21] Various judgments from various jurisdictions form the interpretation of the law relating to cartels to be followed by Indian Competition Law.[22]

Bid Rigging

The next relevant concept to discuss is Bid-Rigging. Rigging a bid occurs when by collusion among the bidders, actual and potential, the members of that group keep the bid amount at a predetermined manipulated level. The substance of the explanation to the Section 3(3) is that 'bid-rigging' occurs when there is an agreement, between the enterprises or persons, engaged in the supply of the identical or similar products and services, which has the effect of eliminating or reducing competition for bids, or adversely affects or manipulates the process of bidding.

Vertical Restraints

Vertical Agreements are the agreements between enterprises at different stages of production, distribution, etc. It is another way in which competition in the supply of a product or a service may be reduced through practices that control or remove the freedom of one of the parties in concluding an agreement in the way in which it would be enough to meet its actual needs that the transaction is intended to procure. Inevitably, the imposing of this unwanted burden will be by the economically stronger of the parties. Where the parties are at the different stages of the production, then this practice is considered as the Vertical Restraint. Section 3(4) of the Competition Act contemplates that it would be anti-competitive only if the agreement providing for this practice causes or is likely to cause an appreciable adverse effect on the competition in India. Examples of such restraints are:

1. Tie-in Arrangement;
2. Exclusive Supply Agreement;
3. Exclusive Distribution Agreement;
4. Refusal to Deal;
5. Re-Sale Price Maintenance.

Abuse of Dominant Position

Dominant position has been appropriately defined in the Act in terms of the position of strength, enjoyed by an enterprise, in the relevant market, in India, which enables it to (i) operate independently of competitive forces prevailing in the relevant market; or (ii) affect its competitors or consumers or the relevant market, in its favour. Section 4 enjoins, No enterprise shall abuse its dominant position. Dominant position is the position of strength enjoyed by an enterprise in the relevant market which enables it to operate independently of competitive forces prevailing in the market or affects its competitors or consumers or the relevant market in its favour. Dominant position is abused when an enterprise imposes unfair or discriminatory conditions in purchase or sale of goods or services or in the price in purchase or sale of goods or services. Again, the philosophy of the Competition Act is reflected in this provision, where it is clarified that a situation of monopoly *per se* is not against public policy but, rather, the use of the monopoly status such that it operates to the detriment of potential and actual competitors. At this point it is worth mentioning that the Act does not prohibit or restrict enterprises from coming into dominance. There is no control whatsoever to prevent enterprises from coming into or acquiring position of dominance. All that the Act prohibits is the abuse of that dominant position. The Act, therefore, targets the abuse of dominance and not dominance *per se*. This is indeed a welcome step, a step towards a truly global and liberal economy. Examples are:

1. Predatory pricing;

2. Directly or indirectly imposes unfair or discriminatory conditions;
3. Limits or restricts production of goods or provision of services;
4. Denial of market access; etc.

Role of Consumer Protection Adjudicating Bodies

Competition Commission of India was established in 2003 with the Government Notification in order to regulate the fair competition in the Indian market. The Commission has taken birth out of the competition policies that have been enacted in the form of the Competition Act, 2002.[23] The jurisprudential rationale behind developing such law can be explained with the fact that government policies should seek to enable consumers to obtain optimum benefit from their economic resources.[24] This enunciates the Roscoe Pound's theory of 'Balancing of Interests' where the law must be a mean to balance the needs of the various groups of the society, here, it can be figured out that such groups can be the Consumers and the Market Regulators or say Producers, which may include manufacturers, firm owners, sellers and many others. Government policies should also seek to achieve the goals of satisfactory production and performance standards, adequate distribution methods, fair business practices, informative marketing and effective protection against practices which could adversely affect the economic interests of consumers and the exercise of choice in the market place.[25] The next assertion that is made in the concern of the Consumer Protection is that Governments should establish or maintain legal and/or administrative measures to enable consumers or, as appropriate, relevant organizations to obtain redress through formal or informal procedures that are expeditious, fair, inexpensive and accessible. Such procedures should take particular account of the needs of low-income consumers.[26] United Nations Conference on Trade and Development (hereinafter UNCTAD) has made numerous recommendations from time to time in order to ensure the prohibition of the anti-competitive activities and enhancing the consumer protection, through facilitating the work of UNCTAD and facilitating the International Cooperation.[27] Thus, the Competition Commission is a result of the international concern over enacting the Competition Laws to regulate the elements to affect the unfair competition in the markets.

Competition Commission of India

Nature, Duties and Jurisdiction: Comparative Analysis

The Preamble of the Competition Act, 2002 itself enshrines the establishment of the Competition Commission of India (Hereinafter Commission), which is deemed to be the sole guardian of the Competition regulation in India. Thus, Competition Act, 2002 provides for establishment of a Commission to prevent practices having adverse effect on competition etc. The duties of the commission can be enumerated as:[28]

1. To eliminate the practices having the adverse effect on the competition.
2. To promote and sustain competition.
3. To protect interests of the consumers.

To achieve the above-mentioned duties, the Commission has been provided with the jurisdiction to regulate certain activities which under the Act, are considered being anti-competitive or the elements retarding competition. The Commission can exercise the jurisdiction to:

1. Enquire into the Anti-Competitive Agreements (e.g. Cartel Formation, Bid-Rigging, etc.)[29]
2. Enquire into the abuse of the Dominant Position (e.g. Predatory Pricing, etc.)[30]
3. Regulating Combinations (e.g. Mergers and Acquisitions, etc.)[31]
4. Undertake Competition Advocacy (including advice on the policy issues, creating public awareness, imparting training on competition issues)[32].

The Competition Commission of India has been empowered for inquiring the anti-competitive activities that are taking place outside the territory of India but have the adverse effect on the competition of India, thereby, ultimately affecting the welfare and interests of the consumers.[33] Thus, this denotes the extra-territorial jurisdiction of Competition Commission. Also, the earlier MRTP Act did not possess any of such provision regarding the extra-territorial jurisdiction.[34] Thus, the Commission can control the offshore combinations and thus, can modify the mergers within various jurisdictions.[35] Here the highlighting point is that the "Redressal Forums" for Consumer Protection under the Consumer Protection Act, 1986 do not possess such extra-territorial jurisdiction when it comes to the question of the consumer protection. The activities that are subjected to the enquiry under the Competition Act, 2002 have not been touched by Consumer Protection Act, 1986. It is submitted in the light of the above analysis that the Redressal Forums under Consumer Protection Act, 1986 cannot save wider consumer interests which are out of the purview of the Consumer Protection Act, 1986 and Competition Commission of India as a regulator of consumer interest can very efficiently address these issues as it is empowered to do so under the Competition Act, 2002. Thus, the Competition Act fills up the voids left by Consumer Protection under certain fields.

Certain exclusions under the Act, include, reasonable rights under Intellectual Property Rights, etc. which are protected under the Act and agreements that are exclusively meant for exports only.[36]

Legal Status of the Commission

The Competition Commission of India has been empowered with the regulatory and the Quasi-Judicial Powers,[37] and it renders its functions through benches.[38] Each bench comprises at least two members, and one of which should be the Judicial Member.[39] Thus, it is in addition to the Adjudicating bodies that have been set up under the Consumer Protection Act, 1986. The difference lies when the subject-matter dealt by these bodies is put to analysis. The Consumer Dispute Redressal bodies are the adjudicating bodies to provide the relief to the consumers, covering all kinds of goods and services that are being covered by the Consumer Protection Act, 1986 which is the governing law of these adjudicating bodies. The Competition Commission of India on the other hand, only applies to the activities which restrict the fair competition in the market thus, distorting the forces of demand and supply and prejudicing the interests of the consumers.[40]

Thus, while analysing the interface between the working of the adjudicating bodies under the Consumer Protection Act, 1986 and the Competition Act, 2002, it is clear that they share a common goal to "save the consumers". Better Competition produces better products. However, in the production of the commodities, the Competition Act, 2002 prohibits certain activities which restrict competition and lead to monopolistic control. Thus no, option or choice is left with the consumer. So "Killing of the Consumer Choice" has taken place. But, if various varieties of a goods are present in the market and the consumer is deceived by the producer, then he can approach the adjudicating bodies under the Consumer Protection Act, 1986. An important difference lies in the fact that the Competition Law leaves unfair trade practices to consumer fora and not to the Competition Commission of India.[41] Thus, it can be submitted that Competition Act, 2002 kills the reason for production of bad product and Consumer Protection Act, 1986 compensates for the ill effects of the bad products.

Area of Operation: Competition Commission of India

Orders of Commission in case of anti-competitive agreement and abuse of dominant position can be enumerated as follows:

1. It can impose a penalty of not more than 10 per cent of turn-over;
2. In case of Cartel – 3 times of the amount of profit made out of cartel or 10 per cent of turn-over;
3. Pass a cease and desist order;[42]
4. Award compensation;[43]
5. Order modification of agreement;[44]
6. Order costs[45] in case of abuse by dominant enterprise, may recommend division of the enterprise to the Central Government;[46]
7. Pass such other order as deem fit.[47]

Orders of the Competition Commission in respect of combinations can be enumerated as:

1. Shall approve the combination if no appreciable adverse effect is found.[48]
2. Shall direct that combination not to take place if it appreciably affects competition.[49]
3. May propose suitable modification as accepted by parties.[50]
4. If not accepted, parties to submit modifications with 30 days.[51]
5. If modifications accepted, combination will be allowed.

Certain penalties are also available for the non-compliance of the orders of the Commission. These are not provided in the Consumer Protection Act, 1986, like for example, the power of *suo motu* enquiry. Commission has *suo motu* power to enquire whether an anti-competitive agreement or abuse of dominant position causes or is likely to cause an appreciable adverse effect on competition.[52] Commission has also the *suo motu* power to enquire whether a combination causes or is likely to cause an appreciable adverse effect on competition,[53] provided this power must be exercised within one year from the date of combination has taken place.[54] This power is absent in the Consumer Protection Act, thus, Competition Act, further proves to be a modified compilation of provisions which are aimed to secure the sacred principles of the Consumer Protection Jurisprudence.

Competition Advocacy

Competition Act, 2002 in the form of the provision for the Consumer Advocacy has secured the basic fibre of the consumer protection jurisprudence which has emanated from these consumer welfare legislations for the protection of the Consumers. This is the responsibility of the Commission to take measures for promotion of competition advocacy, creating awareness and imparting training about competition issues.[55] Advocacy means competition promotion through non-enforcement measures for promotion of competition advocacy and creation of awareness about competition issues, the Commission may undertake the following work:

1. Encourage and interact with the organizations of

stakeholders, academic community etc. to undertake activities, programmes, studies, research work, etc. on competition issues;

2. Encourage the academic/professional institutions to include competition policy and law in the curriculum; undertake appropriate capacity building programmes and arrange training for its officers/staff and stakeholders etc.

Thus, it is clear that Competition Act, 2002 is an advanced legislation when compared to Consumer Welfare Act, 1986, which does not incorporate any provision to ensure Consumer Protection Advocacy.

Anti-Competitive Mergers Affect Consumer Interest

Mergers and Joint Ventures can generate efficiencies and most mergers are either pro-competitive or competitively neutral. But, mergers that are anti-competitive, however, can lead to rise in consumer prices of magnitude at unpredictable intervals.[56] Such questionable mergers might also significantly diminish product quality and output as also consumer choice and innovation. To distinguish between mergers that threaten free markets and those likely to promote them, sophisticated economic analysis and thorough factual investigations are necessary. Constraints put by the Competition Law on mergers and acquisitions are among the least known to the practitioners. Laws in this area are complex; the issues are subtle; and the policies and their enforcement will continue to evolve. But the issues and requirements here deserve more than passing acquaintance, since violations pose a "showstopper" barrier to mergers and acquisitions.[57] The consumer welfare standards concerned with the anti-trust law or competition law are different in different countries and different regions. The term consumer welfare is often misinterpreted in anti-trust analysis. It is sometimes used to refer to economic efficiency or certain consumer interest without defining its real content.[58] The consumer welfare model argues that the ultimate goal of the Competition Law should be to prevent increases in consumer prices due to the exercise of the market power by dominant firms.[59] With a view to prevent combinations, which would cause an appreciable adverse effect on competition in India, the government has made suitable provisions in the Competition Act regulating mergers and acquisitions, excluding the case of the Public Institutions.

For the purposes of evaluating the effect or possible effect of a transaction between enterprises on competition, the ability of an enterprise to compete, it is necessary to ascertain the degree of autonomy it has. The Act uses a composite expression – combination to cover these modes, viz. merger, acquisition of shares, assets, acquiring control of an enterprise. The term 'amalgamation' and 'merger' are interchangeable hence the word 'merger' will be used. Section 5 of the Competition Act wets out when a 'combination' is to be taken as to have resulted. The term 'combination' is wider and will include transactions in addition to a merger. The basic principle of this section is that a combination would result, subject to the other prescriptions of the section, such as the monetary thresholds of assets or turnover of the enterprises specified therein, on: (a) acquisition of control, shares, voting rights or assets of one or more enterprises one or more persons; (b) acquiring of control by a person over an enterprise when such person has already direct or indirect control over another enterprise engaged in production, distribution or trading of a similar or identical or substitutable goods, or provision of a similar or identical or substitutable service; (c) any merger or amalgamation.

Section 6 deals with the procedure for regulation of combinations. For Section 6 to apply, the combination, within the meaning of Section 5, should be one that causes or is likely to cause an appreciable adverse effect on competition within the relevant market in India. Such a combination would be void. Section 20(4) sets out the factors that the Commission shall have due regard to, in determining whether a combination would have such an adverse effect on competition. Section 31 specifies what orders may be passed by the Commission on certain combinations.

The operative part of Section 6 of the Indian Competition Act, provides for the regulation of combination. According to sub-section (1), a combination that causes or is likely to cause an appreciable adverse effect on competition within the relevant market in India is void. According to the relevant provisions of the Act, only those mergers and acquisitions are liable to be regulated that qualify under the definition of combinations under

Section 5. Size is currently the only criteria for stipulating the post-merger review of mergers and acquisitions. Other arguably more valid criteria such as the market size of a particular industry or the market share of an industry player are not included. There exist no provisions for the regulation of those mergers and acquisitions that do not fall within the meaning of combination and yet have the potential to affect competition adversely. There may arise a situation where any merger may not come under the definition of combination, yet may give rise to serious competition concern in a market. Therefore, most enterprises with a lower asset value and turnover would be excluded from this stipulation. Let us suppose a situation where there are only two competitors for a product and they decide to merge. However, their asset values as well as turnover are such that their merger would fall outside the definition of combination as given in the Act. Hence, despite causing clear appreciable adverse effect on competition, the merger would go unregulated.

The threshold values indicated serve only as a trigger for the investigative process and do not render the merger bad by themselves. The CCI would carry out a more detailed investigation before any action is taken against the particular merger. However, in view of the dynamics of the Indian economy and the unstable currency rates the threshold values serve little purpose. It is, therefore, suggested that a suitable compromise would lie in listing several criteria like asset valuation and net turnover, market share, etc., the satisfaction of even one of which could trigger an investigation. The very purpose of Sections 5 and 6 of the Act is to restrict combinations which cause or are likely to cause an appreciable adverse effect on competition. It is, indeed hard to understand how the above can be achieved without considering market share of the merging and the merged entities.

Section 5 of the Competition Act contains provisions regarding acquisitions, acquiring of control, mergers and amalgamations. However, the Act does not delve into the repercussions of arrangements on competition. Section 390(b) of the Companies Act, 1956 defines the term arrangement as "including a re-organization of the share capital of the company by the consolidation of shares of different classes, or by the division of shares into shares of different classes or, by both those methods." This term is of wide import and includes all modes of reorganization of the share capital, takeover of shares of one company by another, including interference with preferential and other special rights attached to shares. Arrangements can have dire consequences on competition and must, therefore, be specifically included in the provisions regarding combinations under the Act.

Section 6(2) of the Act gives enterprises and persons the option to notify the CCI of the proposed combination, but it is subject to Section 6(1) which renders the proposed combination, if it has an adverse effect on competition, *void ab initio*. Thus, a combination falling afoul of the provisions of Section 5 is void in the first instance. Pursuant to Section 29(3) of the Act, the CCI may invite any person or member of the public affected or likely to be affected by the combination, to file a written objection. This section gives the CCI excessive discretion to decide on which persons are eligible to be invited to file their objection against the combination. This section must, therefore, be amended to allow anyone affected by the combination to file a written objection against the combination.

Conclusion

We can conclude that the roots of the Competition Law and the Consumer Protection Law lie in the same place. They form the two wings of the same house. The interface of these two can only be determined on economic terms but the aim should be analyzed in terms of public interest. It is evident from the discussion that the Competition Act, 2002 has been an extension to the Consumer Protection Law in India. It is a branch of Consumer Jurisprudence where the rationale of market regulation affecting the consumer interests is examined in the light of the provisions giving effect to fair competition and leading to establish a market devoid of monopolistic ventures which kill the consumer choice and affect the poor consumer specially in the developing country like India. Thus, Competition Act, as the sister Act of Consumer Protection saves the consumer by prohibiting the anti-competitive activities and thus, articulating the just and noble cause of consumer welfare.

NOTES

1. Thomas Hoehn *et al.*, 'India's New Competition Law: No Longer an Elephant in the Corner', *International Company and Commercial Law*

Review, I.C.C.L.R. 2009, 20(3), 83-87, at p. 83. The need for the introduction and implementation of new competition and merger control legislation in India is due to the increased liberalisation and deregulation of Indian industry and the transition towards a market economy. An effective competition policy is generally recognised to be a necessary element of a market economy. Over 100 countries have introduced competition legislation and more are in the process of implementing new laws. The objective is to promote rivalry among firms and achieve sustained growth in productivity and consumer welfare.

2. James Kirkbride, 'The Law of Unfair Competition: Is there an E.C. Approach?', *Company Lawyer, Comp. Law.* 2000, 21(8), 230-233, at 231.
3. T. Rammapa, *Competition Law in India: Policy Issues in India and Developments* (Oxford Press, ed.) p. 2, New Delhi, 2006.
4. Dr. Pijan Wu, Caroline Thomas, Taiwan's Fair Trade Act: Achieving the right Balance, *Northwestern Journal of International Law and Business,* 26 Nw. J. Int'l L. & Bus. 643, at 643.
5. Preamble to the Competition Act, 2002: *An Act to provide, keeping in view of the economic development of the country, for the establishment of a Commission to prevent practices having adverse effect on competition, to promote and sustain competition in markets, to protect the interests of consumers and to ensure freedom of trade carried on by other participants in markets, in India, and for matters connected therewith or incidental thereto.*
6. Thomas B. Leary, 'Competition Law and the Consumer Protection Law: Two wings of the same house', *Antitrust Law Journal,* available at http://www.ftc.gov/speeches/leary/041022learyarticle.pdf, visited on 5th September, 2009, at 1147.
7. Section 2(nn) of Consumer Protection Act, 1986.
8. Section 2(r) of Consumer Protection Act, 1986.
9. *Supra* note 5 at p. 1148.
10. *Supra* note 5 at p. 1149.
11. Aditi Gopalakrishnan, 'Competition Act and MRTP: One 'Two' Many', *Business Line,* Thursday, August 20, 2009, available at, http://www.thehindubusinessline.com/2009/08/20/stories/2009082050390800.htm visited on 22nd August, 2009.
12. Article 81 of the EC Treaty which is the *Magna Carta* of the Competiton Law in European Union deals with the Anti-Competitive Agreements and thus, is adopted by the Indian Competition Law also. *See* Tarun Jain, *Regulatory Structure under EC Competition Laws: Lessons For India,* available at <http://www.ssrn.com> accessed on 20th August, 2009.
13. *Supra note* 3 at p.50.
14. *Ibid.*, Agreements here referred include all types of agreements. These will be rendered the nature of anti-competitive agreements when

they will breach the provisions of Section 3 of the Competition Act, 2002.

15. Pradeep S. Mehta, *Functional Competition Policy in India* (CUTS International, ed.) p. 56, New Delhi, 2006.
16. Section 2(h) of Competition Act, 2002; Enterprise under the Competition Act can either be a 'person' or a department of the government (as qualified in the sub-section) carrying on the economic activity in the supply of goods and services. Supply of goods would cover production, storage, and distribution or the control of goods and in case of services; it would refer to the provision of the services. Supply at any stage towards selling in the market would be covered.
17. *Official Journal* L 068, 13/03/1992 pp. 0019-0033.
18. *Supra note* 3 at p. 65.
19. *Id* at p. 86.
20. *Id* at p. 52.
21. Vinod Dhall, *Competition Law Today* (Oxford Press, ed.) p. 4, New Delhi, 2007.
22. *United States* v. *Trenton Potteries Co. et al.* 273 US 392 (1927); *The Lombard Club Case* (EC Press Release), *Plasterboard Cartel Case* EC Press Release DN: IP/02/1585; *Arizona* v. *Maricopa County Medical Society* 457 US 332 (1982); *United States* v. *Socony-Vacuum Oil Co.* 310 US 150 (1940); *Sarabhai Chemicals (P.) Ltd. and another, in re* (1979) 49 Company Cases 145 MRTP Commission.
23. CCI is similar to the regulatory body in the European Union, the EC Commission, which acts as the watchdog of the fair competition in that region. *See Supra note*.
24. Roderick Miller, *Doing Business with India*, GMB Publishing Ltd., ed., p. 130, London, 2003.
25. United Nations Guidelines for Consumer Protection (as expanded in 1999), United Nations Conference on Trade and Development (UNCTAD), available at a <http://www.unctad.org/en/docs/poditcclpm21.en.pdf>, accessed on 21st August, 2009.
26. *Id* at p. 9.
27. Recommendations on the Regional Seminar on Consumer Protection, Competition Policy and Competitiveness, UNCTAD, TD/B/COM.1/EM.17/2/Add.1, 5th September, 2001, available at http://www.unctad.org/en/docs/c1em17d2a1.en.pdf, accessed on 21st August, 2009; UNCTAD has been working for a long period in order to enforce the competition policy in the international arena. The Cooperation of the European Economic Community and USA has been widely discussed by UNCTAD, the role of various bilateral treaties and various other international legal instruments like Free Trade Agreements, Mutual Assistance Agreements between various nations has been a remarkable achievement of UNCTAD in order to

enforce international cooperation for the implementation of competition policies to regulate the anti-competitive activities and to promote the consumer welfare, Experiences Gained so far on International Cooperation on Competition Policy issues and the Mechanisms Used, UNCTAD, TD/B/COM.2/CLP/21/Rev.1, 19th April, 2002, available at <http://www.unctad.org/en/docs/c2clp21r1_en. pdf> accessed on 22nd August, 2009.

28. Section 18 of the Competition Act, 2002.
29. Section 3 of the Competition Act, 2002.
30. Section 4 of the Competition Act, 2002.
31. Sections 5 & 6 the of Competition Act, 2002.
32. Section 49 of the Competition Act, 2002.
33. Section 32 of the Competition Act, 2002.
34. Thus, the jurisdiction of the Competition Commission of India has embraces the "*Effects Doctrine*". Under the principles of the competition law and policy, the Effects Doctrine, allows the domestic competition laws to be applicable to foreign firms, but also to the domestic firms located outside the State's territory, when their behaviour or transactions produce an "effect" within the domestic territory. The nationality of the firms is irrelevant for the enforcement of the competition law and effects doctrine covers all categories of firms irrespective of their nationality. This is reflected in the Section 32 of the Competition Act, 2002; Singhda Pandey, *Extra Territoriality and Merger Control: Study from major Jurisdictions and Provisions in Indian Competition Act, 2002*, available at <http://www.cci.gov.in/images/media/Research Reports/concept_20081202123940.pdf>, accessed on 20th August, 2009.
35. Aaditya Mattoo & Robert M. Stern (ed.), *India and WTO*, Oxford University Press, Washington, 2003, p. 222.
36. Section 3(5) of the Competition Act, 2002.
37. Christian Campbell (ed.), *Legal Aspects of doing Business in India and the Pacific*, Yorkhill Publishing Co., Salzburg, 2007, p. 128.
38. Section 22(1) of the Competition Act, 2002; Paul Cook *et al*. (ed.), *Leading Issues in Competition, Regulation and Development*, Edward Edgar Publishing Company, Cheltenham, UK, 2004, p. 409.
39. Section 22(3) of the Competition Act, 2002.
40. S.S. Singh and Sapna Chadah, *Consumer Protection in India—Some Reflections*, available at <http://consumereducation.in/cons_book1_final.pdf> accessed on 21st August, 2009.
41. Vraj Lal Sappovadia & Kandarp Patel, *Competitiveness of Indian Business vis-à-vis Legal Provisions and Judicial Interpretation*, available at <http://www.ssrn.com>, accessed on 23rd August, 2009.
42. Section 27 (a) & (b) of the Competition Act, 2002.
43. Section 27(c) read with Section 34 of the Competition Act, 2002.
44. Section 27(d) of the Competition Act, 2002.

45. Section 27(e) of the Competition Act, 2002.
46. Section 27(f) of the Competition Act, 2002.
47. Section 27(g) of the Competition Act, 2002.
48. Section 31(1) of the Competition Act, 2002.
49. Section 31(2) of the Competition Act, 2002.
50. Section 31(4) of the Competition Act, 2002.
51. Section 31(6) of the Competition Act, 2002.
52. Section 19(1) of the Competition Act, 2002.
53. Section 20(1) of the Competition Act, 2002.
54. Proviso to Section 20(1) of the Competition Act, 2002.
55. Section 49(3) of the Competition Act, 2002; T.N. Ninan (ed.), *Business Standard, 2008*, Business Standard Books, New Delhi, 2008, p. 90; Pradeep S. Mehta (ed.), *A Functional Competition Policy in India*, CUTS International, New Delhi, 2006, p. 61.
56. Aditya Bhattacharjea, *India's Competition Policy: An Assessment*, available at <http://www.ssrn.com> accessed on 23rd August, 2009.
57. Robert F. Bruner (ed.), *Applied Mergers & Acquisitions*, John Wiley & Sons., p. 742, New Jersey, 2004.
58. Katalin Judit Creses (ed.), *Competition Law and Consumer Protection*, Kluwer Law International, The Hague, p. 20, The Netherlands, 2005.
59. *Ibid*.

REFERENCES

Bhattacharjea, Aditya, *India's Competition Policy: An Assessment*, available at http://www.ssrn.com.

Bruner, Robert F., *Applied Mergers and Acquisitions*, John Wiley & Sons., New Jersey, 2004.

Campbell, Christian (ed.), *Legal Aspects of doing Business in India and the Pacific*, Yorkhill Publishing Co., Salzburg, 2007.

Cook, Paul *et al.*, *Leading Issues in Competition, Regulation and Development*, Edward Edgar Publishing Company, Cheltenham, UK, 2004.

Creses, Katalin Judit, *Competition Law and Consumer Protection*, Kluwer Law International, The Hague, The Netherlands, 2005.

Dhall, Vinod, *Competition Law Today*, Oxford Press, New Delhi, 2007.

Experiences Gained so far on International Cooperation on Competition Policy issues and the Mechanisms Used, UNCTAD, TD/B/COM.2/CLP/21/Rev.1, 19th April, 2002, available at http://www.unctad.org/en/docs/c2clp21r1_en.pdf

Gopalakrishnan, Aditi, 'Competition Act and MRTP: One 'Two' Many', *Business Line*, Thursday, August 20, 2009.

Hoehn, Thomas *et al.*, *India's New Competition Law: No Longer an Elephant in the Corner*, International Company and Commercial Law Review.

Jain, Tarun, *Regulatory Structure under EC Competition Laws: Lessons for India*, available at <http://www.ssrn.com>.

Kirkbride, James, 'The Law of Unfair Competition: Is there an E.C. Approach?', *Company Lawyer*, Comp. Law. 2000.

Mattoo, Aaditya & Robert M. Stern, *India and WTO*, Oxford University Press, Washington, 2003.

Mehta, Pradeep S., *Functional Competition Policy in India*, CUTS International, New Delhi, 2006.

Miller, Roderick, *Doing Business with India*, GMB Publishing Ltd., London, 2003.

Ninan, T.N. (ed.), *Business Standard 2008*, Business Standard Books, New Delhi, 2008.

Pandey, Singhda, *Extra Territoriality and Merger Control: Study from Major Jurisdictions and Provisions in Indian Competition Act, 2002*, available at <http://www.cci.gov.in/images/media/Research Reports/concept_20081202123940.pdf>.

Rammapa, T., *Competition Law in India: Policy Issues in India and Developments*, Oxford Press, New Delhi, 2006.

Recommendations on the Regional Seminar on Consumer Protection, Competition Policy and Competitiveness, UNCTAD, TD/B/COM.1/EM.17/2/Add.1, 5th September, 2001, available at http://www.unctad.org/en/docs/c1em17d2a1.en.pdf.

Sappovadia, VrajLal & Kandarp Patel, *Competitiveness of Indian Business vis-à-vis Legal Provisions and Judicial Interpretation*, available at http://www.ssrn.com.

Singh, S.S. & Sapna Chadah, *Consumer Protection in India—Some Reflections*, available at http://consumereducation.in/cons_book1_final.pdf.

United Nations Guidelines for Consumer Protection (as expanded in 1999), United Nations Conference on Trade and Development (UNCTAD), available at a http://www.unctad.org/en/docs/poditcclpm21.en.pdf.

Wu, Pijan, Caroline Thomas, 'Taiwan's Fair Trade Act: Achieving the right Balance', *Northwestern Journal of International Law and Business*, 26 Nw. J. Int'l L. & Bus. 643, at 643.

6
Alternative Disputes Resolution and Consumer Disputes Redressal Machinery

Ramesh Kumar

Introduction

By "consumerism" we mean the process of realizing the rights of the consumer as envisaged in the Consumer Protection Act (1986) and ensuring right standards for the goods and services for which one makes a payment. This objective can be achieved in a reasonable time frame only when all organs of market act together and play their role. The players, in the market, are the consumers, voluntary consumer organizations, the government, the regulatory authorities, consumer courts, organizations representing trade, industry and service providers, the law-makers and those in charge of implementation of the laws and rules. In the present era of consumerism, the transition from a predominantly "sellers market" to a "buyers market" has established new theories of consumerism, hence the doctrine of 'Caveat Emptor' has now shifted to 'Caveat venditor'.

Today due to globalisation and liberalisation the consumer has become very demanding. Consumer literacy is on the rise due to information explosion. As the awareness is increasing more and more complaints are being filed in the consumer redressal agencies. No doubt the disposal is taking place but it is accompanied with a lot of delay. The consumer needs quick and inexpensive justice. This will not only give him relief but also enhance his confidence in the redressal mechanism and rule of law. Keeping in view the need to provide quick justice to the consumers, its time that alternative mechanisms to redress consumers' grievances are thought about. This will help in reducing delay apart from providing alternate platform to the consumers to redress their grievances. This paper basically analyses the existing mechanism of consumer grievance redressal under the Consumer Protection Act, 1986 and explores the alternate disputes redressal mechanism along with specific steps to operationalise the system.

Consumer Protection Act, 1986

It is one of the most progressive and comprehensive piece of legislation enacted for the better protection of consumers. It was enacted after in-depth study of consumer protection laws in a number of countries and in consultation with representatives of consumers, trade and industry and extensive discussions within the Government. Though the CPA is a remarkably focused legislation with minimum legal and technical procedure and easily accessible redressal system, but the system is lacking on several grounds.

Delay in Disposal of Disputes

Even though a time period of 3-5 months has been provided in CPA rules for the disposal of disputes, hardly any Forum or Commission has been complying with these provisions. Delay can be reduced by not permitting adjournments and allowing the appearance of lawyers only with the consent of opposite parties and the Forum.

Narrow Definition of Consumer

Payment of consideration for goods and services is the critical element in deciding with disputes. This narrow definition has left out several service providers out of its ambit. A wider interpretation is required to remove this defect.

Defective Appointment Procedure

Usually, vacancies make the forums non-functional and non-legal members do not have sufficient experience and knowledge of consumerism. In number of cases, such appointments are made for political gains and/or administration bias, not for keeping in view the consumers cause at large.

Non-execution of Orders

In majority of cases orders of the Consumer Forums are not executed in letter and spirit. Consumer Forums have no power to attach properties of such parties who do not comply with the order. In such circumstances, the Forum can issue arrest warrants. To attach the properties, the case is transferred to the nearest Civil Court and process of recovery is very tedious. Power to attach property should be given to Consumer Forums/Commissions with the power to appoint receiver.

Misinterpretation of Law

In many cases, provisions of Consumer Protection Act are not interpreted in letter and spirit. The law is used as per the convenience of its members as non-judicial members are often unable to find the correct interpretation of law. Many a times, cases are filed in appeal only on the ground of erroneous mistake in procedure and conduct of proceedings and as a result the orders lose the sanctity.

Statutory Limitations

Individual consumer cannot take up the matter in the larger interests of consumers. Only registered and recognized associations can take the matter before the Consumer Forum. Moreover, Consumer Forum has no power to take *suo motu* notice on such matters. No power has been delegated to Consumer Forum to refer the matter for consensual disposal. Section 89 of CPC is not applicable.

Administrative and Financial Constraints

Many consumer courts have been facing problems, viz. required space not available for conduct of proceedings, processing deficiencies due to resources, lack of competent staff, long pending vacancies, storage of records and stationery and lack of other amenities.

Complicated Court Procedure

Though the parties have right to present their case in person and there is no need of lawyer to appear on their behalf, but the opposite party (merchant) is always represented by lawyers. As a result, the dispute turn into Lawyers *v.* Consumer which makes the matter more complicated.

Are Consumer Courts Part of ADR?

The provisions of Consumer Protection Act, 1986 sometimes mix with the concept of ADR and adversarial jurisprudence. It is a debatable question whether Consumer Courts are the part of Alternative Disputes Resolution or Not? Consumer Protection Act, 1986 defines these bodies as "redressal agencies". Composition and selection procedure of members is different from civil courts. The objective of CPA is "to provide speedy, simple and inexpensive redressal to consumer disputes through summary trial". Jurisdiction is limited as compared to civil courts. These forums are not referred as "Courts" in CPA as they are not under the supervision/control of judiciary. Having all the above salient features, there forums cannot be placed under ADR mechanism as they are designed to function in an adjudicatory or adversarial manner having same powers as civil courts have. Disposal of matter is in the form of "Order" and there is a provision of appeal against the order. Moreover, participation of lawyers and procedures of filing of complaint, notice, opportunity to respond, evidentiary matters, issuance of findings, appeals and execution are similar to civil courts. In the light of above discussion we need to find answers to following questions: What effect do they have on working for formal civil justice system? Do they improve on the quality and quantity of justice otherwise available? Do they increase access to justice and if so, for whom? Is there any Party Autonomy under this system?

Effect on Civil Justice Procedure

The proceedings are triggered by filing a complaint with the appropriate forum and proceeds much as a civil case would. Notice to the opposite party and an opportunity to respond. Taking evidence and powers of forum are identical to those of civil courts regarding summoning, discovery, affidavits and requisitioning. Disposal of matter is in the form of "Order". There is a provision of appeal against the order. Execution process is also designed similar to regular civil courts. The forum has power to enforce its decisions in the manner as if it were a decree or order made by civil court and if required can take assistance of regular courts in executing its orders. Provision of fine and/or imprisonment for failure to complying orders are alike civil courts.

Quantitative Justice

To reduce burden on civil courts, and to justify ADR, these forums do not have any significant impact on case load of civil courts. Very few cases are filed with civil courts related to consumer disputes even prior to inception of CPA. Prior to the creation of consumer courts people even did not think in terms of filing court cases to resolve these types of disputes, therefore, consumer courts have no quantity effect on formal judicial system.

Qualitative Justice

It includes community empowerment, party participation (party autonomy) and access to justice based on equity. Community empowerment by appointing lay-members (non-judicial members) is limited to possible pool of elite, experts in economics, law and other related areas. Ex-judges or sitting judges being president dominate the proceedings and running the proceeding in the manner as court rooms. CPA was supposed to be a simpler system of redressal mechanism but the lawyers and presidents of consumer courts (most of lawyers appointed as Presidents) preferred the interpretation of legal language more important than the purpose and intention of the Act itself. It is correct that "A consumer dispute can be disposed of in one hearing" but it is allowed to carry on for several years because of complex court procedure. Lawyers are expected to assist the litigant but in such forums litigants are created for the survival of lawyers. Consumer expects relief from the court whereas lawyer tries to linger on the matter only to stop misuse of the law and judiciary. Is it not a mockery of the CPA itself and denying justice to the people at large?

Access to Justice

In a country with more than one billion population, predominantly rural, 1569421 complaints filed in about 15 years means that there are still large potential complainants who do not have access to the redressal machinery due to various reasons. When complex question of fact and law are involved the complainants are encouraged to take the matter to civil court. Therefore, we cannot say these forums are not duplication of civil courts.

Party Autonomy

In adversarial proceedings reliance on lawyers leave very little room for party participation in settlement process. The complainant has little knowledge of substantive law whereas the respondent is usually represented by a lawyer. The adversarial proceedings and common presence of lawyers enhanced the influence of judges. On the other hand, non-judicial-members with lack of working knowledge of court procedure have diminishing role under the presidentship of attached judges. It was proposed in 2001 Amendment Bill of CPA that respondent can be represented by a lawyer only if the consumer engages one is a lawyer himself or if the consumer does not object.

No Consensual Adjudication under CPA

Does the Consumer Disputes Redressal Commission have jurisdiction to refer the dispute pending before it for a consensual adjudication by third person and then make the said decision of the consensual arbitrator on order of the commission itself? In this regard the Supreme Court in one of the cases[1] held that Arbitration clause is not a bar to entertain the complaint by the redressal agency constituted under CPA, since the remedy provided is in addition to the provisions of any other law for the time being in force. Forums/Commissions under CPA are quasi-judicial bodies to provide speedy and simple redressal to consumer disputes. They have been empowered to give relief of specified nature. Commission may refer disputes to Arbitration/Conciliation under the provisions of Arbitration and Conciliaticn Act, 1996 but it would be an unhealthy practice for commission/forum to abdicate their duties and functions and to delegate adjudication of disputes before them to third party. The commission/forum is not applying its mind or adjudication on the dispute, it is merely putting its impremanitive on decisions given by third parties. By doing so, it is abdicating its own functions and duties. Such a procedure is unwarranted and unjustified.

Consumer Forums are not Substitute of Arbitration

Is Consumer Court competent to intervene where there is a contract between the parties to settle any dispute through arbitration? On this question in *Fair Air Engineers Pvt. Ltd.* v. *N.K. Modi*[2] it was held that Section 13 of the CPA provides for the procedure of adjudication. Sub-section 4 provides that forum/commission shall have the same powers as are vested in a civil court under the Code of Civil Procedure, 1908. Sub-Section 5 says that every proceeding before the Forum shall be deemed to be a judicial proceeding within the meaning of Sections 193 and 228 of IPC and shall be deemed to be a civil court for the purpose of Section 195 and Chapter XXVI of the Cr.P.C., 1973. Therefore, proceedings before the Forum/Commissions under CPA are legal proceedings and these Forums and Commissions are judicial authorities falling under Section 34 of the Arbitration Act but Section 34 does not confer an automatic right nor create an automatic embargo on the exercise of the power by the judicial authority under the Act.

It would be appropriate that these Forums/Commissions created under CPA are at liberty to proceed with the matters in accordance with the provisions of the Act rather than relegating the parties to an arbitration proceeding pursuant to a contract entered between the parties. It was held that the dispute under CPA need not be referred to arbitration and the matter could be decided on merits.

Need for ADR in Consumers Disputes

In general, ADR covers all methods of resolving disputes related to obligations resulting from contracts concluded between sellers of goods or service providers. This system includes Arbitration, Conciliation, Mediation and Negotiation. In some countries, ADR systems have been developed by business organizations in order to provide speedier, more informed and more cost-effective dispute resolution. ADR is the priority to resolve consumer disputes in the present open market economy with many international issues:

Globalization

With the advent of globalization and participation of Indian consumers in emerging international market, ambit of consumer protection has increased tremendously. New emerging economic developments and growing controversies in Indian market gives new dimension to consumer jurisprudence. Development of social action litigation and consumer protection, consumer protection and environmental litigations, consumer protection and business, self-regulations etc. are few examples which do not meet the redressal requirements under Consumer Protection Act, 1986.

E-business

Indian consumers are buying goods and services from the businesses based in other countries. Recourse to courts in disputes resulting from international internet transactions is often complicated by the difficult questions of which law applies or which authority has jurisdiction over such disputes. Consumer law, in India, is not strong enough even to protect people from fly-by-night operators or international defaulters. There is lack of self-regulatory international principles and rules.

Emerging Technologies

Innovative use of technology to settle consumer disputes can be very result oriented. Problems such as authentication and security to the application of an appropriate level of confidentiality can be solved through newer technologies. In addition, many safety issues which are still out of the ambit of consumer laws can be covered. Earlier the interpretation of 'right to safety' was limited but now its definition has included safety issues of technologies like GM food. Today, in cross border markets, consumers have no control over where the products they use come from. Consumer has no knowledge or control of manufacturing practices of other countries but rely completely on import regulations. Double standard business practices MNCs have been adopting in Indian market which give birth to many important and critical consumer disputes at large. It is a fact that half of the Indian population has no access to present consumer redressal machinery because of illiteracy, poverty, cost, access to judicial system and other socio-economic factors then how they can get Global access of international rules and adjudication system even through ADR?

Need of Better Public Utilities

Functioning of government controlled public utilities is very irresponsible and consumer biased. These agencies are working under feudalistic administrative environment in an opaque and anti-consumer atmosphere. Such bodies do not respond to consumer complaints. They prefer to wait for court orders and ultimately wasting public exchequer in appealing at various levels to tire out the consumer. On numerous occasions these government bodies do not even care for orders passed by Consumer Courts. There is an urgent need for proactive consumer-friendly ADR services in these government agencies.

ADR on the Basis of Equity or Code of Conduct

ADR system should be on the basis of equity, code of conduct or other rules agreed by the parties. It is experienced that industry has been alleging that CPA is bias against it. An appropriate answer can be found in the ADR as the alternative system aims to solve the dispute between the consumer and the businesses through simple and effective mediation between the two. The system is based on the rationale that producers are eventually consumers; there is no point in going for a direct confrontation in case of grievance. Most of the consumer disputes are arising due to lack of proper communication between the consumer and seller. An urgent attention is required to create win-win situation where both the parties work as partners and complimentary to each other. Only in case of intentional violation of consumer rights, the matter could be brought to quasi-judicial consumer courts for adjudication.

Consumer Activism

Significantly, the CPA and the related legal framework have provided the basis for the statutory authorities to create alternative forum for consumer disputes resolution. Despite the CP Act legislated in 1986, it was only as late as in 1991, the consumer disputes redressal forums were set up. In many districts of the country still we do not have consumer courts. Delay in appointment put a complete halt in the working of CPA. Inadequate support staff, inadequate provisions of office equipment, lack of library facilities—all these indicate the administrative indifference towards the consumer protection. Moreover, Government has not filed complaints, though the government has been empowered to do so under the Act. Government seems to have no interest in taking the Act to the people at large. ADR mechanism can promote consumer activism at large.

What Do We Need in ADR for Consumers' Disputes?

For speedy disposal of consumer disputes, the ADR process may be voluntary, mandatory, binding or adversary if required. Following concepts and forms can be added to the present dispute redressal system:

Pre-Dispute ADR (Amendment in Consumer Protection Act)

There is a need to identify numerous consumer goods and services which could offer ADR to resolve disputes. Companies should be promoted for voluntary ADR system. Consumer dispute redressal process would receive significant attention due to issues related to mandatory pre-dispute binding ADR. To achieve this, reference be made by the consumer court for alternative disputes settlement mechanism at the pre-trial stage and no provision for further appeal. An amendment is required in the present scheme of Consumer Protection Act, 1986.

Consumer Conciliation Committee under CPA

The provision of Consumer Protection Councils under CPA is to promote and protect the consumer rights and such councils have statutory powers to constitute Conciliation Committees for the purpose of providing conciliation and mediation facilities. Disputes can be resolved amicably on agreed terms consented by both the parties through such committees and if the parties agree on the final proposal, it becomes a contract enforceable in its capacity. One such successful ADR system has been initiated in the State of Goa by constituting Consumer Conciliation Committee which has been guiding the parties towards fair compromise.

Facilitation-cum-Information Centres

Though there is a scheme of 'Consumers Information Centre' sponsored by the government to promote consumer rights and these centres can play an important role in development of ADR system for speedy disposal of consumer disputes. In addition, Facilitation-*cum*-Information Centres should also be created and attached to every consumer court to assist consumers in settling disputes through ADR. At apex level such centres should be given powers to receive complaints from consumers on the working of the consumer courts at all levels. Such centres should be empowered to have through review of the functioning of the consumer courts at the district level.

Establishment of Permanent Lok Adalats in Public Utility Services

Generally the consumer courts are flooded with electricity, telephone or insurance disputes and it creates the impression that such courts are not Consumer Courts, instead these are Electricity Courts or Telephone Courts. Such problem can be dealt with the creation of Permanent Consumer Courts or Lok Adalats with Public Utility Services. The system of Lok Adalat is an innovative concept which can provide an effective mechanism for resolving consumer disputes through ADR. It seeks to provide compulsory pre-litigative mechanism system for conciliation and settlement of cases relating to public utility service, viz. transport of goods and passengers, postal and telephonic services, water and power supply to public, sanitation, hospitals and insurance etc. More and more permanent Lok Adalats should be established with such public utility service providers.

In-house Arbitration for Consumer Goods and Services

Arbitration is normally final and binding and thus it may not lend itself to non-jurisdictional world of cross border business to consumer transactions. It may be in the form of contract terms with the proposed possibility of ADR given by the seller or service provider. Encouraging in-house consumer disputes resolution through arbitration is very important, particularly in electronically consumer transactions, e.g. credit cards and internet marking. It should be the duty of the businesses to inform the consumer about the conditions of in-house ADR.

Online Disputes Resolution

E-commerce, especially between consumers in one country buying goods or services from other countries is growing fast. It needs to win consumer confidence by the companies to protect the common interests. We all know that recourse to court annexed dispute resolution in international e-business is raising complicated questions, viz. jurisdiction, court proceedings, cost of suit, execution, appeal etc. Secondly, consumers are not resort to the competency of court and principle courts of other countries as well as the merchants find themselves uneasy in dealing with laws and processes of destination country (consumer's country). The solution is that the internet businesses should be bound to offer attractive extra-judicial procedure, viz. ODR for settling consumer disputes as an alternative to cumbersome court system. Such ODR may be quite successful, effective, quick and efficient for addressing consumer complaints and progressing businesses as well. In addition, the use of ODR would avoid overburden of judicial system. ODR can be more effective in finding solution that satisfies both the parties in the international market.

Encourage In-house Consumer Satisfaction Programme

It should be based on purely internal dispute settlement services that may be offered by merchants as an after-sale service for good commercial sense, rather than as an alternative to court procedure. If consumer wishes to make use of ADR offered by the merchant, he may be invited to submit his complaint first to such a service centre before filing it with the normal system. Such extra judicial procedures for settling disputes is an alternative to the cumbersome and expensive procedure of courts. For example, if a merchant involved in the sale of low priced goods might choose to offer an unconditional money-back guarantee to all customers rather than putting the dispute in litigation channel. The consumer may be requested to have the complaint first to an in-house customer satisfaction system and if not satisfied take the matter to ADR mechanism.

Promotion of ADR through Consumer Organizations

In India, more than 2500 government as well as voluntary consumer organizations have been working for the last two decades to promote and protect the consumers' rights. Government of India has also been encouraging such organizations by providing support to take up numerous field programmes for consumer protection. It is found that many such organizations have high level of calibre and capacity to conduct mediation and negotiation in consumers' disputes and following ADR related programme.

Consumers Disputes Mediation Centres

Instead of presenting consumer complaint in courts, each side should meet personally with the mediator available with Mediation Centre in joint sessions as well as separately. It can be used to resolve the disputes between businesses and consumer in particular. Mediation should not intervene in negotiation but register the final agreement between the parties. The successful result of mediation between consumer and merchant should be legal contracts and would be enforceable by law. Mediation is currently used worldwide to resolve disputes related to various other issues with successful results and in consumer disputes it needs to be promoted.

Negotiation Helpline Services

Through such helpline service, consumers as well as merchants can bargain for individual or collective advantage and come to the result which serves their mutual interest. In this process the consumer organizations can play a very important role in many ways. The outcome of the negotiation may be a compromise, satisfactory to both the parties in a win-win situation.

Conclusion

ADR covers all the methods of resolving consumer disputes related to obligations resulting from contract even concluded electronically, between seller and consumer. This system includes Arbitration, Conciliation, Mediation and Negotiation. Through ADR consumers' disputes can be resolved fairly and in timely. ADR allows both parties to avoid the delay and the cost of appealing to either statutory agencies of the government or the courts. In addition, the use of ADR avoids overburdening judicial system, while at the same time, preserving the consumers' rights to seek legal redress should they be dissatisfied with the results of the ADR process. Finally, ADR can be more flexible and creative in finding solutions that satisfy both parties, while consumer protection agencies and courts may offer only limited remedies in resolving disputes, particularly where those remedies are prescribed by law or regulations.

NOTES

1. *Skypack Couriers Ltd.* v. *Tata Chemicals Ltd.*, 2000 AIR SCW 1866.
2. Civil Appeal No. 11459 of 1996.

7
Consumerism in Manipur: An Overview

G.P. Prasain

Introduction

The term 'Consumerism' literally means the protection of rights and interests of consumers. This word is neither new for our country nor for the remaining world. Consumer protection, therefore, has a global concern. The necessity of the establishment of separate Consumer redressal system was due to the industrial revolution and the development in the international trade and commerce. This led to the vast expansion of business and trade, as a result a variety of consumer goods appeared in the market to meet daily requirements of the consumers and variety of services have been made available to the consumer like insurance, transport, electricity, housing, entertainment, finance and banking. A well organised sector of manufacturers and traders with better knowledge of market has come into existence, thereby affecting the relationship between the traders and the consumers, making the principle of consumer sovereignty almost inapplicable. The advertisements of goods and services in television, radio, newspapers and magazines influences the demand for the same by the consumers though there may be manufacturing defects or imperfections or shortcomings in the quality, quantity and the purity of the goods or there may be deficiency in the services rendered. Sometimes, consumers suffer due to many reasons. The aggrieved consumers approached to the Civil Courts before the establishment of the Consumer Courts to get relief or redressal for the loss they suffered.

But few people could do so as it took much time and was expensive also. In order to remove all these difficulties to provide for better protection and the interest of the consumer, the Consumer Protection Bill, 1986 was introduced in the Lok Sabha· on 5th December, 1986. The Bill was passed by both the Houses of Parliament on 24th December, 1986 and came on the statutes book as the Consumer Protection Act, 1986 on 15th April, 1987.

Due to rapid growth of industrialization in India after the independence, the Indian market was flooded with consumer goods and services which almost changed the relationship between the consumer and the trader. Since the establishment of the Consumer Protection Act, 1986 many consumer cases could be solved by this Act. The nature of the consumer forums is quasi-judicial. The consumer forum in India is at three tier levels, namely (a) District Forum, (b) State Commission, and (c) National Commission. The Act provides that there shall be one District Forum in each of the District and any complaint of goods and services which is less than ₹ 20 lakh should be claimed in this forum. There shall be one State Commission in each of the state and any complaint of goods and services which is more than ₹ 20 lakh but less than ₹ 1 crore and appeals against the orders of District Forums should be entertained in this Commission. And there shall be one National Commission where the value of the goods or services and compensation, if any, claimed exceeds rupees one crore and appeals against the order of any State Commission should be entertained in this Commission. Under this Act, the complainant is exempted from paying the court fees and is capable of getting relief within a period of 90 days except where test report of laboratory analysis is required for which a period of 150 days is prescribed. Besides the Consumer Forums, there are also Consumer Protection Councils in each State and at the Centre. The Minister in-charge of the Consumer Affairs in the Central Government shall be its Chairman. The Central Council shall meet as and when necessary, but at least one meeting of the council shall be held every year. The objective of these Consumer Protection Councils is to promote and protect the rights of the consumers.

It seems that the purpose of the Act is to remove the unfair trade practiced by the manufacturers, traders, sellers and professionals as well as to protect the aggrieved consumers from being cheated by trading community who indulge in unfair trade practices provide or deficient or negligent services. The legislative enactments reveal that that protection of the consumers has been high governmental priority. Legislatures, judges, law reformers, academics, lawyers and consumer activists have to formulate positive schemes for the effective implementation of the basic rights of consumers and should work together for creating welfare of the consumers and in this way, promote consumer welfare in the country.

National Scenario – A Brief

Even though it's nearing 25 that the Consumer Protection Act came into effect, few people approached the consumer courts for redressal of their grievances. Only three out of 2000 people approached consumer courts with complaints during the last 15 years, says the study conducted by Consumer Action and Network Society (CANS). The State-wise analysis found that around 16 lakh cases were registered in various consumer courts in India. On the basis of average registration of maximum complaints with consumer courts, Chandigarh topped the chart with two in every 100 consumers approaching the courts, Nagaland with only one in every 25,000 people preferring to approach consumer courts is at the bottom of the chart.

According to the report by CANS up to the year 2001, the large number of complaints, i.e. more than 2.43 lakh complaints were lodged with District Forum in Andhra Pradesh and the lowest 41 complaints in Dadra and Nagar Haveli during the last 15 years. In disposal of cases, Lakshadweep was found to be at the top with cent per cent clearance of cases. Pondicherry follows next with 97 per cent clearance, followed by Kerala, Manipur, Sikkim, Punjab, Karnataka, M.P., Andhra Pradesh and Andaman and Nicobar. In fact, there are about 1400 NGOs in India working for this cause. Various factors can be traced out for the weak performance of the NGOs.

(a) Lack of devoted members. Most of the members of these NGOs are busy in their own schedules and they join these NGOs only as part time members and are mostly unable to devote their time and efforts for the cause.

(b) Lack of funds is another important factor responsible for the poor performance of the NGOs.

(c) Insensitive attitude of the Government is another factors contributing to poor performance of the NGOs.

Most of the consumers in India—whether rich or poor, literate or illiterate, urban or rural often become the victims of adulterated, spurious, hazardous and substandard goods as well as wrong measurement and high prices. Shortage in the supply of several commodities, unethical and deceptive advertisements, enables the businesses to make quick money at the cost of consumers. Even the goods/services of state undertakings, nationalized banks, state electricity boards, telephone departments, etc., are not exceptions. Despite a number of laws passed to protect the interests of the consumers, the Indian consumer is mostly unaware of his rights. The methods for seeking redress are often felt to be cumbersome, costly and time-consuming with little hope to secure justice.

As against this scenario, the consumer in the developed countries enjoys far more protection. The governments in these countries give as much importance to protecting the interest of consumers as it does with the trade and industry and the consumer himself is well aware of his rights. In spite of the various price controls and the strict enforcement of regulation for printing the maximum retail price on most of the products, the traders usually resort to different dubious methods to get still higher prices. Even knowledgeable people are cheated in a sophisticated way without becoming aware of it.

One way to improve the situation is to keep the consumer informed of his rights and privileges and the various legislative measures available to him. Some of such legislative measures are:

1. Agricultural Produce (Grading and Marketing) Act, 1937
2. ISI Certification Marks Act, 1952
3. Prevention of Food Adulteration Act, 1954
4. Essential Commodities Act, 1955
5. Standards of Weights and Measures Act, 1976
6. Standards of Weights and Measures (Packaged Commodities) Rules, 1977 and 1990
7. Monopolies and Restrictive Trade Practices Act, 1969 (Specially the part dealing with RTPs and UFTPs)

8. Environment (Protection) Act, 1986
   (a) Air (Prevention and Control of Pollution) Rules, 1989
   (b) Hazardous Wastes (Management and Handling) Rules, 1989
   (c) Water (Prevention and Control of Pollution) Rules, 1989.

The public distribution system and the law enforcing the display of stock position and price lists outside the shop are well known. The latter measure is not taken seriously by the trader or the consumer or even by the law-enforcing authorities due to various practical impediments. Most of the laws have not succeeded because of several inadequacies in them and the existence of corruption among the law-enforcing authorities. Unscrupulous businessmen take advantage of these inadequacies and manage to avoid penal action. Moreover, a large number of consumers are indifferent to the reality of the situation. As a result, they are not even acquainted with the privileges they are entitled to enjoy and the legal protection available to them. The average consumer usually thinks only in terms of his individual and immediate interests. There are very few who would take the trouble to protest individually or even collectively. The traders are aware of this tendency on the part of the consumers and so are encouraged to resort to various malpractices.

The institutional measures instituted by the government have also not worked well. For example, the fair price shops and co-operative super markets have been opened essentially to rationalise distribution and to control prices. But in actual practice, they deal in a limited number of goods and the services offered are so poor that most of the consumers find that private shops are better in many ways. There should be safeguards for the consumers to enable them to keep the businesses in check from resorting to malpractices. Such safeguards and checks are found even in developed economies where competitive market conditions prevail and literacy levels are high. There is much to be done in a country like India. Consumer education through which the consumer is made to understand his rights and the steps he could take in the event of the rights being affected is essential in this context. The recognition of the rights of the consumer, therefore, is an important step in the effort to protect consumer's interest.

Implementation of CP Act in Manipur

Manipur is a land locked state connected to the Indian mainland through the peripheral states of Nagaland and Assam by National Highway—39 and 53 respectively with an international transit point at Moreh for transaction of foreign goods between Manipur and Myanmar. Imphal, the capital city of the state is the centre of market activities among the producers, sellers, and domestic consumers. Consumer/customer oriented organization like Bharat Sanchar Nigam Ltd., BSNL, Inter State Surface Transport and Air Transport, and public sector unit like Indian Oil Corporation Ltd. etc. interact with consumers, the process of their service utilization by the consumers and need based consumption of petroleum production respectively. Thus, consumerism is the profit oriented game play of traders, sellers and service providers in respective markets. Due to this process consumers in particular have to face many hardships in the form of unsatisfactory return for which they make satisfactory payments. As such, consumer issues are bound to emerge in any consumer market activities and Manipur.

It was mainly through the efforts of a hard working social worker—Shri Akoijam Chaoba Singh that a Consumer Protection Society of Manipur was established and registered in 1986. There were about 100 founder members, and by unanimous choice, Shri Ak. Chaoba Singh and H. Harideva Sharma became the Secretary and the President respectively of the society. Various posters, pamphlets and handouts indicating rights and privileges of consumers of various goods and services were distributed or displayed at strategic points. An office of the society was opened in Paona Bazar, Imphal for extending assistance to the individual consumers and various societies/clubs engaged in consumer assistance programmes. Surprise checks with the assistance of departments like Weights and Measures, Imphal Municipal Office, etc. were done to check two widespread enemies of consumers, viz. cheating in weighing and adulteration, both in food and non-food items. With the spread of consumer movements all over the country including Manipur, the need for establishing consumer courts, both at the district and the state level arose for settling consumer disputes mainly between producers of goods and services and the consumers.

The State Government set up the State Commission in 1988 and Mr. H. Harideva Sharma was appointed as a Member of the State Consumer Disputes Redressal Commission, Manipur. The other member was Km. Kh. Promodini Devi. The State Commission was headed by Justice S.N. Phukan of the Guwahati High Court. Initially, the district level court was established at Imphal only. The first members of the Consumer Disputes Redressal Forum, Imphal were Shri C. Upendra Singh (Retd.), District and Sessions Judge, Manipur and Shri Ak. Chaoba Singh the founder secretary of the Manipur Consumer Protection Society. A lady member was also appointed after some time.

Justice Sema succeeded Justice Phukan who became a judge of the Supreme Court. The State Consumer Commission was set up in the Library Room of the Imphal Bench of the Guwahati High Court. Justice Sema was subsequently succeeded by the (Retd.) Justice Y. lbotombi Singh and they worked together for about a year prior to retirement after serving a full term. Km. Kh. Pramodini Devi retired a few months earlier. Justice Y. lbotombi Singh also resigned after a few months and a new team of judges were appointed for the State and the District level courts. The State Commission could not play a major role in protecting the consumers.

Now the State Commission is situated within the campus of the Civil Supplies Directorate. One must be wondering whether the court was protecting the interests of the Civil Supplies Department—supplier of goods and services or of the general public—a consumer of goods and services. Moreover, the place is not centrally located. There is still another point to be looked into. Although, consumers can approach consumer courts without the assistance of advocates, but there are advocate entailing heavy expenditure on poor consumers.

Manipur was one of the leading State in North East India regarding the consumer movement and consumer education up to the early part of 2001. The largest number of cases were disposed of at the District Forum, Imphal, and followed by Thoubal and Chandel District and few cases came in Bishnupur, Ukhrul and Senapati District. The remaining districts did not have any complaints. The main reason was the non-appointment of the Presidents and Members of the State Commission and District

Forums since 2001. Therefore, there is a dire need to look into the matter and to activate the Consumer Courts as early as possible in the interest of the consumers. It is also important to impart consumer education to different stakeholders particularly the pressmen or media persons. Because it is the media persons who can easily give any kind of information or message to the general public. Therefore, consumer education should be given priority. There are so many stories about the negligence and carelessness by the providers of goods and services in Manipur. To mention a few, surgeons leaving surgical instruments inside the body, worms found in tap water meant for drinking, glass pieces found in soft drinks, airline authorities not delivering luggage thereby creating serious difficulties for the passengers concerned.

The position today is that large number of traders and businessmen, in order to become millionaire in a short period, are busy cheating the consumers by way of charging excessive prices, supplying defective goods or providing deficient services. In fact, consumer exploitation has become the fashion of the day because the producers, suppliers, manufacturers and retailers are in much superior position. This is not an exaggeration but only a glimpse of consumers' woes. Furthermore, backlog of consumer disputes due to lack of funds, shortage of staff and non-payment of their salaries, often for months, led to the closure of Forums. In fact, consumers have to wait for years to get redressed and the concept of speedy justice has gradually melted out. If this situation remains for long, the very purpose of the Act will be defeated. The consumers continue to be exploited owing to multiplicity of reasons, namely:

1. Lack of awareness on the part of the consumers.
2. Lack of initiative to fight for the cause.
3. Lack of confidence of the consumers in the redressal mechanism.
4. Pending backlog of cases and long delay in the disposal of cases.
5. Economic constraints.
6. Procedural complexities.
7. Un-organised consumers owing to the weak strength of NGO are fighting for their cause.

Challenges Ahead

At present, consumerism in Manipur is very poor. With the non-functioning of District Forums as well as State Commission, consumers are left with no other alternatives. There were three NGOs in Manipur working for the cause of consumers, viz. (i) Consumer Protection Society, Imphal established in 1986, (ii) Consumer Club, Imphal established in 1990, and (iii) Consumer Guidance Society, Imphal established in 1995. But unfortunately, all these NGOs are not functioning any more.

Since 2001, the District Forums are not functioning due to the apathy shown by the concerned authority. After a long time the State Government appointed Hon'ble Gauhati High Court, Justice (Retd.) H.K.K. Singh as Chairman of the State Commission in March 2006. It has not started functioning yet due to the delay in the appointment of two other members. It is quite disheartening to know that no consumer related cases are filed in the state since 2001 due to the non-functioning of District Forums and State Commission.

Future Prospects

Keeping in view the importance of consumer protection and welfare, the attention of the general public and more particularly, the State Government is drawn for collective endeavour to protect the rights and interests of the consumers. Consumer movement, even though slow in Manipur, needs to gather momentum with growing consumer awareness. It is an admitted fact that consumers are the most important agents in the market economy. Public awareness and the role of the government to guarantee and ensure the legitimate rights of consumers is the need of the hour. Consumers rights education should, therefore, form an integral part of the academic curriculum so that consumers do not become victims of poor quality, unsafety, under measurement, adulteration and false promises made by unfair trade practices.

Conclusion

Consumer education is a prerequisite for the success of consumerism in Manipur. Consumer should be made aware of their rights and responsibilities and the utility of consumer movement. Proper consumer education and motivation would help change the stoic attitude of the helpless consumer. Consumers should be convinced that things could be made better if they have the determination to complain against anomalies and fight for justice. There is an urgent need for both formal and informal consumer education in Manipur. The formal consumer education can be imparted through schools and colleges. Consumer education should form a part of the school curriculum. Informal education can be imparted to those who are not regular students of the educational institutions. Consumer forums, consumer co-operatives, social service unions, etc., can play an important role to impart informal education to the consumers to make them conscious of their rights and their role in protecting their rights.

Unless the consumers are aware of their rights and powers through the people's participation programmes such as awareness campaigns and mass education on consumer related issues, the welfare of consumer may not be of much use. The Consumer should come forward with a written complaint to the concerned authorities, only then the frauds will be taught a lesson. The Consumer Protection Society of Manipur, Consumer Club, Imphal and Consumer Guidance Society of Manipur should be activated by filling up the vacant position of the office bearers at the earliest so that the consumer movement be activated in the state.

REFERENCES

Consumer Protection and Trade Practices Journal, Vol. 10, April, 2002.
Consumer Protection and Trade Practices Journal, Vol. 13, July, 2005.
Consumer Protection and Trade Practices Journal, Vol. 14, February, 2006.
Ghose, P.K., *Business Policy*, New Delhi, Sultan Chand & Sons, 1990.
Kotten Philip, *Marketing Management*, Prentice Hall of India, New Delhi, 1979.
Literature published by Ministry of Consumer Affairs, Govt. of India.
The Consumer Protection Amendment Act, 2002.

8
Strengthening Consumer Movement

G.C. Mathur and *Gauri Modwel*

Introduction

Consumers' community slogan "Jago Grahak, Jago" has done tremendous service to consumers by making them aware of their basic rights as customers and guiding them to how to get redressal of their complaints. But sustained consumer-movements are essential for spreading awareness among consumers about the market trends and tactics. The national standards like ISI, AGMARK, Hallmark, Woolmark, etc. play a great role in identification of quality products. The idea is, however, defeated unless these standards are publicized in the media on regular basis. Here again the role of the States becomes important. States do not have any planned programmes or budgetary provisions to work on propagation of such Standards.

We need to take the advantage of technology advancement for converting the National Consumer Helpline into a web based centre with a Chat Room for experts, officials, consumers in the street, and even the members of the consumer forums besides others for a regular interaction. It will greatly boost the level of awareness, particularly implementation of consumer protection policies and procedures in the tooth of opposition from the anti-consumer lobby. Implementation, of course, depends upon how serious are the authorities particularly in the States.

For the purpose of giving a boost to the consumer movement the role of Consumer Clubs (C-Clubs) and Voluntary Consumer

Organisations (VCOs) is to be understood and appreciated by the implementing agencies. In these days of out-sourcing implementations through non-governmental organizations, C-Clubs and VCOs are the only reliable communication links between the policy makers and the beneficiaries. If nursed properly and empowered these will prove extremely advantageous to the society. There is no dearth of public spirited individuals to lead these organizations. It is not a bad idea if the States' Department handling Consumer Affairs let the Education Departments to independently handle C-Club projects with VCOs as Nodal Agencies. The States' Education Department could apply and receive CWF grants directly for the first two years initially. Though it will be under intimation to Department of Consumer Affairs of the State but operations of C-Clubs will be the responsibility of the Department of Education.

In spreading consumer protection messages these VCO/C-Clubs could also be linked to local community radios. VCOs can function as Nodal Agencies because the State Department of Consumer Affairs is not in a position to guide and lead the C-Club activities for the simple reason that the incumbents there hardly have any interest. Firstly, because they are prone to transfers and retirements and secondly, their interests lay elsewhere—in controlling funds. The concept of C-Clubs in schools and colleges stipulates the following:

1. A Teacher is named for running the C-Club.
2. C-Club has its name and logo.
3. C-Club has its own letterhead with school's name and address.
4. C-Club has its separate S/B Account in a Nationalised Bank and maintains financial statements immaculately with audit of accounts.
5. C-Club is provided with basic infrastructure—at least a table, 2-3 chairs, a computer system with necessary accessories and attachments, an almirah for records and another for its library.
6. C-Club is held in reckoning at the time of drawing a schedule of curriculum/calendar each year at the beginning of the academic session.

7. C-Club membership is open to the entire school strength of teachers and students.
8. On transfer/leaving the school, the principal/teacher in-charge must hand over a proper charge of the C-Club either to the incoming principal or the teacher named.
9. A book on the teachers' training was developed by the Central Board of School Education (CBSE) jointly with National Council of Education, Research and Training (NCERT) and Voluntary Consumer Organisations in the nineties. The book was distributed widely among the libraries/schools in the country by CBSE. That book is very useful for guiding teachers on consumer education and the same be updated and a second edition printed.

In India consumer awareness is as much a challenge as is education. Several myths prevail in Indian consumer's mind. For example, there is a popular myth that "*Bohni* time is retailers' prerogative to charge any rate". Many consumers including literates feel that they can't bargain with a shopkeeper if they are the day's first set of customers in the shop. What a wonderful myth to the delight of the retailers! Maybe the first sale of the day signify the *Bohni* time for the shopkeeper, but certainly not our time, rather consumers' time, to get stripped. There is another popular myth that the customer must bear all the taxes, again and again even when not due at the stage because no statute provides for the same. These myths are nothing but the symptom of maladies that afflict the consumer's mind-set.

Consumer Education

Prolonged unfair market conditions have forced the pressure on us to impress upon the government and the academicians to give serious thought to developing consumer education courses that lead to professional "Consumer Protection Management" (CPM) degree for the public spirited individuals. CPM degree will be incomplete if it does not educate about the application of Consumer Protection Act, 1986, (CPA) along side the information on various market forces that affect the physiology of transactions. If CPA is the right hand of the Consumer Protection, Right to Information Act, 2005, (RTI), is the left hand. RTI is a wonderful tool chiselled to remove the knots in the governance, provided it is used diligently—not with any revenge to harm, but for correcting the maladies. Consumer education is to protect consumers from market hazards, defective goods and services and to educate about grievance redress mechanism besides products' and services' usage/utility. While academic education (distinctly different from CPM) is for earning livelihood. This distinction is desirable in the given conditions and remembered at all stages of consumer protection.

Education is about issues that affect consumers. For example, one issue is about effecting refund of consumers' unclaimed money in billions, rather trillions, of rupees lying with Banks, insurance companies, Ministry of Chemicals and Fertilizers (read National Pharmaceutical Pricing Authority—NPPA) (recovered from pharmaceutical companies), so on and so forth. The issue is better understood when explained quoting an example; in one case the Reserve Bank of India, Mumbai, *vide* its letter No. DAPM. CO.RIA.1792/07.50.01/2008-07 dated 27.9.2006 had informed Binty that the amount lying in "unclaimed deposits accounts" with the urban cooperative banks alone was ₹ 19,294.23 lakh. Figures of the State Bank of India and Associates stand at ₹ 1,40,26,81,242.2—accumulated after waiting for more than ten years for consumers of banking services to claim refund. In respect of pharmaceutical sector it was ₹ 98.72 crore in 2006.

Another serious issue about which consumers need to be educated by VCOs is the Sales Tax, a State subject, a subject that needs to be tackled at State level only: Traders deposit Sales Tax (now VAT) after collecting from consumers. At times, on assessment by the authorities, it is found to have been deposited in excess in the due course, after collecting from consumers. It is ordered to be returned to the traders who in turn are expected to refund it to the individual consumers which is practically not possible. For example, in response to an RTI enquiry the Delhi Government's Department of Trade and Taxes had informed in November 2006 that the refundable amount lying with a particular branch of the department for the period 1997-98 to 2006-07 (September 2006) tops up to ₹ 102.82 crore.

Solution lay in legislation for creating a separate Consumer Welfare Fund in MoCA-DoCA where this refund could be deployed for consumer welfare by an institution, like forum created with Public Private Partnership (PPP). A directive could be inserted in the policy statement for the States to have their own CWF where such refunds of the over charged Sales Tax to consumers could be deployed. This entire process falls within the ambit of consumer protection.

Addressing Key Issues

Consumer Protection Councils

On a wider scale the Consumer Protection is achieved through government plans, policies, procedures and regulations besides the judicial and quasi-judicial recourse. One of the procedures for protecting consumer interests enshrined in CP Act is the setting up of Consumer Protection Councils (CPCs) at the Centre and the States. While at the Centre it is lackadaisical, in the States mostly these are non-existent. Even where they exist, the functioning is purely in name. It is submitted that the Ministry of Consumer Affairs, Government of India should push hard the State Governments for setting up the CPCs and making them operational. It is probably because the Department is overworked. But the MoCA can at least encourage VCOs to undertake Capacity Building of the States implementing authorities like Department of Consumer Affairs, Education Department and principals of schools where C-Clubs are working or going to be launched to educate the benefits of the CPC.

Another wayout is by reviving judicial activism and putting in force with vigour the system of penalizing the officials causing injury, instead of the state exchequer. It will be pertinent to make a mention here of the Chief Justice of India, K.G. Balakrishnan who emphasised, while speaking at a seminar on 12.9.2009 on corruption organized by Central Bureau of Investigation (CBI) and the National Institute of Criminology and Forensic Science, that it is not the question of punishment but the certainty of punishment which proves to be an effective deterrent against corruption[1].

Mediation

Another area of concern is that the volume of consumer grievances/ complaints has gone up manifold in every sector of economy that has clogged the redressal system. Alternative suggestion is being made for arbitration (*Madhyakshta*). The decision of the Hon'able Supreme Court ending the jurisdiction of the Consumer Courts to entertain disputes relating to telecom services and putting it in the lap of Indian Telegraph Act, 1885, (BSNL, Calicut *v.* M. Krishnan) has not resolved the dispute. It would have been better if the Supreme Court (SC) had advised the Government of India to appoint Ombudsmen for settlement of such disputes. Competition under Regulatory Framework is an effective tool to protect consumer interests. We need to understand that while competition is the mainstay of the free market, search for market 'Imperfections' and 'Failures' is the mainstay of Consumer Protection.

VAT and the Consumer

It is unfortunate that prior to Value Added Tax (VAT) coming into effect in 2005, when the Sales tax was chargeable at the First Point of Sales on certain items, was in fact charged from consumer (when not due) at the Last Point of Sales (by the retailer) on Maximum Retail Price (MRP) and that too without mentioning it in the cash memos. This phenomenon at least in the case of chemists' trade in India was widespread. One cannot believe that such a huge imperfection at the hands of the bureaucracy and failure at the hands of the VCOs could have happened in full glare of the authorities in the States and the Centre and, also the Comptroller and Auditor General of India (CAG).

It was expected that the introduction of VAT will bring relief to the buyers in the market. VAT is a wonderful scheme and perhaps has no parallel in so far as the equal distribution of the burden of tax on sales among the manufacturer, the wholesaler, the dealers (retailers), and the consumers is concerned. But, trade has failed to honour the commitment of respecting the values ingrained in the VAT Scheme. Market is charging VAT additionally from consumers on MRP though the rules provide it to be inclusive of all taxes particularly in respect of packaged commodities. VAT Scheme provides for setting of the value on which VAT has already been paid by the seller on the earlier purchase/sale. Accordingly, the retailer has to set of the value on which he has already paid the VAT. That is, he can charge consumer the VAT only on the value difference between his purchase and sale prices. But, the retailer charges VAT on MRP without setting of the values of VAT paid earlier.

Government of India's Department of Consumer Affairs will do justice to the implementation of VAT and the consumers if it amends Section 2(r) of the Packaged Commodity Rules (that allows MRP to be inclusive of all taxes) making it VAT compliant and fulfilling of the Right to Information given in the CPA. It is linked to another deliberate imperfection which relates to the involvement of the State authorities in devising procedures and practices for collection of taxes on sales under VAT Scheme. In Delhi, the Department of Trade and Taxes has introduced two sets of invoices; one is called the Tax Invoice and the other Retail Invoice. In the presence of a Tax Invoice, relevance of Retail Invoice is not understood. While filing the Monthly Returns the dealers in Delhi are required to submit commodity-wise Taxable Turnover and Tax as per the details in form DVAT-16, which is an open invitation to conceal turnover and the actual Tax collected.

An illustration will help in understanding this problem

Here the taxable turnover of a dealer is the total of the difference between his purchase price and the sales price on which he can charge the VAT at the prescribed rate. The Tax (VAT) here is one that is calculated on the total value of the 'difference' between purchase price and the sale price and collected on the basis of the Tax Invoice. How Retail Invoice is in the reckoning is not understood. In Maharashtra the dealer will give the bifurcation of the VAT and price, provided one asks for the same. As explained above, procedure for collecting VAT/Sales Tax varies widely from State to State. In the banking sector, the interest rates could vary but the procedure for lending or opening of accounts should be uniform as also the minimum balance in accounts. It is suggested that while undertaking the exercise for preparing Budgets at the Centre and States, it is strongly recommended, to take into confidence the views and suggestions of various consumers' representatives. Any commercial, industrial, and business plans developed by the concerned ministries or departments both, at the Centre and the States, must insure that consumer interests have been taken care of.

**Illustration*: MRP of a packaged commodity printed on the label = ₹ 1, 000. VAT is @ 12 per cent. (Figures of MRP and VAT %age are at random.). Under the Rules MRP is inclusive of all taxes.

1st Point Sale (From Mfrr to Wholesaler)		2nd Point Sale (Wholesaler to 1st Dealer)	
	Sale Pr	**Pur Price**	**Sale Pr.**
	500.0	500.00	675.00
* VAT	60.0		21.00
Total	560.00.		696.00

3rd Point Sale (1st Dealer to 2nd Dealer)		4th Point Sale (2nd Dealer/Retailer to Consumer)	
Pur Price	**Sale Pr.**	**Pur Price**	**Sale Pr.**
675.00	875.00	875.00	1,000.00
	24.00		15.00
	899.00		1,015.00

***Value after set off for VAT calculation:** *** 175.00 *(675-500)** ***200 *(875-675)** ***125.00 (1000-875)**

Total VAT collected by the government = ₹ 60+21+24+15 = ₹120.00.

Total VAT illegally collected from consumer by the retailer = 60+21+21.48+24.42 = ₹ 126.90 (₹ 127/-) and not deposited in the state exchequer unduly enriching the retailer.

Reason is that the Packaged Commodity Rule 2(r) says that the MRP is inclusive of all taxes, and the Department of Consumer Affairs in the GoI vouches the same, whereas the Department of Trade & Taxes of Delhi Government says that the retailer can charge VAT on MRP. And, further, there are separate invoices for tax and retail.

In practice mostly VAT is charged extra, i.e. over and above the MRP by the retailers, except in the case of medicines. The Department of Trade & Taxes of Delhi Government says that the retailer can charge VAT on MRP.

Consumer and Health Care

One area where the government has miserably failed in developing consumer policy that protect consumers interests relate to health care, especially relating to tobacco growing, manufacturing, processing, beedi rolling, and distribution, besides consumption (Agriculture, Industrial, Commercial, and labour policies). Various warnings to consumers about the ill effects of tobacco have not yielded any results because of the addiction to nicotine. The Government of India knows very well that tobacco is a health hazard product yet it has not done anything significant or appreciable. Ban on smoking in public places in India was imposed on 2.2.2008. But it has been boldly reported by *The Times of India* in its issue of 2.10.2009, "A year on, smoking ban just on paper".

The expenses on treatment of diseases like cancer caused by tobacco smoking and chewing are much higher than the revenue yield. The Courts in India right up to the top know that tobacco consumption is health hazardous, yet they appear to be government-policy-compliant. The governments at the Centre and States have not shown any inclination to curb tobacco growing and use—earning undue revenue and vote bank policies. There are solutions to check tobacco consumption. On consumers' demand one solution given to the government is phasing out the growing, manufacturing, processing, packaging and distribution over a period of 15-20 years. During this period alternatives suggested elsewhere to rehabilitate the manpower employed today in this sector could be undertaken. Cess on tobacco has been imposed and is being collected to rehabilitate the beedi workers particularly. But how many consumers and beedi workers know about the rightful utilization of this cess is unknown.

Another solution to tobacco-curb lay with the consumers themselves by making the 'phase out' demand a spectacle and an election issue. Realisation has to be drilled deep into the minds of consumers that tobacco is a consumer issue and must be addressed with all seriousness.

Advocates and Consumer Courts

Last but not the least is the issue of forcing lawyers on consumers by the consumer courts. Consumer complaints are simple to resolve for which no lawyer is required. *Jago Grahak, Jago* has carried the message again and again that there is no need of engaging a lawyer, but it has no impact on the functioning of consumer courts.

It will be a good idea if a country-wide study is made on the types of complaints resolved at the levels of District Forum, State Commission and National Commission in the last five years for determining the roles of lawyers—whether their presence was required or not and the issue of undue adjournments. There is no hesitation in saying that the lead is taken by the National Commission which has even removed the consumers' rest room and provided one air-conditioned room for the Advocates' Bar. This is discriminatory and must be protested by all VCOs. Our short-term mission will be achieved if the Government of India firms up its industrial, commercial, agricultural, and environmental policies by making Consumer Protection-friendly so as to enable the consumers to access the market without fear of being cheated. These are small suggestions to strengthen the consumer movement. But if these steps are taken the benefit to the consumers will be immense. These suggestions are based on the authors decades of experience as an activist in the field of consumer protection, education and awareness.

Prevailing market practice which is that the retailer is charging consumers MRP + VAT, i.e. ₹ 1000+120 = ₹1120 instead of ₹ 1015 putting consumer to a net loss of ₹ 105. The Department of Trade and Taxes of Delhi Government says that the retailer can charge VAT on MRP. Exception is in the case of medicines which are presently exempted from application of Packaged Commodity Rules. The Packaged Commodity Rule 2(r)[2] says that the MRP is inclusive of all taxes, and the Department of Consumer Affairs in the Government of India vouches the same, whereas the Department of Trade and Taxes of Delhi Government says that the retailer can charge VAT on MRP. And, further, there are separate invoices for tax and retail. MRP inclusive of all taxes violates the very Right to Information enshrined in the Consumer Protection Act, 1986, and the solution lay in making the VAT charged transparent, accountable and VAT Scheme compliant.

NOTES

1. *The Times of India,* dated 13.09.2009.
2. The Standards of Weights and Measures (Packaged Commodities) Rules, 1977.

9
Food Standards in India: Need to Integrate with International Standards

Megha Neelakshi Katheria and *Pragya Singh*

Introduction

> "Amidst of an active propaganda machinery, controlled by the world's largest corporations constantly reassuring that consumerism is the path to happiness, governmental restraint of market excess is the cause of our distress, and economic globalization is both a historical inevitability and a boon to the human species, a consumer is a shopper who is sore about..."

This is a famous saying by David Edward which holds immense relevance in the modern context of globalization, liberalization and consumerism in India. Over the past decade the visibility of the forces of globalization all over the world cannot be denied. On going back in history it is seen that *Kautilya* in his treatise *Arthashastra* has made references to the concept of consumer protection against exploitation by the trade and industry relating to measurement and adulteration and punishment for these offences. Advancement in time-line along with the sky rocketing achievements of mankind in science and technology has also changed the species consumption patterns. The arena of consumption not only sees new products daily on the market shelves but also witnesses the fresh diaspora of complications of the modern consumer world.[1]

Today at the dawn of the new millennium in the era of globalisation the primary concern for every human being is the consumption of food. People at present are extremely conscious of their health and looks, both of which are highly dependent on the food consumed. The National Sample Survey Organization (NSSO) has computed the monthly per capita consumption expenditure during 2004 to find that rural Indians spend roughly 57 per cent on food-related items, while urban Indians spend 46 per cent. The statistics are even more surprising when it comes to the purchase of packaged food such beverages, refreshments and processed food. The same reports show that while rural India spends ₹ 37 on packaged food, which is 10 per cent of its food expenditure in the month, urban India on the other hand spends ₹ 101 which is roughly 20 per cent of its food expenditure.[2]

This change in the market trend for packaged food is also marked by a desire to be informed by a smart consumer. The population living on border poverty line is also increasingly making informed choices when it comes to food. They too have understood the meaning of nutritious and safe food in its holistic sense. One is now able to recognise stale or tasteless food at a glance and hence discards it immediately. People are conscious of the fact that any cure requires time and money which has to be endured along with deep suffering. This repugnant realization has awakened the consumers to the need of safe, pure and nutritious food.[3]

As a result of this developing countries are consciously focusing on food safety in order to cater to the growing realization of its potential impact on public health among the masses. The increasing scientific understanding of public health and the consequences of unsafe food amplified by the rapid global transmission of information regarding public health threats associated with food-borne and zoonotic diseases (such as E. coli, salmonella and H5N1virus) through various forms of media has alerted consumers to food safety risks and raised public health concerns in many developing countries.[4]

Hence while formulating national policies with regard to food quality standards the governments should take into account the domestic socio-economic scenario and accordingly adopt the standards as laid down by the Food and Agriculture Organization of the United Nations and the World Health Organization in Codex

Alimentarius or, in their absence, other generally accepted international food standards.[5]

What is CODEX?

The Codex Alimentarius (Latin for "food code" or "food book") is a collection of internationally recognized standards, codes of practice, guidelines and other recommendations relating to foods. food production and food safety. Its texts are developed and maintained by the Codex Alimentarius Commission, a body that was established in 1963 by the Food and Agriculture Organization of the United Nations (FAO) and the World Health Organization (WHO). The Commission's main aims are stated as being to protect the health of consumers and ensure fair practices in the international food trade. The Codex Alimentarius is recognized by the World Trade Organization as an international reference point for the resolution of disputes concerning food safety and consumer protection.[6]

Problems of Consumer

Meaning of Adulteration

Adulteration of food stuff has become one of the most formidable social problems of our times. This evil has deleterious effects on the health of people. It has often led to large human tragedies. Adulteration of food stuff is an activity in which a large number of trading men and business concerns are busily engaged in pursuits of easy money.[7] Adulteration in simple words is the mixing of something inferior or superior to any commodity which reduces its purity or makes it harmful for use. Any material which is or could be employed for the purposes of adulteration is called an adulterant. If an article of food is not of the quality demanded by the purchaser or is not of the quality which it purports or represents, it can be said to be adulterated. Section 2(ia) of the Prevention of Food Adulteration Act defines adulterants and further lays down the conditions that would amount to adulteration of food.[8] Adulteration of food stuff happen's everyday before our eyes but it is we who choose to turn blind towards it. The main offences under law relating to adulteration of food are:

1. Rendering food injuries to health.
2. Selling food not complying with food safety requirements.
3. Selling food not of the nature etc. demanded.
4. Falsely describing or presenting food[9].

Misbranded Food

The term "misbranded," as used in this chapter, applies to all drugs or articles of food, or articles which enter into the composition of food, the package or label of which bears any statement, design or device regarding such article or the ingredients or substances contained therein which is false or misleading in any particular, and to any food or drug product which is falsely branded as to the state, territory or country in which it is manufactured or produced.[10]

In *Public Prosecutor* v. *K. Satyanarayana* the sample of uddi pappu taken from the respondent's shop on analysis was found to contain 1.76 per cent of talc. Consequently the respondent was prosecuted under Section 2(ix)(d) read with Sections 7 and 16 for selling misbranded article of food. But the lower courts relying on Appendix B, A-18.06 of the Act acquitted the accused.

In *Kailash Chandra* v. *State of UP*, the applicant was convicted by the trial court for false and misleading statements in labels, because the quantum of salt found by the analyst was marginally in excess from the quantity shown on the label. In appeal, the applicant was acquitted of the charges as the excess being on the marginal and not harmful. It is clear from various cases that many of the accused get acquitted on revision by the higher courts on multifarious considerations.[11]

Genetically Modified Food

The facts and figures show that our country's population has crossed the 1 billion mark and more than 400 million people are living below the poverty line. Many people die a gruesomely starved death due to shortage of food and it is said that this is on account of our inability to produce food in sufficient quantities. This bitter truth is the driving force behind genetic engineering.

The modification done in genetically modified food is basically a change in the characters of a particular crop.[12] The most contentious debate around the world is whether GM foods are different in safety/nutritional value or not? Proponents of GM foods will swear that they are "just the same" as traditional ones but the gene manipulation behind the process is a clear departure from what farmers have been practicing.[13]

Consumers' Interest and Genetically Modified Food

An appropriate labelling system of genetically modified food is one of the cornerstones in resolving the current controversy concerning the application of biotechnology to food. The information regarding the GM food should be given explicitly on the label of the food product as it is a consumers basic right to know about the kind of food or food products that is about to be consumed so that one can make an informed choice with respect to safety and health.

FAO and WHO advocate the concept of Substantial Equivalence to address the safety evaluation of GM foods. This approach states that if a new food or food component is found to be substantially equivalent to an existing food or food component, it can be treated in the same manner with respect to safety. However, this equivalence to a traditional one is difficult to establish. One has to keep in mind that substantially equivalent is not the same as really equivalent.[14]

Prevention of Food Adulteration Act, 1954

The Prevention of Food Adulteration Act, 1954, is concerned with eradicating the evil of food adulteration which is rampant in the present times. To some extent the Act regulates consumer supplier relations. It tries to ensure that the food is prepared, packed and stored under sanitary conditions and accordingly made available to the people. The Law Commission of India found the Prevention of Food Adulteration Act, 1954 to be the most adequate statute which regulates a socio-economic offence with the special provisions required for combating these offences.[15] In fact the problem here lies not with the lack of the arenas regarding food safety that it covers but the wider interpretation given both in terms of powers conferred and the scope of the law laid down.

Drawbacks

Mandatory Procedures

Under Section 13(2) of the Act, the accused has the right to get the samples tested at the Central Food Laboratory. The stringent procedure laid down along with a mandate makes the requirement of sealing, fastening and dispatch of the samples compulsory. Even a slight glitch in the procedure followed such as incorrect sampling, delay in the delivery of report to the accused, damaged samples and even the question of the authenticity of the report by the public analyst are seen under the view of the frustration of the rights of the accused.

Under Section 13(4) of the Act, the certificate issued by the CFL Director supersedes the report of the public analyst. If the report is in favour of the accused then he or she is discharged immediately. The fact of the matter is that the path from the laboratory to the courtroom is a long way during the course of transit the report often gets tampered as money changes hands. Hence the accused manage to delay the trials by resorting to these errors which makes the entire trial a lengthy affair.

Statutory Interpretations

The statute lays down rigid standards as a result of which even the slightest deviation or non-compliance with these standards would attract prosecution. However, this does not render the food article "adulterated" as such. For instance, if the defendants plead that the food article was not "meant for human consumption" he could not be held guilty for the crime of adulteration. This shows that manufacture and storage of such articles is not prohibited unless they specifically sold or attempted for sale for human consumption.[16] Under Section 19 of the Act, if the accused claims warranty, then he has committed no offence and can show receipts of sale to be discharged. This does seem to be logical since they bought the goods unknowingly and it was not their fault. However, in reality this is an easy recourse to acquittal. Another recourse that the manufacturers often adopt is that of denial which ensures that the trial is delayed.

The Act does not define or govern certain products such as energy drinks which began manufacturing post the enforcement of the Act. Manufacturers use this loophole to challenge the categorization of the product as a carbonated drink.[17] They claim that energy drinks are non-alcoholic proprietary food and the Act does not lay specific standards and regulations for proprietary food products except that their labels ought to display nutritional content of the product.

Judicial Interpretations

Northan v. *Raj*[18] the food inspector purchased from the appellant some chilly powder which was found to be containing ash 8.38 per cent by weight. The accused was acquitted by the Apex Court on the ground that there was margin of error in the test analysis. On the other hand, in *Gauranga Aich* v. *Assam*[19] addition of salt to chilly powder was held to be adulteration in the view that the "quality and purity of the article had fallen." Another paradoxical judgment is that of *Kailash Chandra* v. *State of Maharashtra* where in the accused was acquitted by the High Court despite the presence of salt in slight excess from the quantity shown in the label. In *Raj Kumar* v. *UP*[20] a *heeng* sample was found to be adulterated but the conviction by the lower Court was reversed by the High Court. In a number of cases the benefit of doubt doctrine has been used to grant acquittal.[21] Generally legal "technicalities" have prevented conviction. Minor excesses are overseen and technical lapses by the prosecution prove fatal to conviction of the accused. An overview of the judicial decisions under the Act reveals that the trend of the courts has been to interpret it in ways that allow successful prosecution.[22]

Suggestions

Single Food Law and Enforcing Agencies

The multiplicity and complexity of the laws that govern this sector gives rise to multiple harassment and corrupt practices. Keeping this in view, there should be only one law governing the quality of food products and a single enforcement body.

Redefining Terms

The laws as well as certain terms need to be relooked at and reframed so as to remove the ambiguities and avoid the various possibilities of interpretation. This will ensure that the judiciary does enter into too many technical interpretations which many a times leads to acquittals.

Fixation of Time Limit

In most cases, the trial takes around five years to release a judgment. By the time the trial gets over the sample spoils and hence has to be destroyed. Many accused get discharged on some similar ground or the other. The law should frame a maximum time limit for all the adulteration cases to avoid lengthy trials.

Gradation of Punishment

Gradation of punishments for adulteration and misbranding offences should be according to the severity of offence. The fine imposed must ideally be based on the turnover of the company.[23]

Systematic Procedure for Sample Collection

Though the department does take cognizance of different factors while going for sample collection, they are not effectively followed and the samples are largely drawn on lottery basis. The department should take more samples from the street vendors, as the percentage of adulteration in their samples is high. Inspection of food items should be done at the manufacturing point, as it is there that adulteration cases generally start.

Allocation of Funds and Equipments for Laboratories

Most of these shortcomings, including too few and under-equipped laboratory facilities for analyzing food samples and a shortage of food inspectors, are a direct result of the limited funds allocated to implementing the Act. The apparatus for enforcement is also inadequate. Other suggestions for improved government enforcement suffer from the same shortcomings: dependence on government financing and implementation by a somewhat corrupt bureaucracy. Licensing and inspection at all levels of the food distribution chain would be expensive and cumbersome.[24] Requiring standardized packaging is impractical and too costly in this economy.

Food Safety and Standards Act, 2006

The food sector is governed by various laws each complimenting and supplementing the other, including the previously examined prevention of Food Adulteration Act which aimed to safeguard the health of the Indian consumer. However, due to variations in the specifications, standards and pragmatic administration by the different Ministries of the various laws there emerged implementation hurdles and apathy towards safety standards. The sector faced problems as different products were governed by different laws and Ministries making the implementation of laws all the more haphazard and hence an urgent need was felt to consolidate these laws into one uniform code.

President, APJ Abdul Kalam in his address to the Parliament in 2005 also emphasized on the need for a single integrated food law to replace the myriad of laws that were stalling the growth of this sector.[25] The view was echoed by in the report by the Standing Committee of Parliament on Agriculture in its 12th Report submitted in April 2005.[26] Subsequently the Ministry of Food Processing Industries (MoFPI) took a keen interest in the drafting of the food bill with the aim to consolidate and integrate the existing food laws. The President of India signed the Bill on August 23, 2006 and was finally enacted as, The Food Safety and Standards Act, 2006 (No. 34 of 2006). The Government of India notified the enactment in the Official Gazette on August 24, 2006.[27]

This Act consolidates the laws relating to food and establishes the Food Safety and Standards Authority of India (FSSA) with the purpose of laying down "science-based standards for articles of food and to regulate their manufacture, storage, distribution, sale and import, to ensure availability of safe and wholesome food for human consumption." It also aims to establish a single reference point for all matters relating to food safety and standards, by moving from multi-level, multi-departmental control to a single line of command.

The FSSA regulates the use of food additives, processing aid, contaminants, heavy metals, insecticides, antibiotics and certain other residues. The FSSA also constitutes scientific panels and scientific committees to address various technical issues such as food additives, pesticides and antibiotics, genetically modified foods, functional foods, biological hazards, contaminants, labelling and methods of sampling.[28]

The Act makes it mandatory for every business food operator to hold a licence which is to be issued by the Designated Officer.[29] It is also required by the distributor of a food article to identify the manufacturer or the seller of a food item.[30] Food products such as genetically modified food products, organic food, health supplements and proprietary foods cannot be manufactured, stored, processed or sold unless they adhere to the regulations of the Act. The designated officer mentioned before is to be appointed by the State Commissioner of Food Safety.[31] The DO has the power to cancel licences, prohibit the sale of any food article, serve an "improvement notice" and investigate complaints against food safety officers.

The Act also provides for the food recall procedures an aspect that was absent in the Prevention of Food Adulteration Act,1954. Henceforth, if a food business operator considers the food item to be unsafe and not in compliance with the specified standards he can initiate procedures to withdraw the food article in question and inform the competent authorities accordingly.[32]

Drawbacks

The unorganized/informal sector includes a large number of street food vendors, hawkers and also certain small scale industries. Unorganized food sector would face difficulties in following the rules laid since the rules are uniform for both the organized and unorganized sector especially with rules regarding specifications on ingredients, traceability and recall procedures.[33] The application of the same regulations and procedures is impractical especially in short term. The road side hawkers are generally illiterate and shall not realize or know about the regulations and procedures that are supposed to be followed and mostly lack the supportive systems required for providing the food to the levels prescribed. With regards to labelling laws it would be very difficult for a small entrepreneur to print such detailed information as an MNC may. Also the term adulterant is defined as "any material which is or could be employed for making the food unsafe or sub-standard, mis-branded or containing extraneous matter."[34] It holds a very wide connotation which may work against many of the small entrepreneurs.

What needs to be addressed here is not a high "quality" of food but basic hygiene and cleanliness for which efforts shall have to be made to provide them with the necessary supportive systems.

The bill remains silent on the definition for water. As examined under the Prevention of Food Adulteration Act, 1954 the definition of food either needs to be expanded to include water or the term it self needs to be defined so that quality checks can be imposed on this too. Although standards are specified for water used as an input in manufacture/preparation of food, the Act does not require any specific standards for potable water.[35] There is a need to bring the word 'water' under the definition of food so as to ensure the availability of potable water as well as use of quality water in the manufacture of other products. For instance, in the case of the aerated drinks wherein top notch companies such as Coca-Cola and Pepsi were accused for the use of toxic pesticides, one of the major loopholes was that while the Act prescribed that potable water must be used for the manufacture of aerated drinks it did not define "potable water".[36]

The Act also mentions certain terms like 'Food Safety Management System' whose definition calls for adoption of 'Good Manufacturing Practices', 'Good Hygienic Practices' and 'Hazard Analysis and Critical Control Point'. However, it is not clear from the Act what these terms imply and whether the CODEX definition of such terms is to be followed.[37]

The bill does not cover the area of pre-production such as prior harvesting and animal feed. Hence, the amount of pesticide and antibiotics that enter into food at its source cannot be regulated.[38] It will be difficult for processing industries to take the onus for ensuring that such standards are within the acceptable levels in processed food when raw material fails to meet these standards. Also unlike other countries in India home-cooked food is a major source of consumption and hence the need to have quality raw materials increases even more. Another point to be noted is its effect on the consumption of genetically modified food. The law does not make the labelling of GM foods mandatory[39] and since GM food, the seeds and crops, are not covered by this law while it is proven that GM food majorly affects consumer's health and food safety.

The local level officer, i.e. the DO has been given the power to suspend any food operator's licence[40] or institute inquiry or even ban the sale of some product. This wide ambit of the power gives the DO the scope to harass the food operators and opens the doors for corruption. The Bill does not specify details about labelling, and leaves it to the regulations which will be issued by the FSSA. However, there is a view that certain items are important enough to be specified in the Bill such as labels identifying Genetically Modified Food and labels detailing nutrition content in packaged food.

In case of recall procedures, the Bill does not require the food business operator to inform consumers about a product recall, especially if some of the products have already been sold. The information has to be conveyed only to competent authority. This is unfair for those consumers who have already purchased the goods unknowingly and may even suffer damages.

With regard to the Codex guidelines, traceability of an article covers the whole chain from the farm to the consumer. However, in India, many items such as grain and vegetables are sold at *mandi* (wholesale) markets.[41] If a food product contains grain or vegetables with pesticides above the permitted level, it would not be possible to trace back the contaminant beyond the *mandi*. This makes it difficult to take any corrective action in this regard. With respect to the composition of the FSSA there must be adequate representation of authority in this autonomous body. There should be a wider representation from various industry sectors (such as fruit and vegetables; meat and poultry products; milk and milk products; marine products; pickles and jams) as well as from restaurants and street vendors. Only one member each from a consumer organization and agribusiness companies have been slated to be on the Authority.[42] However, a valid counterpoint to this would be that a regulatory should not have people from business since that would result in conflict of interest and hence should comprise independent experts and bureaucrats.

Another criticism of the Act is that unlike the Prevention of Food Adulteration Act, 1954 which is socio-legal Act, the Food

Safety and Standards Act, 2006 aims to be a science based regulation and hence serves to the benefit of the industry. Since Industry has always aimed to use the controversies and uncertainties of scientific findings as an excuse to stymie tough regulatory standards the Act only furthers their purpose. The objectives of the proposed food laws appear to be directed at eliminating the competition from informal food sector including the *dhabas* and tiffin carriers which pose a threat to the agribusiness companies.[43] As long as food is being sold at such cheap prices, the agribusiness companies will find it difficult to gain a strong foothold in the Indian market. This is probably because the food laws are being prepared in consultancy with the agribusiness consultants and officials.

Conclusion

Consumers have sought protection through legislation because the general laws and market forces had failed to provide it. By the time market forces have time to operate, far too many consumers are dead, maimed, or impoverished.[44] The Indian food industry is single handedly ruled by multinationals as a result of which many local players have been eliminated. In the absence of domestic players, the Indian consumers are forced to buy products of multinationals priced at exorbitant rates. In such circumstances the dire need to protect their health and ensure safety becomes an even more important arrangement. Strange as it may seem, most consumers do not even know that the law is on their side. Certainly, if consumers perceive certain goods as hazardous they will not choose this alternative. Consequently, there will be a strong motivation for reputable business to observe high commercial standards of behaviour. It is for the consumers to enforce the provisions of law by vitalizing enforcement. The machinery is available but it has to be used effectively.

The present challenge before the Ministry of Food Processing is first to build up consumer confidence before embarking on its path to 'harmonize' food laws.[45] At the same time there is an urgent need to step up monitoring of food imports. It is a well-known fact that much of the agricultural commodities and food imports into India are of poor quality. Ground realities need to be fixed before the full implementation of Act. Quality control mechanisms need to be put in place and the focus should be amended from protecting the commercial interests of the agribusiness companies.

The Food Safety and Standards Act, 2006 is a competent Act but not devoid of its own flaws. The government must ensure that the interests of small entrepreneurs, farmers and the consumers are not compromised. The provisions must not adversely affect the innocent manufacturers for some of the stringent provisions, apt for the giant companies, would impose high penalties on him for no fault of his. The laws that were in force in the West cannot be directly applied in India. They should be taken as a standard and be adhered to while keeping in view the economic conditions of domestic manufacturers, food habits and lifestyles of people. Laws should be made more flexible in terms of procedures. The law should recognize the distinction between sub-standard food and adulterated food. It is also practically impossible to infuse costly technology into the food industry all of a sudden.

We believe that more tough guidelines are required because there are always two sides of a coin, each instance of Consumer affairs could be easily termed as another 'Consumer mistreatment'. Within a nation-state, national laws may prevent some of this harm, but once national boundaries are crossed, their effectiveness is limited, and consumers can hope for very limited protection.[46] If such trade proliferates and consumer fraud becomes a major problem, nation-states and commercial interests that provide access then fairly restricted action may be taken to curb unacceptable and deleterious practices.

NOTES

1. Pankaj Bansiwal & Jitendra Bansiwal, *Consumerism in the Globalized World*, http://www.legalserviceindia.com/article/l75-Consumerism- in-the-Globalized-world.html, Last Accessed on 30th September, 2009.
2. Report no. 454, "Household Consumer Expenditure in India, 1999-2000", (Ministry of Statistics and Programme Implementation—Government of India).
3. Mary Katherine Schmidl and Theodore P. Labuza, *Essentials of functional food*, 1st ed. 2000, pp. 99-118.
4. Dina Umali and Mona Sur, *Food safety in globalized economy: opportunities and challenges for India*, (paper presented at International Association of Agricultural Economist Conference, Australia, held on August 12-18, 2006).

5. United Nations Guidelines for Consumer Protection.
6. http://www.codexalimentarius.net/web/index_en.jsp (last visited on 27th September, 2009).
7. United Nations Food and Agriculture Organization Report on Food Adulteration in India (May 1975).
8. Section 2 (I a) of Prevention of Food Adulteration Act,1954.
9. *Supra,* n 7.
10. http://delcode.delaware.gov/title16/c033/index.shtml (last visited on 28th September, 2009).
11. V.K. Aggarwal, *Consumer Protection Law,* 5th ed., 2003, pp. 345-356.
12. http://www.consumer-voice.org/Department/food/gmfood.asp (last visited on 26th September, 2009).
13. *Supra,* n 8.
14. http://www.consumer-voice.org/Department/food/gmfood13.asp (last visited on 26th September, 2009).
15. The Law Commission of India, Report on the Trial and Punishment of Social and Economic Offences (Forty-seventh Report) pp. 125-144 (1972).
16. Kumar Gaurav and Mayank Singhal, Delhi's Food: How Safe?, http://www.ccsindia.org/ccsindia/interns2003/chap3.pdf, Last accessed on September 30, 2009.
17. Nidhi Jamwal, "Caffeine hits energy drinks", Down to Earth, May 15, 2009, http://www.downtoearth.org.in/full6.asp?foldername=20090515&filename=news&sec_id=4&sid=1, (Last accessed September 30, 2009).
18. 1995 Cri. L.J. 2661.
19. 1990 2 F AC 41.
20. 2001 Cri. LJ 2093 (All.)
21. *Ghansu* v. *MP,* 1999 Cri LJ 2843 (Mad).
22. The Law Commission of India, Proposal to Include Certain Social and Economic Offences in the Indian Penal Code (Twenty-ninth Report) 72 (1966); Prem Varma, Law of Adulteration and Pollution 10 A.S.I.L 89 (1974).
23. *Supra* n.16, at p. 33.
24. A'an M. Katz, "The Law against Food Adulteration", *Journal of Indian Law Institute,* Vol.19, 1977, p. 73.
25. APJ Abdul Kalam, Address to the First session of Union Parliament, 17th February, 2003, http://archives.indiainfoline.com/bu05/apjk.html, (Last accessed on 30th September, 2009).
26. M.R. Madhavan and Kaushiki Sanyal, PRS Legislative Brief on Food Safety and Standards Act, 2006, India Together, http://www.indiatogether.org/2006/feb/law-foodsafe.htm, (Last Accessed 30th September, 2009).
27. The Ministry of Food Processing Industries. Industry Specific

Information, http://mofpi.nic.in/industryspecificinformation/index.htm. (Last Accessed 30th September (2009).
28. *Supra*, n 26.
29. Section 31(3) of Food Safety and Standards Act, 2006.
30. *Supra*, n 26.
31. See Section 30(3) of Food Safety and Standards Act, 2006.
32. Section 28 of the Food Safety and Standards Act, 2006.
33. *Supra* n. 26.
34. 'Hasty' implementation of new law on food safety opposed, *The Hindu*,5th August, 2009, Madurai, http://www.thehindu.com/2009/08/05/stories/2009080555500200.htm, (Last accessed 30th September, 2009).
35. M. Prasad Palthur, S.S. Sajala Palthur, Suresh Kumar Chitta, "The Food Safety and Standards Act, 2006: A Paradigm Shift in Indian Regulatory Scenario.", *Pharmaceutical Review Articles*, Vol. 7 Issue 5, http://www.pharmainfo.net/reviews/food-safety-and-standards-act-2006-paradigm-shift-indian-regulatory-scenario, (Last Accessed 30th September, 2009).
36. Gaurav Choudhury, *"Crippling Colas"*, *The Tribune*, August 13, 2003, http://www.tribuneindia.com/2003/20030816/windows/main1.htm, (Last Accessed 30th September, 2009).
37. *Supra*, n. 35.
38. *Supra*, n. 35.
39. *Supra*, n. 26.
40. Section 31(4) of Food Safety and Standards Act, 2006.
41. *Supra*, n. 26.
42. Devinder Sharma, "Food Safety bill may Hurt Hawkers", *India Together*, 10th February, 2005, http://www.indiatogether.org/2005/feb/dsh-safefood.htm, (Last Accessed 30th September, 2009).
43. *Ibid*, n. 42.
44. *Supra*, n. 1.
45. *Supra*, n. 42.
46. *Supra*, n. 1.

REFERENCES

A Treatise on Consumer Protection Law, A book by the Indian Law Institute, Delhi.

Alan M. Katz, The Law against Food Adulteration, *Journal of Indian Law Institute*, Vol. 19, 1977.

Kumar Gaurav and Mayank Singhal, *Delhi's Food: How Safe?*, CCSINDIA.

M.R. Madhavan and Kaushiki Sanyal, PRS Legislative Brief on Food Safety and Standards Act, 2006, *India Together*.

M. Prasad Palthur, S.S. Sajala Palthur, Suresh Kumar Chitta, "The Food

Safety and Standards Act, 2006: A Paradigm Shift In Indian Regulatory Scenario.", *Pharmaceutical Review Articles*, Vol. 7, Issue 5.

Mary Katherine Schmidl and Theodore P. Labuza, *Essentials of functional food*.

Pankaj Bansiwal & Jitendra Bansiwal, "Consumerism in the Globalized World", *Legal Service India*.

Paper food safety in globalized economy

Prem Varma, *Law of Adulteration and Pollution* 10 A.S.I.L 89 (1974).

Ronaldo porto nacedo jr, "Globalization, Regulation and Consumer Law", (islandia.law.yale.edu/sela/macedoe.pdf)

S. Sivakumar, "Central Legislations", *Annual Survey of Indian Law*, vol. XLII, 2006.

The Law Commission of India, *Proposal to Include Certain Social and Economic Offences in the Indian Penal Code* (Twenty-ninth Report) 72 (1966).

The Law Commission of India, *Report on the Trial and Punishment of Social and Economic Offenses* (Forty-seventh Report) 125-144 (1972).

UN guidelines for Consumer Protection.

United Nations Food and Agriculture Organization Report on *Food Adulteration in India* (May 1975).

V.K. Aggarwal, *Consumer Protection Law*, 5th ed., 2003.

www.ccsindia.org

www.codexalimentarius.net

www.consumer-voice.org

www.delcode.delaware.gov

www.downtoearth.org

www.indiatogether.org

www.legalserviceindia.com

www.mofpi.nic.in

www.thehindu.com

www.tribuneindia.com

10
Expanding Media Market, Shrinking Consumer Choice

D.S. Poornananda

Introduction

The growth of media in the last two decades has been unprecedented. Media ownership and control have changed drastically. This has implications for democracy and public discourse. By providing accounts of the contemporary world and images the media plays a pivotal role in shaping social consciousness. The media are important in a situation where most of the citizens never meet their fellow citizens and the media serve as a kind of proxy.[1] They provide a link to the larger society and in varying degrees a sense of connectedness and solidarity. They not only provide information and entertainment but also play a central role in working of democracies. They create what Habermas[2] calls 'public sphere'[3] enabling discussion and debate on issues vital to the community. A society can claim to be democratic only when people make informed choices. If citizens cannot make informed choices they will be led to badly formed choices.[4]

The public has to know what is going on and the options that they should weigh, debate and act upon. If they are wrongly or inadequately informed about the choices they may make, may not be in their own interest or in the best interest of democracy. A public sphere works well when there is a wide range of media. The crucial factor is that there are no restrictions on the range of choices available to the media consumers. 'Uses and gratifications' approach assumes that people are relatively active communication participants who choose media or content.[5] People take the initiative in selecting and using communication vehicles to satisfy felt needs or desires.[6] Media use may not only be a response to basic needs, but may also satisfy wants or interests such as seeking information to solve a personal dilemma. People intentionally participate and select media or messages from communication alternatives in response to their expectations (Katz, Blumler, and Gurevitch[7]). Using media and gratifying one's needs is possible only when true choices are available to the media consumers.

The choices that the uses and gratifications approach sees are hardly found in a market dominated by huge media corporations. Studies have shown that the media has lost diversity and ability to present different points of view. Instead, there is homogeneity of news and a regurgitation of the same news stories on every channel and headline. Media conglomerates encourage popular tastes to become more uniform.[8] They have argued that television blurs traditional social distinctions, blends otherwise divergent groups into the mainstream and bends the mainstream in the direction of the medium's interests in profit, populist politics and power. Multiplicity of TV channels is not an expansion of viewers' choice; it is expansion of advertisers' space.[9]

The first person to see rapid decline of choices to the media consumers was Upton Sinclair, best known for his book *The Jungle* (1906), which exposed labour and sanitary conditions in the Chicago stockyards. Sinclair made a systematic and damning critique of the severe limitations of the "free press" in his book *The Brass Check* (1919). It was a groundbreaking critique of the structural basis of U.S. journalism, arguably the first such systematic critique ever made. Sinclair explained the predicament of the media audience in a four-part systemic model emphasizing the importance of owners, advertisers, public relations, and the web of economic interests tied into the media system, and invested in its control of public opinion.

In fact, many of the concerns Sinclair had about commercial journalism did not disappear with the rise of professionalism and "objectivity"—a development he witnessed and regarded with disdain as a sham solution.[10] Moreover, as commercial pressures on the integrity of journalism have intensified over the past two decades, much of Sinclair's critique now appears startlingly accurate. Researchers such as Todd Gitlin, Herbert Schiller, Gaye Tuchman, Ben Bagdikian, Michael Parenti, Herman and Chomsky have continued his tradition of media criticism. They have shown incompatibility between a corporate run news media and the rights of the audience.

Several decades ago a major city might have ten to twenty daily newspapers, or more, each representing a distinct political viewpoint. No single paper dominated the market, and if someone was dissatisfied with the existing range of viewpoints, it was not impossible to launch a new newspaper. The market was relatively competitive. All that changed by the late twentieth century as newspaper markets became vastly less competitive. The "barriers to entry" have made it much more difficult for new entrepreneurs to find competitors. Advertising has become the largest source of revenue which has greatly enhanced the concentration process. Advertisers tend to flock to the paper or papers that offer the most readers at the lowest "cost per thousand". This tends to drive marginal papers out of business, strengthening the monopolies.

Content choices and open space for discussion are hard to find in the monopolistic media. The agenda-setting hypothesis[11] argues that ideas and images that mass media disseminates largely determine what citizens think about and the importance they give to the issues. Studies have shown that those problems that receive prominent attention in the media become the problems the audience regards as the most important. The agenda that the dominant media sets may not have anything to do with the issues that the ordinary confront everyday.

A few corporations that dominate media market build up a dominant discourse leading to widening of the 'spiral of silence' on issues critical to the people.[12] Because of people's fear of isolation or separation from those around them, they tend to keep their attitudes to themselves when they think they are in minority. The media controlled by the dominant economic forces tend to present one side of an issue to the exclusion of others which encourages those people to keep quiet without registering their apposing viewpoint. If various viewpoints about an issue are ignored, marginalised, or trivialized by media reports, then people will be reluctant to talk about them. As the time passes, those viewpoints will cease to be heard in public and therefore, cannot have impact upon political decision-making (Herman and Chomsky, 1988). Instead of encouraging people to speak the corporate media silence them.

Growing Media Empires

Before the 1990s, media systems in many countries were largely composed of domestically owned radio, television and newspaper industries. A global commercial media market began emerging in the 1990s. Radical improvements in communication technology have made global media empires feasible and lucrative in a manner unthinkable in the past.[13] As one of the world's largest and fastest growing industries, mass communications shares the characteristics of the other fields of enterprise to which it often has important economic links.

Concentration is a universal feature of today's industrial world. In the oil, automotive, soap, tobacco and drug industries, a smaller number of companies wield ever-greater market power. Propelled by growing capital requirements and by the incessant demands of capital markets for larger profits companies in every field or enterprise buy out, merge and consolidate. They cut deals with competitors, seek to preempt or crowd out upstart rival, exploit new technologies, identify and co-opt new ideas and fresh talent. With corporate profits increasingly dominating decisions concentration of ownership endangers plurality, diversity, risk taking and dissent.[14]

When Ben Bagdikian examined growing concentration of media ownership in his book 'The Media Monopoly', in 1983, he had found that 50 corporations controlled half or more of the media business. By the time he published his 2000 edition, the number had fallen below ten. The number came to 29 in 1987, 23 in 1990, 14 in 1992, 10 in 1997, 6 in 2000 and 5 in 2004. Only five media corporations—AOL Time-Warner, News Corporation, Disney, Bertelsmann and Viacom—account for more than half of the media business. These five largest media firms are major producers of information, entertainment and media software and have global distribution network[15]. The media industry had never witnessed such vertical integration before. There is now a phenomenon of the single owner paying money to the writer of the novel in the form of book advance and royalties, and then paying the screenwriter to write the feature film which is produced at the owner's studio. The owner's magazine does features about actors, producers, directors and other celebrities to promote the movie, while his television network that has the late night talk show on which these folks appear as guests. He owns the theatres in which the movie is shown, the cable networks on which the rerun is provided, the pay-per-view services where people watch it in hotels and the video rental stores where others go to rent it. This has created the possibility of an incredible multi-media, multi-national hype of a product which left on its own might very well have gone nowhere. A few such media firms dominate what we read in books, see in feature films, read in magazine articles and so forth.

This trend towards media concentration is linked to the spread of neo-liberal economics, technological developments and the emergence of global and regional agreements on multi-lateral trade.[16] The emergence of such a highly concentrated media system in the hands of a few huge concerns violates the basic principle of a free market in any liberal democracy.

Corporate media depends on advertising revenue and must, therefore, compete for advertisers' attention and serve advertisers' interest to prosper. In fact the prime objective of media is to deliver affluent consumers to advertisers. Advertisers decide what people should see or read. Audience service is a mean, not an end. Everything works within a framework of private cost and benefit calculations. They exclude materials that the audience might want to watch but which might stir up controversy objectionable to advertisers. Advertisers don't support media that regularly criticize their products or discuss corporate wrongdoing. This results in a preference for entertainment over controversy, serious political debate, and discussions and documentaries that dig deeply, inform, and challenge conventional opinion.[17] There is more entertainment but little useful information. Surveys conducted during the wars have shown more television news coverage of the war people watched, less they knew about the war and more they supported the government policy.[18]

Those who defend commercial media argue that the market gives people what they want. Whether the market for mass communication is exactly comparable to the market for toothpaste, chocolates or other consumer products, in which the manufacturers either make what the public will buy or perish, is a big question. The consumption of ideas and images are different from the consumption of goods. The ideas and images that mass media disseminate shape collective life, form social values and determine the course of history. The information that individual absorbs becomes part of the culture that everyone shares in ways that have different consequences than choices in toothpaste or soft drinks. The fact is that the most important transaction in the media marketplace does not involve media companies selling content to audiences, but rather media companies selling audiences to sponsors. Market forces could conceivably cripple the media performance of watchdog function. Profit-oriented pressures could lead media entities to abandon expensive, investigative journalism and replace it with cheaper and routine beat reporting.

Forces resisting market domination are too few and too weak. Within the developing countries including India, citizens' resistance to domination of media market can hardly be seen except for the sporadic protests by some social activists and fundamentalist groups. Since media activism is still in its infancy it is difficult to say for sure what course it will take.

The Myth of Competition

The present media system is not the result of free markets or natural law; it is the consequence of a number of important state policies and manipulation of the market by giant corporations.[19] Media corporations have greatly benefited from subsidies, and favourable regulations. The largest media firms are all built on top of the profits generated by government gifts of monopoly rights to broadcasting spectrum or monopoly cable franchises.

Media industries are barely competitive in the economic sense of the term. These major media conglomerates are often more cooperative than competitive, with an increasing number of strategic alliances and joint ventures. Given the small number of media players, there is very little competition in the media industry and the major media companies use a variety of strategies to try to reduce the limited competition that does exist. Inter-corporate investments and interlocking of directorships between the media companies have been common. The giants do compete ferociously, but they do so under the oligopolistic markets, meaning they have far greater control over their fate than those in truly competitive markets. It means that it is extremely difficult, if not impossible, for newcomers to enter these markets as viable players.

Such a concentration of media power into few hands is disastrous for the free marketplace of ideas, the bedrock upon which informed self-government rests. The concept of free market of ideas presupposes that every type of idea will get into the market. If free access is denied to any idea then the competition of ideas becomes limited. The key to making markets work in the consumers' interest is that they should be open to newcomers, but the present conglomerate dominated markets are not even remotely competitive in the traditional sense of the term.[20]

The constitutional provisions with regard to free speech protect an idea when it comes into the market but have been indifferent in creating opportunities for its expression. There is a romantic notion of freedom of speech that the market place is freely accessible.[21] The constitutional issue generally is whether the expression already uttered should be given protection, not creation of an environment in which citizens can freely express themselves. Thus the constitutional imperative of free expression becomes the very instrument of repression of competitive ideas. There should not only be protection of expression after publication but also for its emergence by publication. But the media system dominated by a few firms hinders emergence of newer voices of expression. An established newspaper with large circulation has a stable volume of advertising revenue. Starting a new newspaper requires huge investment. One should have the ability to absorb losses for a period of one or two years. Those who cannot mobilize huge capital cannot enter the market because newspaper is a product that is sold at a price far below the cost of production.

Price cuts set new entry barriers by making it unattractive for new players, make newspapers vulnerable to pressure by advertisers, threaten the survival of smaller newspapers and in the long run affect the media's diversity and plurality.[22] Throughout the twentieth century, not more than a few upstart newspapers have successfully entered established markets.

More importantly, the price war will result in concentration of more power in the hands of only those newspaper owners who have the financial strength to withstand the effects of a prolonged price-cutting strategy. This will block arrival of new newspapers and marginalize other newspapers forcing some of the weaker newspapers to close down. For a healthy and vibrant democracy, it is not only important to have a free press—free from both governmental and corporate control—it is also essential to have as many different views on any subject as possible. Inevitably, a price war of the kind being witnessed in India can result in a loss of diversity and pluralism. Many small newspapers representing different voices are closing down in the wake of big newspapers cutting prices and launching district editions full of local news.[23] The district editions with localised advertising have become money spinners for the publishers (Sinha, 2002). The strong moral and creative impulses that fire journalism have been subordinated to the demands of the quarterly earnings statement.

Everyone has equal opportunity to put forward his opinions only when a truly free market exists. Newcomers should have an opportunity to start new publication with fair chance of achieving success. Fixing a minimum price at which newspapers of a particular size could be sold was suggested as an effective measure to bring about an atmosphere of fair competition by the First Press Commission and the Second Press Commission. But these suggestions have come into conflict with the constitutional guarantee of freedom of speech and expression[24]. Over the years revenue from circulation has been decreasing while the revenue from advertising has been increasing. The newspapers that are dependent on advertising revenue may have no obligation to be responsive to readers' needs and interests.

Democratization of Media

There have been movements around the world for media reform which have been stressing on media independent of both state and private control. One of the measures needed for democratization of media is imposition of restrictions on cross media ownership[25]. Since corporate control of the media is the biggest hurdle to the democratization of communication it is important to look for alternatives that provide space for all. Media democratization expands the range of voices accessed through the media, builds an egalitarian and participatory public sphere, promotes the values and practices of sustainable democracy outside the media, and/or within the media, and offsets the political and economic inequalities found elsewhere in the social system. Autonomous and non-profit entities can provide alternatives to market-driven or exclusively governmentally dominated media systems. There is a burgeoning global grassroots resistance of individuals, groups and organizations who perceive their interests ignored, damaged and threatened by the commercialization of the media and communication. The non-commercial media has the potential of providing diverse news and opinions.[26] There are communication technologies which can help democratize media in a manner unimaginable some decades ago.

Community radio has emerged as an alternative medium that is developing into a tool of participatory communication. Since it is cost-efficient, it can be used for disseminating information among the marginalized, especially in developing countries. Its language and content can be made most suited to local needs. It is also relevant to local practices, traditions and culture.

After the initial investment is made, sustainability of the project is feasible, and community participation can be depended on. In terms of outreach and geographic coverage too, radio has a strong advantage. The convergence between radio and internet is providing new strengths to community and has enormously increased networking opportunities.

Non-profit and development organizations have been lobbying in India to get affordable permission to broadcast information that could help the "information poor" get an understanding of issues critical to their lives. An increasing number of communities in India are exploring whatever avenues are open to them to get their voices and messages heard. Communities are taking communication and information matters into their own hands and exercising greater control over their access and services. It is harder to democratize television because production and distribution costs are very high. But, proliferation of cable channels seems to hold forth new democratic possibilities. Many cable networks in Indian cities and towns provide programmes on local events and issues. Television cooperatives in Honduras that have installed cable systems and transmit programmes on community activities appear to be a possible way of democratizing television.

The fall in the price of video equipment has enabled amateur and semi-professionals to venture into video production. Their productions are distributed through cable systems and to organizations and groups for use in meetings, and public and private showings. There are thousands of non-governmental organizations, colleges and schools which seek alternative video programmes. An alternative video movement has sprung into existence to meet this demand. The *youtube* has provided unlimited opportunities for individuals and organizations to broadcast their videos.

The fact that the mainstream media are annoyed at the very idea of alternative media is evident in their reaction to a suggestion made by the Press Council of India[27] (PCI) in 1998. The Council identified private ownership of newspapers as one of the factors impeding press freedom and advocated a system of cooperative ownership as an alternative ownership structure. The Indian Newspaper Society (INS), the Forum of Newspaper Proprietors and Publishers, condemned PCI's suggestion and also complained to the Vienna-based International Press Institute (IPI) which advised the Press Council to refrain from "interfering in matters that should be determined by the market". The Council's argument was that the Constitution of India permitted cooperatives as it did individual proprietorships, partnership firms, trusts, companies and corporations. The Council suggested that *Jan Morcha* which is run by a cooperative in Faizabad for the last four decades could be a model. The paper has always fearlessly fought against the anti-people policies of the government and the vested interests. The paper has shown that cooperative ownership can shield newspapers from proprietary pressures. Although India has shining examples of well-run cooperatives there has not been a single nationally circulated newspaper or magazine brought out through cooperative effort.

Because of the Internet's ability to cheaply and quickly distribute vast amounts of information, in addition to its ability to facilitate communication, it has been described as the "new technology of democracy,"[28] capable of reinvigorating the depressed public sphere. Around the world democratic forces and insurgent groups have been able to bypass the media systems controlled by corporations and governments and communicate among themselves through the Internet. The Internet is providing a mechanism for individuals and groups marginalized by the commercial media system to communicate and share information quickly, in large quantity and on global basis. The Internet may serve as public space where the marginalized groups can practice their discourse before engaging in debate with dominant groups.[29] Internet petitions and symbolic web protests expand the range of political participation options open to citizens.

Since the Internet was originally established as a cooperative, non-hierarchical, communication system, it was designed to facilitate the sharing of information both between individuals and among groups of individuals. This capability, plus the fact that the underlying digital technology supports the whole gamut of multi-media communications, has made the Internet the first general purpose, interactive medium available to the average person. As such, it seems natural that it has a propensity to foster activity in the public sphere.

Although the Internet has the potential to provide a qualitative and egalitarian type of journalism, politics, media and culture colonization of cyberspace by state and economic interests is limiting the extension and autonomy of online discourse. The largest computer, telecom and media firms are doing everything in their considerable powers to see the Internet is brought within their empires. Thus, interception and surveillance possibilities are many as it is an open system. Governments around the world are removing all privacy protection from Internet users.[30] Once seen as censorship-proof, the Net is facing several restrictions. And, a majority of the people in the world still can't afford the technology needed to access the Internet. In India there are only around 45 million Internet users for a population of more than a one billion. These limitations have to be understood while advocating the concept of cyber democracy.

Conclusion

The concentration of ownership of media endangers plurality and diversity. Although the number of media channels has grown in the recent past the number of corporations that own them has shrunk reducing the choices media consumers have. There is a need to bring in media reforms in order to ensure that a few conglomerates do not dominate the media market. Regulations have to be introduced to place reasonable limits on the number of channels, newspapers and magazines a single corporation can own in a specific region.

Citizens groups, media activists have been calling for a movement for asserting the rights of media consumers. They have also advocated bringing media services under the consumer protection law. Establishing a well-funded viable and healthy non-profit and non-commercial media sector, independent of big business and government is crucial to make freedom of speech and expression meaningful and to provide a choice of diverse ideas and opinions. It is also important to maintain a strong and vibrant non-commercial public broadcasting service that provides a full range of programmes to the entire population. Newer ownership and public interest regulations are needed for media firms that are granted broadcast or cable licences. Policies that promote the creation of small commercial media are needed so that the media consumers will have greater choices. These reforms would go a long way towards democratizing the media systems and ease the corporate grip over our economic, political, social and cultural spheres. They are important in creating more egalitarian, democratic and humane world. This cannot be achieved overnight. It has to develop into a movement as part of the consumer movement.

NOTES

1. Herman, E.S. & McChesney, R., *Global Media: The New Missionaries of Corporate Capitalism,* London: Cassell, 1997.
2. Habermas, J., *"The Public Sphere"* in C. Mukerji and Schudson (Eds.), *Rethinking Popular Culture,* Berkeley: University of California Press, 1991.
3. Public sphere includes all the places and forums where issues of importance to a political community are discussed and debated and where information is presented that is essential to citizens' participation in community life. Habermas' work relies on a description of a historical moment during the 17th and 18th centuries when coffee houses, societies and saloons became the centre of debate, and extends this to an ideal of participation in the public sphere for today.
4. Bagdikian, B., *The New Media Monopoly,* Boston: Beacon, 2004.
5. Fisher, B.A., *Perspectives on Human Communication,* New York: Macmillan, 1978.
6. Katz, E., Gurevitch, M., & Hass, H., "On the Use of Mass Media for Important Things", *American Sociological Review,* 38, 164-181, 1973.

7. Katz, E., Blumler, J.G., & Gurevitch, M., "Utilization of Mass Communication by the Individual" in J.G. Blumler, & E. Katz (Eds.), *The Uses of Mass Communications: Current Perspectives on Gratifications Research* (pp. 19-32). Beverly Hills: Sage, 1974.
8. Gerbner, G., Gross, L., Morgan, M., and Signorielli, "Charting the Mainstream: Television's Contribution to Political Orientation", *Journal of Communication*, 32, (1982) 100-127.
9. Deshpande, S., Of Consumers and Kings, Seminar, 455, 23-26, 1997.
10. McChesney, R.W. and Scott, B., "Upton Sinclair and the Contradictions of Capitalist Journalism", *Monthly Review*, 54(1), 2002, 33-42.
11. Cohen, B.C., *The Press and Foreign Policy*, Princeton: Princeton University Press, 1963.
12. Noell-Neumann, E., *The Spiral of Silence: Public Opinion—Our Social Skin*, Chicago: University of Chicago Press, 1984.
13. Ambirajan, S., "Globalisation, Media and Culture", *Economic and Political Weekly*, July 17, 2141-2147, 2000.
14. McChesney, R., Rich, *"Media, Poor Democracy: Communication Politics"* in *Dubious Times*. Illinois: University of Illinois Press, 1999.
15. Except for Bertelsmann which has started its operation in India recently the other companies dominate the Indian television market.
16. Hackett, R.A and Carroll, W.K. (2004). "Communication Rights: Critical Social Movements and Media Reform", *Media Development*, 1/2004, 24-29.
17. Postman, N. Amusing, *Ourselves to Death*. Public Discourse in the Age of Show Business. New York: Penguin Book, 1985.
18. Postman, N., *Technopoly: The Surrender of Culture to Technology*. New York: Vintage Book, 2000.
19. McChesney, R.W., "Global Media, Neoliberalism and Imperialism", *Monthly Review*, 52 (10), 57-68, 2001.
20. Baker, E.C., *Media, Markets and Democracy*, Cambridge: Cambridge University Press, 2002.
21. Government of India, *Report of the Second Press Commission*, Vol. I. New Delhi: Controller of Publications, 1982.
22. Mohan, R., "Moving With the Times, Competition in Indian Media", *The Hindu*, February 12, 2001, p. 12.
23. Ninan, S. & Malaviaya, S., "Rural Newspaper Revolution", *The Hindu* Sunday Magazine, June 27, 2004, p.4.
24. The First Press Commission of India had suggested fixing of newspaper price based on the number of pages of a newspaper published as one of the measures to ensure that there was multiplicity of voices in the media market. But in the *Sakal Newspapers* case the Supreme Court of India struck down the Newspaper (Price and Page) Act, 1956 declaring it unconstitutional as it violated Article 19(1)(a)

that guarantees freedom of speech and expression to all citizens. The Second Press Commission recommended a re-examination of the case in view of the monopolistic growth of the press.

25. The Associated Chambers of Commerce and Industry of India (Asso Cham) has disfavoured cross media ownership on companies to manage print, broadcasting and electronic media, arguing that it will create monopolistic tendencies. Canada, United Kingdom, France and Australia have placed restrictions on cross media ownership.
26. Parthasarathi, Vobodh, *Alternative Communication*, Seminar, 455, 1997, 12-15.
27. The Press Council of India was set up with the objective of preserving the freedom of the press and maintaining and improving the standards of newspapers and news agencies.
28. Carey, J., "The Press, Public Opinion, and Public Discourse", in T. Glasser and C. Salmon (Eds.) *Public Opinion and the Communication of Consent*. New York: Guilford. 373-403, 1995.
29. Hunter, C.D., *"The Internet and the Public Sphere: Revitalisation or Decay?"*, 1998, http://www.asc.upenn.edu/usr/chunter/public_sphere.html
30. Evan, C., *"Host Not Responding Presumed Censored"*, 2007, http://www.netfreedom.org/news.asp?item=171.

REFERENCES

Bagdikian, B., *The Media Monopoly*, Boston: Beacon, 1983.

Chomsky, N., and Ramachandran, V.K., "Iraq is a Trial Run", *Frontline*. 20(07), 21-25, 2003.

Cohen, B.C., *The Press and Foreign Policy*, Princeton: Princeton University Press, 1963.

Herman, E.S. and Chomsky, N., *Manufacturing Consent: The Political Economy of the Mass Media*, New York: Pantheon, 1988.

Iyengar, S., & Kinder, D.R., *News that Matters: Television and American Opinion*, Chicago: University of Chicago Press, 1987.

McCombs, M.E. & Shaw, D.L., "The Agenda Setting Function of Mass Media", *Public Opinion Quarterly*, 36, 1972, 176-187.

Parenti. M., "Monopoly Media Manipulation", *Mediterranean Quarterly*, 13 (2), 2002, 56-66.

Rubin, A.M., "Uses, Gratifications, and Media Effects Research" in J. Byrant & D. Zillmann (Eds), *Perspective on Media Effects* (pp. 281-301). Hillsdale, NJ: Lawrence Erlbaum Associates, 1986.

Sinha, A.K., "Inroads into the Districts", *Advertising and Marketing*, 13 (1), 2002, 64-67.

Section II

Consumer Protection: Case Studies

11
Protecting the Rural Consumers: Need to Reorient Policies

Suresh Misra and *Sapna Chadah*

Introduction

Rural areas currently are home to nearly 70 per cent of India's population and have historically accounted for more than half of Indian consumption. Even with increasing urbanization and migration, it is estimated that 63 per cent of India's population will continue to live in rural areas by 2025. In terms of economic output, rural India accounts for almost half (48%) of the country's economy, and the rural markets have the potential to reach $500 billion by 2020. Globalisation, liberalisation and privatisation have enabled the entry of several private traders, including large multinationals, who have transformed the Indian economy into a vibrant, rapidly growing consumer market. The rural markets are now flooded with different kinds of goods and services, substantially effecting and changing the purchasing pattern of the consumers. The rural markets, which were earlier ignored by most of the big international market players, are now being seen as a land of great business opportunity and they are all targeting the rural consumers.

An analysis of available literature reveals that the impact of globalisation is being felt in rural India as much as in urban but the process is slow. However, in the long run it will have its impact on target groups like farmers, youth and women. In some states the affluent farmers, today 'keep in touch' with the latest information and maximise both ends. Animal feed producers no longer look at Andhra Pradesh or Karnataka. They keep their cell phones constantly connected to global markets. Surely, price movements and products' availability in the international market seem to drive their local business strategies. The estimated annual business from rural markets is around ₹ 1, 23000 crore, comprising ₹ 65000 crore of FMCG, ₹ 5000 crore of durables, ₹ 45000 crore of agricultural inputs including tractors and ₹ 8000 crore of two wheelers and four wheelers. Similarly the retail sector has a huge potential for growth and the opportunities in retail sector is expected to touch $43 billion by the year 2010.

The 61st Round NSS data shows that the share of expenditure in 2004-05 on food in rural India was 55 per cent of the total expenditure, while non-food expenditure was 45 per cent, thus the growth of food related expenditure has been much lower than the growth of non-food expenditure. The increase in monthly per capita expenditure on food was of 18.8, while on non-food was of 53.83. The fastest growing non-food expenditure categories are education and healthcare. Consumer durables are another category that is growing fast. Rural consumers are now opting for life improving products and services of real quality or durables that enhance productivity and increase earnings. As the disposable income of the rural masses is growing, more and more corporate houses are entering into the rural markets with their new goods and products. Due to this marketing for rural consumers is becoming more complex. According to experts, the four factors which influence demand in rural India are—access, attitude, awareness and affluence. Some companies have successfully used these to influence the rural market for their products.

In a country like India, where a substantial number of the rural people are living below the poverty line, having high level of unemployment and poor literacy level; consumer awareness continues to remain low. Several studies have shown that rural consumers are generally ignorant and they are also unorganised. Under these circumstances, the sellers or the manufacturers, exploit the consumers. Though, the consumers in India have been provided with various safety measures against their exploitation, but still the situation remains quite grave. Rural markets are full of sub-standard goods and duplicity of branded goods is another major problem in rural areas. As there is no check on production and sale of such products in the rural markets, many products have become a health hazard and threat to life. The expansion of service sector has added to the problem as services like insurance, banking, electricity and medical have expanded in the rural areas without any checks and balances and the rural consumers continue to be exploited by the service providers. Deficiency in services is a major area of concern as in most of the cases no adequate information is provided to the consumers. The low quality of medical services coupled with widespread of spurious drugs are causing major health hazards. The vulnerable sections are generally women, children and farmers. It is common to find that farmers are supplied defective seeds, adulterated pesticides and other commodities with no appropriate mechanism to redress their grievances. The expansion of mass media has further aggravated the situation and given impetus to consumerism in the rural areas.

Therefore, it has widely been held that the fate of the rural consumers cannot be left to the market forces. In the present situation, consumer protection, though as old as consumer exploitation, has assumed greater importance and relevance. In view of this the Government of India has taken a number of legal measures to protect the consumers by widening the scope of consumer protection. Now there exist laws and policies which focus on consumer protection and welfare. Special emphasis is being given to consumer education so that people become aware about their rights and responsibilities as consumers and know how to redress their grievances. Even before the enactment of the Consumer Protection Act in 1986 various Acts intended to protect the consumers directly or indirectly against different forms of exploitation were enacted from time to time. However, except for the Monopolies and Restrictive Trade Practices (MRTP) Act, 1969, all the other Acts were mainly punitive and preventive in nature. In spite of these Acts the consumers did not have any effective mechanism or institutional arrangements for the speedy redressal of their grievances. Moreover, the lack of effective popular movement isolated the consumer and his plight only increased. Seeing the pressure mounting from various consumer protection groups and the consumers themselves the Parliament enacted the Consumer Protection Act in 1986 and at present this is the principal legal remedy available to the consumers. This is an important Act which seeks to provide better protection of the interests of the consumers.

Lack of Consumer Awareness

The best way to empower the consumers is to educate them and enhance their awareness about their rights and obligations. Consumers must be aware about the market mechanism and how to protect their interests. Various stakeholders need to come together to educate the consumers. The media campaign *'Jago Grahak Jago'* is an important step towards consumer empowerment. The consumer clubs in schools and colleges are also playing a important role in consumer education. But in spite of all these efforts a very small segment of the population is aware of the legal remedy that is available to them.

After the enactment of the Consumer Protection Act in 1986, the first independent evaluation study of the implementation of this Act was done through a study conducted by IIPA in 1994. It was found that large majority of the consumers belonging to various categories and income groups were completely ignorant of the existence of the CPA and the redressal agencies created under it. Eleven years later, according to a survey commissioned through ORG Centre for Social Research by the C&AG, the position had improved only marginally. The survey was conducted in July-August, 2005 in 25 States/UTs covering 48,732 consumers, 6237 complaints, 249 manufacturers/service providers, 39 NGOs and 34 laboratories. The report of ORG-MARG revealed that:[1]

- Sixty-six per cent of the consumers interviewed were not aware of consumer rights and 82 per cent were even unaware of the Act.
- Nearly 49 per cent of the aware consumers had come to know about the Act only in the last 4 years though the Act had been in existence for the past 18 years.
- Overall, only 13 per cent of the consumers reported to have been aware of the existence of any redressal agency.
- A majority of the complainants came to know about the redressal agencies through electronic media (48%), print media (61%) and friends/relatives (68%), NGOs were not a popular source of awareness as only 4.9 per cent of the complainants attributed their awareness to the work of NGOs.
- The consumers were not aware of the features of the simple

> and inexpensive system of lodging complaint in the absence of any focused awareness programme launched by the Ministry or the States in this regard. The beneficiary survey carried out by ORG–MARG revealed that 78 per cent of the respondents were carrying a negative opinion of the efforts made by the government or had no idea about the same and were not aware that they could directly represent themselves in the Consumer Forums. It is pertinent to note that lack of awareness in this regard had deprived the consumers of the benefit of the adjudication mechanism as out of the total expenditure of ₹ 3387 incurred by the consumers on each case in the Consumer Forum on an average, as much as ₹ 2787 (82%) was the expenditure on advocates.

Therefore, one of the major hindrances on the consumer movement in the country is the lack of awareness among the consumers. The consumers apart from being unorganized do not have the mechanism to understand their rights and responsibilities. The problem is more acute in the rural areas. A lot more needs to be done on this front. The right to consumer education has been recognised under the Consumer Protection Act, 1986. However, unless awareness increases realizing this right remains a distant dream. In fact, an educated and aware person is an empowered consumer. Education equips a person with the skill to make discerning choices, to sort out problems effectively and to seek further information and help appropriately.

Rural Consumers

The Indian rural consumer lives in around 600,000 villages across the country and they account for over 70 per cent of the population of the country. While the rural consumer is generally seen as the less affluent, as compared to his urban cousin, things are changing in rural India over the last ten years. Like any market that has seen a demand and awareness boom, rural India has been witnessing considerable rise in purchasing power. A change in consumption patterns and access to communication media have made rural market a vital cog in the sales-growth wheel, especially with demand for many categories of products and services plateauing in the urban markets. In spite of increasing number of rural consumers, provisions for consumer protection and welfare are often based on the general standard and circumstances of those living in big cities and towns. Although consumers as a whole are in an equal bargaining position, there are certain recognizable groups which are disadvantaged in more ways than the others. Disadvantaged consumers are those who are less able to assert their rights and rural consumers comprise one such group. Rural consumers remain disadvantaged as their right to information, choice, redress, and consumer education are not sufficiently fulfilled. Consequently, such consumers need support in maintaining their rights so that they can bargain equally with the producers or the service providers.

Marketing and Research Team (MART) an organization involved for decades in rural marketing research, has over the years built up a veritable trove of research on rural consumers and their consumption patterns. Some of the findings were presented by the President, MART at the Rural Marketing and Communication Conference organized by the Federation of Indian Chamber of Commerce and Industry (FICCI) at Delhi held in 2003. The following are the findings of MART:

The rural consumer may not be very educated, but he is certainly astute, with a lot of common sense and practical experience of handling the vagaries and uncertainties of life. He displays great ingenuity and adaptability as evidenced by his learning to repair his tractor, hand pump and motorbike, and finding a host of local solutions in everyday life. Though low on economic resources, he does not go in for only 'cheap' products but looks for value for money. Perception of a premium product is not yet relevant in rural markets, with consumers more concerned with functionality than unnecessary 'frills' with a consumer durable. Too many features with a product tend to confuse the rural consumer.

Rural consumers are generally mistrustful and wary of urbanities and turned off by their patronizing attitudes. It is not easy for a rank outsider to get the rural consumer to spend money. Brand adherence is high among village consumers. This may not necessarily be on account of loyalties. Limited access to alternatives and lack of information about possible choices do make them 'stick' to tried and tested brands. Brand recognition is often on the basis of logos, symbols, colours rather than the exact brand name. This tendency is partly responsible for the widespread menace of spurious products in rural markets, as it is easy to deceive the rural consumer with look-alikes. A very high degree of involvement characterizes purchase of expensive products like consumer durables. A lot of checking and counterchecking is done to seek reassurance on the soundness of the buying decision. Marketers must embody reassurance and provide opportunity to 'see and touch' the product in their marketing communication processes.

Routine is important to a rural consumer's life as a lot of time consuming activities characterize his everyday life. The routine is governed by nature and seasons, not by the calendar or the clock. Sunday is not typically a holiday. In buying processes, the consumer is not in a hurry and cannot be pushed into a hasty purchase for these segments. Rural incomes show a great seasonality for the segment of large farmers. The segment of petty farmers, farm labour, non-farm workers and the salaried class show a greater regularity of income patterns so the consumption cycles are also more regular and predictable. On account of far higher degree of inter-personal communication characterizing village life and relatively low penetration of mass media, word of mouth is a very effective medium of influence generation. Existing users, dealers, village influential, youth studying or working in urban locations are all consulted before making purchases.

Among the households with TV ownership, TV viewing is the highest among women and children who in contrast to the traditional, household head dominated decision scenario are fast emerging as demand generators for the household goods. Decisions on durables like radio, TV and two wheelers are still male dominated decisions, taken in consultation with other people in the community. The rural youth are increasingly becoming more exposed to urban lifestyles on account of their frequent visits to urban locations either for higher education or for work. Their media exposure to television is also much higher. This makes urban lifestyles an inspirational model for them and their preference for national brands is on the rise. While culture and social norms have a greater hold on rural consumer than urban ones, perceptions, traditions and values vary from state to state, sometimes from region to region. It is, therefore, difficult to work with a pan rural

Indian communication package. Two-step flow of communication, using opinion leaders and mass media both, seems to work better in rural settings. These observations made on the basis of a host of research based inputs make it very clear that rural marketing effort cannot be visualized as a simple extension of the urban marketing process. It is a different market and presents a different set of premises on the basis of which suitable marketing.

Rising Rural Prosperity

A number of studies have revealed that the rural consumers have acquired importance as India is now seeing a dramatic shift towards prosperity in rural households. Rural India with its traditional perceptions has grown over the years, not only in terms of income but also in terms of thinking. The purchasing power in rural India is on steady rise and it has resulted in the growth of the rural markets. The market has been growing at 3-4 per cent per annum adding more than one million consumers every year. According to a study by the National Council for Applied Economic Research (NCAER), there are as many middle incomes and above households in the rural areas as are in the urban areas. Moreover, there are almost twice as many lower middle income households in the rural areas as in the urban areas. At the highest income level there are 2.3 million urban households against 1.6 million households in rural areas. As per the NCAER projections, the number of middle income and high income households in rural India was expected to grow from 80 million to 111 million by 2007. In urban India, the same is expected to grow from 46 million to 59 million. Thus, the absolute size of rural India is expected to be double that of urban India.

Exploitation of Rural Consumers

Rising prosperity and growth in rural markets has also lead to an increase in consumer exploitation. Due to poor knowledge about their rights and lack of skills to take a rational decision based on information about the product or services, the rural consumers in India are being exploited in many ways. They have been made to endure sub-standard products and services, adulterated foods, short weights and measures, spurious and hazardous drugs, exorbitant prices, endemic shortages leading to black marketing and profiteering, unfulfilled manufacturing guarantees and host of other ills. The rural consumers who generally depend on weekly markets to purchase essential things are often cheated due to lack of choice. Moreover, the rural consumers are generally ignorant and they are also unorganized. Thus, they are exploited by the manufacturers, traders and the service providers in different ways. The rural consumers are not only scattered but also diverse and heterogeneous thereby making them easy prey for exploitation.

Fake Brands and Spurious Products

One of the major problems being faced by the rural consumers is that of fake brands and spurious products. The brand image of a number of successful FMCG majors has been imitated by some of the small regional companies and the markets are flooded with such products and these fake brands have been sold mostly in rural areas. Fake products are of two types—one, counterfeit products and two, pass-off products. Counterfeit products are fake products that bear identical name of a product/packaging/graphics/colour scheme and even same name and address as the genuine manufacturer. Some one produces these to look exactly like real products other than the legal owner of the real product, trademarks and product packaging. Sometimes, it becomes difficult to tell which the real product is. A rural consumer is brand loyal and understands symbols better and this also becomes a problem as it is easy to misguide the rural consumer. The FMCG industry alone has been facing losses of over ₹ 5,000 crore per year, due to counterfeit products, of the ₹ 113,000-crore FMCG market in India. Counterfeit products result in an annual loss of approximately ₹ 30,000 crore to the industry and ₹ 15,000 crore to the Government exchequer.[2]

On the other hand, pass-off product uses similar sounding or is similar in spelling. They use similar type of packaging or colour or design. These are look-alike products that resemble the original products, mainly through misspelling of the trademark. For example, Sunslik instead of Sunsilk, Clemic Plus or Climic Plus instead of Clinic Plus, Golcate for Colgate, Vips Rub or Vives Rub as a pass-off for Vicks Vaporub. They come out with the motive to mislead and cheating ordinary consumers who are uneducated or in a hurry to purchase the products.

A study conducted by AC Nelson, a leading research agency reveals that FMCG industry loses around ₹ 2500 crore annually to counterfeits and pass-off products. It is also estimated that top brands in India are estimated to lose up to 30 per cent of their business to fake products. Besides the loss of revenue, the trading companies also face the loss of damage to brand image and brand loyalty to consumers. Apart from the loss of revenue and brand image fake products cause immense damage to consumer's health. 10 per cent of all major soft drinks sold are spurious, while 10-30 per cent of cosmetics, toiletries and packaged food are counterfeits. Fake gold and precious metals are worth ₹ 60 billion in India.

Another interesting point is that FMCG counterfeit products only come in smallest size of packing. In the rural segment where fake products thrive, the consumer's low purchasing power makes sachets and smaller packs popular. It is in the case of these small packs that consumers are duped more easily as the quantity is not large enough for the buyer to discern its quality. This is especially so in sachets of shampoo, hair oils, and detergents and so on.

Misleading Advertisements and Role of Media

The media has a greater responsibility towards the vulnerable sections of the society. The rural consumers are one such. With the advent of modern technology, rural consumers today have access to diverse media of which advertising is the major or even the main sources of information about many new products or newly introduced products. The changes in advertising are in part a response to the rapid growth in markets due to globalization. Due to the entry of a large number of players in the rural market and also due to stiff competition there are large numbers of misleading advertisements in the print and electronic media resulting into exploitation of the consumers.

The advertising firms are studying consumer behaviour to design effective communication strategies without caring for the welfare of the consumer. In most parts of the rural areas in the country there is considerable awareness on various latest products that are available in the market. This has been possible due to the penetration of cable and satellite channels that have brought down the world at the finger tips of the common man. The media has influenced the mindset of the rural consumers to such an extent that people who have money start purchasing the products unmindful of the costs, just to satisfy their needs as well as their ego.

The problem is that there are no effective sanctions against misleading advertisements. What needs to be emphasized is that the poor, uneducated consumers in the rural areas are most likely to be harmed. More generally, as a recent World Development, Report rightly emphasized, 'information problems are often at the core of the difficulties that poor people in developing countries encounter in their daily struggle to survive and to improve their lives.'

Field Study

The above scenario reveals the pathetic situation of the rural consumers. To evaluate the extent of the problem and the level of awareness among the rural consumers the Centre for Consumer Studies conducted a study in five states of India. Based on the research we have made some recommendations which will be useful to the policy makers is designing specific policies to protect the consumers.

Objectives of the Study

The main objectives of the study were, to study the level of awareness, of rural consumers on various consumer protection measures initiated by the Government of India and other agencies, to evaluate the rural consumers' current knowledge, attitudes, behaviour and practices while purchasing goods or availing services, to examine the nature of unfair trade practices in the rural areas, to assess the level of satisfaction of the rural consumers on various products and services available in the rural areas and to draw conclusions from the study and suggest remedial measures for better protection of the rural consumers.

Methodology

The present study was an empirical research, based on both

primary and secondary data. It was a blend of both descriptive and analytical methods of study. The information regarding level of satisfaction, awareness, attitude and behaviour of rural consumers at individual and household level was gathered. For the purpose, an interview schedule was prepared. Besides focus group interaction was also done. The sample areas were selected in a way that they can best represent the entire geographical regions of the country. Consequently, five states from different regions of India were selected for the study. They were: Uttarakhand, Meghalaya, Gujarat, Tamil Nadu and Madhya Pradesh. The sample was selected from these five states using the random sampling technique. From each State two Districts and from each district two blocks were randomly selected. From each block four villages were randomly selected. It was not difficult to identify a consumer as everyone is a consumer and either buys a product or avails of a service for consideration. The households from these villages were selected by random sampling technique. Total sample of 2000 households was taken for investigation from 80 villages (25 household from each village) spreading across twenty blocks of five selected states. The data so collected was analyzed and tabulated. Appropriate statistical methods were applied to classify and analyze the data, collected on the subject.

Without going into greater detail we will be discussing the major findings of the study and based on the finding the recommendations that would be in useful in protecting the rural consumers. The major findings of the study are as follows:

Findings

1. The respondents covered various strata of the society so as to make it a representative sample. Males constituted 68.6 per cent of the sample size whereas 31.5 per cent were females.
2. As far as the educational level of the respondents is concerned, 23.1 per cent had no schooling, 17.9 per cent of them had attended school up to the primary level, 26 per cent had middle schooling, 16.3 per cent had studied up to high school, 10.3 per cent had schooling up to intermediate level and 6.6 per cent were Graduates. Post-graduates and Professionals consisted of 1 per cent of the respondents.

3. 1.6 per cent of the respondents were below 20 years of age. 23.7 per cent belonged to the age group between 20-30 years, 38.5 per cent were from the age group of 30-40 years, 22.6 per cent were within 40-50 years of age and 13.7 per cent of the respondents were above 50 years of age.
4. As far as their occupational status is concerned, owner/cultivators constituted 9.9 per cent of the respondents while marginal farmers constituted 16.2 per cent. The major segment of the respondents, which is 25 per cent, consisted of labourers. Among the respondents, self-employed constituted 12.9 per cent, unemployed 13.8 per cent and housewives 13.8 per cent.
5. The survey revealed that majority of the respondents (44.4%) had an annual income of less than ₹ 24,000. The group with annual income between ₹ 24,000-60,000 consisted of 40.1 per cent. 11.4 per cent of the respondents had income between ₹ 60,000–1,20,000. Those whose income was above ₹ 1,20,000 constituted 4.15 per cent of the sample size.
6. As far as the monthly expenditure of the respondents is concerned, 43.5 per cent spent below ₹ 2,000, 45 per cent spent between ₹ 2,000 to 5,000, 8.45 per cent of the respondents' expenditure was between ₹ 5,000 to 10,000. Those whose expenditure was above ₹ 10,000 constituted 2.6 per cent of the sample size.
7. The survey reveals that a major portion of the respondents (34.9%) depend upon the local *haat* or weekly markets, 34.8 per cent depend upon nearby town or *kasba*. Only 18.15 per cent depend upon village shops and 13 per cent go to city for shopping.
8. As regards the inquiry into terms and condition of the goods/services before transaction was concerned more than half (58%) did not make any enquiry 23.1 per cent of the respondents enquired about it sometimes and only 19 per cent made enquiry frequently.
9. Enquiry into various aspects before purchase was directly connected to the level of education. Only 7.7 per cent of the respondents who had not attended schools inquired into the terms and conditions before purchase. On the other hand, 63.3 per cent of the graduate respondents

sought information before purchasing goods or availing a service. Among the sample respondents only 17.8 per cent insisted on taking a cash memo regularly, 31.5 per cent asked for it only sometimes while purchasing costly goods and the majority 50.8 per cent never insisted for cash memo.

10. While purchasing goods 32.8 per cent of the respondents always checked the available choice of the product, 25 per cent checked it sometimes and 42.2 per cent did not do that. 50.8 per cent of the rural consumer did not bother to know about the contents and the expiry date of the product. They are conscious only about the price of the product and sought information about the price. 83.7 per cent of the rural consumer did not think it important to seek information about the nutritional value of the product. Respondent consumers were price conscious 87.4 per cent of them inquired about the price of the product.
11. 73.9 per cent of the rural consumer did not see the expiry date only 21.4 per cent checked it sometimes. 40.7 per cent of the survey rural consumers knew about MRP. Only 24.4 per cent knew that one could bargain on the MRP and more than half (51.2%) did not know about the fact. 40.3 per cent of the rural consumers are aware about ISI mark, 11.9 per cent knew about AGMARK, 10.0 per cent about HALLMARK, 1.2 per cent about FPO and 1.6 per cent about BEE markings.
12. Amongst the various ways of exploitations, 40.2 per cent were overcharged, 14 per cent were victims of food adulteration, 12 per cent complained about poor quality of products, 7.5 per cent about deficiency in services and 7.4 per cent complained about lesser weights. On being cheated/exploited 28.50 per cent respondents ignored the problem, 16.3 per cent tried to get back the money or replace the goods and some respondents (0.8%) tried to mobilize people to put pressure on seller to address their grievances.
13. 92.4 per cent of the respondents were not aware about the CP Act. 34.2 per cent of the respondent knew about *Jago Grahak Jago*. Of the respondents who were aware about the Act, 34.2 per cent received the information from the electronic media, i.e. TV/Radio 6.5 per cent gathered

information from newspapers/journals and 6.5 per cent from NGOs. Of the respondents aware about CP Act only 22.6 per cent were aware about the redressal mechanism under the Act whereas 77.4 per cent were unaware about it. Of the total respondents aware about the Act, 83.7 per cent did not know as to who can file a complaint, 13.5 per cent knew that the complaint can be filed by consumer and 1.7 per cent said that any VCO can file a complaint.

14. Only 9.2 per cent of the respondents agreed that the consumers were aware about their rights and 90.84 per`cent answered in negative. 32.6 per cent respondents said that the consumers were well protected by law while 67.4 per cent could not answer this question. Only 15 per cent agreed that consumer welfare schemes are well implemented by the government and 85 per cent respondents answered the question in negative.
15. Awareness about *Jago Grahak Jago* was quite high. 34.2 per cent of the respondents knew about the slogan. However, majority of the respondents (65.8%) did not know what was being conveyed through the advertisement. 83.2 per cent of the respondents agreed that there is a need to create awareness among the consumers. To the question as to who should be given the responsibility of educations consumers 62.6 per cént of the respondents were of the view that it should be responsibility of the gram panchayats, 20.9 per cent of the view that this task should be carried by the government and 9 per cent felt that the educational institutions can play a role in this.

Recommendations

1. Rural Markets are flooded with substandard goods, adulterated food items and unsafe products. The rural markets are dumped with look alike and pass-off products. The quality of service being provided is not only poor, but lacks transparency resulting in consumer exploitation. Therefore, there is a need to prioritize the protection of rural consumers by strengthening the enforcement mechanism.

2. Lack of choice is a major problem in the rural areas as the consumers do not have access to a variety of products. The dependence of the rural consumers on the neighbourhood shops, who sell on credit, is adding to the problem. Therefore, standardisation of products and availability of packed commodities will help the rural consumers to a large extent.
3. The consumers in the rural areas lack awareness about various measures taken by the government. The multimedia campaign has not been able to educate the consumers to a large extent. The government should launch vigorous campaign to educate the consumers with the involvement of local NGOs, schools and colleges. Awareness about the consumer rights and obligations should be emphasised in such programmes. The Panchayati Raj Institutions should also be involved in the consumer movement and the Gram Sabha should play an active role in generating consumer awareness. The Panchayats must be encouraged to celebrate at least the National Consumer Day. Organisations like Nehru Yuva Kendras, NSS and NCC should be involved in consumer education at the grassroots level as they can play an important role in enhancing awareness. The strategy should be to use various organisations to take forward the consumer movement.
4. Rural consumers are not aware about various standardisation marks and therefore, unable to read and understand the labels on the products. Both print and electronic media must be used to propagate this message among the rural consumers.
5. The consumers in the rural areas lack awareness about various measures taken by the government. The multimedia campaign has not been able to educate the consumers to a large extent. The government should launch vigorous campaign to educate the consumers with the involvement of local NGOs, schools and colleges. Awareness about the consumer rights and obligations should be emphasised in such programmes. The Panchayati Raj Institutions should also be involved in the consumer movement and the Gram Sabha should play an active role in generating consumer awareness. The

Panchayats must be encouraged to celebrate at least the National Consumer Day. Organisations like Nehru Yuva Kendras, NSS and NCC should be involved in consumer education at the grassroots level as they can play an important role in enhancing awareness. The strategy should be to use various organisations to take forward the consumer movement.

6. The rural markets are mostly unorganised. Therefore, there is also a need to regulate the rural markets in terms of quality, safety and weights and measures. The balance used in the rural markets is not of standard quality. Stones are still being used to weight the products and in most of the cases the balance is never calibrated properly. The Department of Legal Metrology (Weights and Measures) in the states has to play a proactive role in this. Pamphlets and leaflets should be distributed in the rural markets periodically highlighting these points and what the consumers can do to prevent being cheated.
7. The SIRDs (State Institute of Rural Development) have the mandate to organise training programmes for the elected representatives and other local functionaries of various departments implementing programmes and schemes. The SIRDs should include a module on consumer welfare in their training programmes to educate the participants on the need and importance of consumer protection.
8. Its time that rural consumers are not viewed as a homogeneous group. Rural women, children and farmers have specific problems and specific policies should be in place to educate and protect them.
9. The District Forums should play a more active role and the members should be involved in consumer literacy. The consumers must be made awareness about the various decisions of the consumer forums so that their confidence in the redressal mechanism can be enhanced. The District Forums should have circuit benches at the block level so that the rural consumers can have easier access to justice and the redressal mechanism.
10. Preference should be given to rural areas while setting up consumer advisory and mediation centres. The rural consumers should also have the benefit of ADR as it will

save both money and time. Such centres should be funded by the State/Central Government and set up at each block headquarters to start with. The local VCOs can be involved in managing the advisory centres. This will help the rural consumers to a large extent.

Rural Consumers: Need for Education and Empowerment

In the emerging scenario it is necessary to protect the rural consumers by educating them about their rights and empowering them to make decisions based on information about the goods and services. Awareness has to be created among the rural consumers. So far the consumer movement has largely been confined to the urban centres, and with the expanding rural markets now the focus has to shift to protect the rural consumer.

Consumer organizations and similar civil society groups have an important role to play in consumer education. They have the means to provide consumers with information and help them to make informed choices. Consumer information needs to be available at the right time and in the right place before or when purchasing decisions are made. Several NGOs are very active in the rural areas in advocating for consumer rights but due to their limited ability to put enough pressure on policy makers, they lack consumer support. This is the dilemma of NGOs in consumer protection. Regardless of these limitations consumer empowerment programmes through regular training and education are very crucial. It is also time to consider consumer education as part of the school and college curriculum.

There is also a need for the effective implementation of various provisions of the legislations enacted to protect the consumers from fake and adulterated products from entering the markets so that the consumers' interests could be safeguarded. Various business houses, NGOs and the governmental agencies have to come together to join hands to combat counterfeiting.

Strengthening Redressal Mechanism

Redress of complaints is a major concern for consumers. Having a right to access the redressal mechanism is of prime importance. For the right to redress to have a practical value, a mechanism must exist to ensure that it can be exercised effectively. If consumer confidence is to be built up they need assurances that if things go wrong they can seek redress. The District Consumer Disputes Redressal Forums which act as the first point of contact in case of a complaint have to play a proactive role in building consumer confidence. The district forums should be strengthened and initiatives aimed at promoting access to simple, swift, effective and inexpensive legal channels be taken up. In many states the District Forums are short of members and also lack the required infrastructure. The State Governments should address the problems of District Forums as well as the consumers to make the redressal mechanism more effective and also responsive. Moreover, it becomes difficult for a rural consumer to go to the district headquarters to file a complaint and then pursue his complaint. It will be better if the concept of circuit benches for the District Forums is also introduced as in the case of National Commission and the State Commissions so that access to justice is ensured for the rural consumers. There is also a need to set up more than one district forum in a district to clear up the pendency of complaints, which has increased substantially. Any further delay in disposal of the complaints will only shatter the faith of consumers in the redressal mechanism.

Role of Panchayati Raj Institutions

To reach the rural consumers, it is imperative to involve the Panchayati Raj Institutions in not only educating consumers but also ensuring that fake and spurious products are not sold in the rural markets. These institutions can play a meaningful role in consumer protection and consumer welfare and this has been recognised by the policy makers. The recommendations contained in the 20th Report of the Standing Committee on Food, Consumer Affairs and Public Distribution (14th Lok Sabha) on the subject 'Consumer Movement in the Country' needs to be effectively implemented. It recommended that the Department of Consumer Affairs should take the desired initiatives to involve Panchayati Raj Institutions in various programmes related to consumer awareness. The publication of the Department specifically 'UPBHOKTA JAGARAN' should be brought out in regional languages and distributed to the elected representatives of the PRIs.

The Committee further recommended that the best forum to educate the rural masses about their rights as consumers as well as the techniques to redress to their grievances is the meetings of the Gram Sabha. It is felt that the Department of Consumer Affairs in consultation with the Ministry of Panchayati Raj should take desired initiatives to have mandatory meetings of the Gram Sabha on 24th December (National Consumer Day) where the villagers could properly be educated about their rights as consumers. No doubt some initiatives have been taken in this direction and capacity building and awareness programmes are being organized through the State Institutes of Rural Development. But to reach such a large number of rural consumers, a vigorous campaign with the involvement of the panchayats needs to be taken up. Specific capacity building programmes for the elected members of the PRIs are to be developed with adequate financial sanctions. All stakeholders need to coordinate their activities and ensure that adequate literature is also made available in the local languages. Street plays and folk songs can be meaningful instruments to create awareness in the rural areas. Apart from these there is also a need to formulate appropriate policies and strategies to protect the rural consumers particularly the farmers, women and children.

Conclusion

The rural consumers are one of the most disadvantaged consumers in the country. The findings of the study suggest that due to ignorance and lack of consumer awareness the rural consumers are exploited. No much progress has been made in providing specific safeguards to them even though their problems are different. We need to design specific policies and programmes aimed at educating them and also enhancing their awareness. The rural consumers are looked upon as a homogeneous entity but the farmers, women, children and elderly consumers have different needs and the resulting exploitation is also different. Unless the rural consumers are taken care of the consumer movement will remain weak. There is a need to involve the Panchayati Raj Institutions and build the capacity of the local level officials/VCOs and other stakeholders. The media also needs to be involved in enhancing the awareness through various educative programmes.

NOTES

1. CAG, *Performance Audit of the Implementation of the Consumer Protection Act and Rules—Report of the Comptroller and Auditor General of India for the year ended March 2005*, Union Government (Civil), Performance Audit, 2006, p. 9.
2. *India PRwire*, February 2, 2010.

REFERENCES

Ambi, M.G. Parameswaran; "The Great Indian Rural Consumer", *Business Standard*, February 15, 2008, New Delhi.

D.K. Bose; "Marketing in Rural India", *Horizon*, October 7, 2007, IIM, Kozhikode.

"Enforce Stringent Laws to Check Spurious Products", *The Hindu*; February 19, 2004.

India PRwire, February 2, 2010.

K.V. Kannan, *"Strategies for Chocolate Companies to Kill Fake Products in Indian Rural Market"*, www,indianmba.com/Faculty.

Kaptan, S.S., *"Rural Consumer and Consumer Protection"*, Sarup & Sons Publication, 2004 (pp 19, 83), New Delhi.

Preeti, Mehra, "Crusade against Counterfeit", *Business Line*, Monday, July 2, 2001.

Pushma, Girimaji, Misleading Advertisements and Consumer, IIPA, New Delhi, 2008.

Ram, Bijapurkar and Rajesh Shukla, *Spotlight on Rural Consumers*, livemint.com, December 4, 2008.

S. John, Mano Raj and P. Selvaraj, *"Social Changes and the Growth of Indian Rural Markets: An Invitation to FMCG"*, International Marketing Conference on Marketing and Society, April 8-10, 2007, IIM, Kozhikode.

Sarangapani, A., *A Textbook on Rural Consumer Behaviour in India—A Study on FMCGs*, University Press, 2009, New Delhi.

"The Great Indian Rural Consumer", *Business Standard*; February 15, 2008.

Venkatesh, Tamlurkar, *Assessing the Marketing for Rural India*, www.indianmba.com/Faculty.

12
Package Labelling in India: Impact on Consumer Welfare

Savita Hanspal and *Sri Ram Khanna*

Introduction

The package of a product is important not only because it protects the contents, prolongs shelf life and helps in selling goods in distant lands but also because it serves as the primary contact point between the manufacturer and the consumer after advertising. It attracts the buyers and provides information that is used for purchasing brands like information on the identity of the brand and its manufacturer or packer or marketer, its ingredients, usage, disposal, quantity, quality and price. So important is this labelling function for the consumers that the Indian Government has promulgated the Standards of Weights and Measures Act, 1976 and the Packaged Commodities Rules, 1977 to ensure provision of fair and accurate information to them. The Rules have been amended from time to time to keep them up with the changing trade practices.

Major amendments have been made to the Packaged Commodities Rules, 1977 by the Government *vide* GSR 425 (E) dated 17th July, 2006, requiring the industry to modify packaging and labelling of the brands manufactured by them. One part of the Amendment came into effect from 13th January, 2007 and the other part from 13th January, 2008. During the first half of 2008, there was a major coverage in the press in India on how some companies had quietly changed the quantities in packages without correspondingly changing the prices, giving a misleading impression to the consumers that they continue to get the same quantity for the price they were paying earlier. Britannia Marie Biscuits, for example, were packed in 188 g instead of 200g; Goodday Biscuits in 92g instead of 100g; Kelloggs Chocos packed in 475g instead of 500g; Maggi in 115g instead of 125g; Red Label tea in 245g instead of 250g; Wheel detergent in 800g instead of 1kg and Lifebuoy in 115g instead of 125g.[1] The consumers failed to notice the changed quantities or the declaration regarding the package being a non-standard pack size and the phenomenon left a large number of consumers disappointed. Many felt cheated as they realised the reduction in net weight only after the matter was widely reported in the print and electronic media. It was felt that the manufacturers or packers have used this strategy to circumvent the reporting of price increase. In the light of the widespread feeling of mistrust, it was felt that there was a need to examine the law.

This paper discusses how consumer welfare is influenced by permitting products to be packed in non-standard pack sizes, the requirement of mentioning MRP and the deletion of Unit sale price, the format of information appearing on the label influences consumer welfare.

Non-Standard Pack Sizes

The Standards of Weights and Measures Act, 1976 establishes the uniform standards of weights and measures based on the metric system to regulate inter-state trade and commerce in weights and measures as well as matters related to other goods which are sold or distributed by weight, measure or number. Section 39 (1)(c) of the Standards of Weights and Measures Act clearly stipulates that in the case of pre-packed commodities, among other things, the package must bear a definite, plain and conspicuous declaration, made in the prescribed manner about the following:

(i) the identity of the commodity in the package;
(ii) the net quantity in terms of the standard unit of weight or measure of the commodity in the package;
(iii) where the commodity is packaged or sold by number, the accurate number of the commodity contained in the package;
(iv) the unit sale price of the commodity in the package;
(v) the retail sale price of the package;

(vi) the name and address of the manufacturer/packer/importer.

The explanation to this sub-section further clarifies that "unit sale price" means the price according to such unit of weight, measure or number as may be prescribed. Under Section 39(5), the Government has the power to specify standard quantities and numbers on packages to avoid confusion for consumers in case of proliferation of package sizes. According to the provision, if such a proliferation is likely to impair the reasonable ability of the consumer to make a comparative assessment of the prices after considering the net quantity or number of such commodity, the Government may direct the manufacturers to sell, distribute or deliver such commodity in such standard quantities or number as may be prescribed.

The Standards of Weights and Measures (Packaged Commodities) Rules, 1977 (Packaged Commodities Rules), apply to commodities in the packaged form which are or are intended/likely to be sold, distributed, or delivered or offered or displayed for sale, distribution or delivery, or stored for such purposes. Prior to the Amendment, Schedule III in the Packaged Commodities Rules mandated fast moving consumer goods to be packed in standard weights;[2] for example, biscuits had to be packed in the following quantities—25g, 50g, 75g, 100g, 150g, 200g, 250g, 300g and thereafter in multiples of 100g up to 1 kg. Similarly, non-soapy detergents were mandated to be sold in packs of the following specifications: below 50g no restriction, 50g, 100g, 200g, 500g, 700g, 1 kg, 1.5 kg, 2 kg and thereafter in multiples of 1 kg. Tea was required to be sold in 25g, 50g, 100g, 125g, 250g, 500g, 1 kg and thereafter in multiples of 1 kg.

The rationale for having standard pack sizes containing commodities packed in round quantities such as 100 ml, 500g, 5m etc. was to enable the consumers to make the calculations and comparison of prices easily, simply and quickly. A consumer can compare price by mental calculations while he is at the retail point surveying competing packages and deciding on a brand he would purchase.

If the same commodity is packed in a large variety of sizes, it results in confusing the consumers as to the economics of his purchase by depriving him of the facilities of quick and easy comparison of prices of packages. This proliferation of weights or measures in which a commodity is available is detrimental to the interests of the consumers, and therefore, requires regulation in such a way that the more commonly used commodities are packed in sizes of uniform denomination so that the consumer can make price comparisons not only against weights—like if 100g costs *x* and 500g costs y, what is more economical to purchase 100g or 500g but also to compare prices across brands, as for example if 100g of brand A is available for ₹ 10 and a similar quantity in brand B is available for ₹ 15, the consumer can find out for himself whether he needs to purchase A or B. In the above situation, when quantities in packages are 88g or 232g, the consumers cannot make quick and easy price comparisons either across quantities or across brands.

Packaged Commodities Rule 5 (as amended by G.S.R. 425(E), dated 17th July, 2006), lays down that specific commodities mentioned in the Third Schedule shall be packed for sale, distribution or delivery in such standard quantities as are specified in that Schedule. The 2006 amendment to Rule 5 has added a proviso that, "provided that if a commodity specified in the Third Schedule is packed in a size other than that prescribed in that Schedule, a declaration that "not a standard pack size under the Standards of Weights and Measures (Packaged Commodities) Rules, 1977 or non-standard size under the Standards of Weights and Measures (Packaged Commodities) Rules, 1977" shall be made prominently on the label of such package. There appears to have been little public debate when the amendment was finalised. The consumer viewpoint perhaps was not adequately represented. The efforts and time spent to have Schedule III standard packages implemented over the years have been brought to naught. This Amendment appears to have undone all the good work done in the interest of the consumer over the past.

Unit Price

The amendments to the Rules have also done away with the mandatory requirement to mention the Unit price on the package. Amendments were made to this provision declaration regarding unit sale price of the package *vide* GSR 521 dated 17th May, 1995; and the Maximum Retail Price (MRP) was instead required to be mentioned. The intention in specifying the unit price in the pre-amendment rules was to enable the consumer to compare the unit price stated on different packages with a view to compute comparative prices to enable the consumer to give him a price advantage. Compliance with the provision of mentioning the unit sale price on the package would also have helped consumers in tracking price changes in case of non-standard packages as well.

Further, in making the comparison between prices charged and the quantities purchased, the consumers should not be expected to make complicated calculations. The manufacturers and packers should not expect them to be number crunchers or great mathematicians especially in a country which is not yet having 100 per cent literacy and where more than 60 per cent of the population is still living in rural areas. The existence of multiple languages compounds this problem further.

Maximum Retail Price

Up to December 1990, manufacturers of packaged commodities in India, had the option to print the price of the commodity on the package in two separate ways—retail price ₹ ..... (local taxes extra) and maximum retail price ₹..... (inclusive of all taxes)[3]. In the year 1990, the Department of Legal Metrology, decided to change the Standards of Weights and Measures Act (Packaged Commodities' Rules) so that all manufacturers had to print the max/retail price, inclusive of all taxes[4], because it was very difficult for consumers to check whether retailers were actually charging the correct amount of local taxes on the products they sold. Section 39(1)(c)(iv) of the Standards of Weights and Measures Act, 1976 requires that the unit sale price should also be declared on the package. Amendments were made to this provision declaration regarding unit sale price of the package *vide* GSR 521 dated 17th May, 1995. Maximum Retail Price at which the commodity in packaged form may be sold to the ultimate consumer was defined to include all taxes local or otherwise, freight, transport charges, commission payable to dealers and all charges towards advertising, delivery, packing, forwarding and the like as the case may be.

It is physically not possible for manufacturers to manufacture and price their products specifically for anyone market which has a unique tax rate or unique retail margins. Consequently, they produce and price the product with one single rate that covers rates applicable all over the country. In order to deal with the varying rates of tax, the manufacturer prints the price prevailing in the market with the highest tax rate. This is detrimental to the interests of the consumers as it means that consumers in markets with lower tax rates have to pay a higher price. The traders, therefore, stand to gain in such a scenario. Sometimes, of course, they pass on a part of this additional margin to the consumers by charging them a price lower than the print price.

Prices also vary from state to state, due to variations in accepted retail margins. Retailers in large cities, with very high overhead costs due to municipal taxes and land prices, require a higher percentage margin than retailers in smaller towns. Since manufacturers are not permitted to charge differential rates when making their sale, they build-in a margin normally equivalent to the higher required margin, into their product prices. Retailers in smaller towns or those willing to work with a lower margin, then sell to consumers at prices lower than the printed price.

Advertisements are aired for creating awareness amongst the consumers that they could bargain at the MRP and can bargain with the retailer to accept a price lower than the MRP. Many consumers have reported that either the retailers refuse their requests for negotiating the prices or reduce the price of the products by a negligible amount like a meagre 50 paise or a rupee on an item worth ₹ 50. Recently, a shopper compared the prices at the local retailer and Big Bazar. The sales and claims of *'sabse sasta'* made by Big Bazar were true as they were selling at prices lower than other retailers to the tune of a rupee maximum. A big deal indeed! I wonder how many consumers have ever seen through this strategy!

There is no uniformity in the negotiation and all depends upon a consumer's skills and persistence in negotiation. Recently, when at the local retailer, a shopper pointed to him that MRP was negotiable, he was "informed" that no bargain was possible on brands sold by MNCs; and if people buy from big stores, the bargaining is not possible at all. A consumer purchased Nuttella from the local retailer who quoted a price of ₹ 275. Another retailer in the same area sold the same for ₹ 200. Just compare the margins and the discounts offered at MRP. Whose interests are being protected? Certainly not the consumers.

Moreover, even in allowing rebates to consumers, the retailer exercises control on how much price he is willing to reduce. There are no guidelines as to how much reduction the consumers can expect or how much they can ask for. The only action they can take is to change their retailers or pay the MRP if bargaining fails. Where the same products are bought in a different ambience, like cinema halls and restaurants, the companies have come out with an innovative strategy in order to circumvent the requirements of the law. While claiming to charge only the printed price, the companies are printing a higher MRP. So a one litre bottle of water available for ₹ 12 outside was available in a restaurant with an MRP of ₹ 20 mentioned on it. At another restaurant, a 750 ml bottle of water was available for ₹ 18. The practice thus, complies with the requirement that brands can be sold at a price not higher than the MRP and legally, different MRPs for different packages of the same commodity are permitted under excise law. The net effect of these provisions is that in the end, it is the consumer who is being short changed.

The arguments that brands should be priced differently because they are being sold in an ambience, or require special selling efforts are cause for a lot of consumer heartburn. The MRPs fixed by the manufacturers already take into consideration these variations and costs involved. The retailers purchase such supplies at bulk prices and discounts from their suppliers for further sale. A margin to profitability is added there too. Moreover, the decision to provide an ambience is that of the seller, and also an expenditure for selling his wares; and this is already built into the cost of selling. How many times should such costs be considered in fixing the prices and why then should the consumers be required to pay higher prices for all such decisions of the sellers where they have no decisive role? Therefore, even in such situations, there should be a cap on how much excess the consumers can be charged for the ambience—10 per cent per item, or 50 per cent or 100 per cent or even more. The charges could be linked to the stars allotted to hotels and restaurants. Cinema halls already charge a premium price for the movie tickets so why should consumers pay twice for purchasing eatables in the same ambience? Why should retailers always think of excuses to increase prices unnecessarily and not think of reducing the high profit margins they build into MRPs?

Impact of Non-Standard Pack Sizes, MRP and Absence of Unit Price

The result of the situation is that amended provisions provide an escape route to the manufacturer/packer to package the commodities specified in the Third Schedule in non-standard sizes and get away with it by a simple declaration required to be made on the package. However, because of the provision regarding non-standard package sizes, the consumers can be easily taken for a ride if they are not discerning or are illiterate. A market survey was conducted by the authors for seven products in October 2008 to identify the weights and corresponding prices. The results of the survey on biscuit packages of up to 250 grams a small value item purchased by consumers belonging to diverse socio-economic profiles are discussed.

The survey highlights three things: Firstly, it emphasized that in spite of the public outcry, the practice has become more popular than before with more manufacturers joining the bandwagon of those packaging in non-standard weights (the packages are reporting the date of manufacture as June 08 and beyond). Secondly, there is a proliferation of package sizes; for example, in less than 100g category, you can find packages for 66g, 70g, 71g, 75g, 86g, 88g, and 92g. Each manufacturer appears to be choosing a different package weight. Thirdly, the difference in weights for say in 50g to 100g category ranges from a measly 8g to as much as 34g.

The Consumer Protection Act, 1986, seeks, *inter alia* to promote and protect the rights of consumers such as

(a) The right to be protected against marketing of goods which are hazardous to life and property;
(b) The right to be informed about the quality, potency, purity, standard and price of goods to protect the consumer against unfair trade practice;
(c) The rights to be assured wherever possible access to goods at competitive prices;
(d) The right to be heard and to be assured that consumers interests will receive due consideration at appropriate forums;
(e) The rights to seek redress against unfair trade practices or unscrupulous exploitation of consumer; and
(f) Right to consumer education.

The amendment has jeopardized the exercise of two basic consumer rights—the right to be informed and the right of access to goods at competitive prices.

Another legislation, the Food Safety and Standards Act, 2006 (FSSA), consolidates the laws relating to food and establishes the Food Safety and Standards Authority of India for laying down science based standards for articles of food and to regulate their manufacture, storage, distribution, sale and import, to ensure availability of safe and wholesome food for human consumption and for matters related to them. Sections 23-25 of this Act prescribe provisions regarding packaging and labelling of foods.

Through these provisions, the Act, only specifies that the packages and labels should not contain anything that misleads the consumers. They should not be misbranded and should not contravene the provisions of any other Act, rules and regulations. The provisions of the Act are not invoked if the packages are marked and labelled and do not mislead the consumers. In the current scenario, these provisions have been reasonably complied with, except that the package sizes mislead the consumers in believing that the quantities available to them have not changed if they fail to read the declaration regarding the quantity.

Deceptive Package

The explanation to Packaged Commodities Rule 28 defines a deceptive package as one "which is so designed as to deliberately given to the consumer an exaggerated or misleading impression as to the quantity of the commodity contained therein, except where bigger dimensions of the package can be justified by the manufacturer or packer as the case may be, on the ground that such dimensions are necessary for giving protection to the commodity contained on such package or for meeting the requirements of the machine used for filling such package."

It is needless to say that a small variation in the quantity in a package may not necessarily require a change in the size of the package in case of all products. If the quantity in the package is changed, without prior notice to the consumer, or without the label "non-standard pack size", the consumer may be misled into believing that the quantity in the package continues to remain the same as before. In such cases, the packages will become deceptive. Packages for many brands were found to be violating this provision as well. In the absence of wide publicity of the changed provisions, the consumers did not even know that they should look out for these labels. The practice is, therefore, an unfair trade practice.

An "unfair trade practice" under Section 2 (r) of the Consumer Protection Act, 1986 means a trade practice which, for the purpose of promoting the sale, use or supply of any goods or for the provisions of any services, adopts any unfair method or unfair or deceptive practice. Clause (ix) of this section states that an unfair trade practice includes "materially misleading the public concerning the price at which a product or like products or goods or services, have been, or are, ordinarily sold or provided, and, for this purpose, a representation as to price shall be deemed to refer to the price at which the product or goods or services has or have been sold by sellers or provided by suppliers generally in the relevant market unless it is clearly specified to be the price at which the product has been sold or services have been provided by the person by whom or on whose behalf the representation is made."

The trade practice of doing away with mentioning the unit sale price and allowing the possibility of packaging in non-standard sizes by the amendment clearly has the effect of making price and quantity comparisons difficult for consumers. The sizes of the packages should enable the consumer to make reasonable comparisons of prices across brands as well as across the quantity of purchase. If they are unable to make such comparisons, the right to make an informed choice is clearly violated.

However, though the practice may not have contravened the provisions of the laws as they stand today, it certainly raises some ethical concerns. The market impact of this amendment to Packaged Commodities Rules throws up the question of whether it is ethical for business to pack products in irregular sizes, especially when the consumers have been used to purchasing products in standard sizes. Is it worth taking the risk of losing consumer confidence by resorting to such a practice rather than come out clearly with a higher MRP on the package upfront? Alternatively, would the insignificant change in the quantities in packages (e.g. from 100g to 88g) have increased the prices so much as to adversely impact sales?

It can be argued that it does not make a big difference to a single consumer; but it cannot be ignored that such a practice makes a huge difference to the profits earned by the manufacturer/packer, as he benefits on the total turnover, which is huge. Just consider for example, that a firm markets 5000 kg of biscuits in a month in a package of 100 g at the cost of Rupees 10 per packet. At this rate it is able to sell 50,000 packets of 100 g each in a month. This is not a very big number considering the size of the Indian Market. Suppose the company decides to reduce the quantity in the package to 90 g each for a price of ₹ 10. The 5000 kg of biscuits would now be sold in 55,555 packages at the price of ₹ 10. Thus, a reduction of 10 g in the weight per pack in this case yields a gain of ₹ 55,555 per month to just one marketer, without any corresponding increase in costs. This is by no means a small amount! Should a manufacturer be allowed to unjustly enrich himself by creating confusion for the consumers? If the decrease in the prices must be hyped, the increase in the prices should also be communicated in a similar fashion.

From a business ethics and consumer perspective, there is no reason why a manufacturer should want to sell in non-standard weights. The situation created by this amendment has amply demonstrated that by selling non-standard weights in packages which are deceptively similar to the standard weight packages, the manufacturers have practised deception. The packages of non-standard weights are deceptively similar to the standard weights specified; thus leading to deceive consumers in to believing that the price of the product has not changed. In order to prevent such deception, the rules should be amended to disallow non-standard packages restoring the pre-amendment position.

Applicability only to Packages Intended for Retail Sale

Another area that merits attention is that the provisions of the Packaged Commodities Rules apply only to packages intended for retail sale. Rule 2 A (b) has been inserted to clarify that the provisions of Chapter II of the Packaged Commodities Rules shall not apply to the Packaged Commodities meant for 'Industrial Consumers' and 'Institutional Consumers'. The *two* are defined below:

> "(a) Institutional Consumer means those consumers who buy Packaged Commodities from the manufacturers and packers for service industry like transportation (including Airways and Railways), Hotel or any other similar service industry.
> (b) Industrial Consumer means those consumers who buy Packaged Commodities directly from the manufacturers/

packers for using the product in their industry for production etc."

However, there may be consumers who could be buying in bulk and directly from the manufacturers in case there is a sizeable consumption of a particular product (say for example, in big or high consumption families, marriages or social and religious celebrations, festivals etc.); in many circumstances to save money. With the changes in retailing formats, the big retailers may purchase brands as institutional buyers and so the packages sold to the individual consumers may not be mentioning all labelling information required by law. Even if the products are to be used as further inputs by others, should they not be complying with the provisions of the Law to ensure that outdated ingredients for example, are not used in manufacturing?

To talk of Institutional consumers are some of them not buying these products for further use by consumers; say for example, people travelling through railways and airways or staying in hotels or hospitals? A part of the cost of travel covers the expenses on providing these accompaniments to the travellers. Do such consumers not have a right to the information on packages? It is also not uncommon to find such packages in retail sales or their use as samples. Are such consumers not vulnerable due to the amendment requiring non-compliance of the provisions by the 'Industrial Consumers' or 'Institutional Consumers'? Some companies may simply distribute their outdated products as free samples, especially to the poor and vulnerable consumers?

Font Size for Declarations

In buying medicines and cosmetics, many consumers have often complained that they are not able to read label information with their reading glasses and have to carry a magnifying glass! It is often seen that the declarations that are required under the rules are made in very fine print which the consumers find very difficult to read. Packaged Commodities Rule 7 dealing with the principal display panel its area, size and letter specifies the minimum height of numerals in terms of mm. In this era of technical advancement, these specifications can be prescribed in font sizes that are easy to read.

Amount of Information on the Label

The culprit for fine prints is also the amount of information appearing on the label. Often so much unreadable information is presented that it serves no useful purpose. There is, therefore, a need for reorganizing the information that must appear on the package. While important warnings and information (e.g. for ingredients see leaflet, in case of complaints see leaflet, usage instructions—inside; side effects inside, etc.) may appear on the package, the additional information (e.g. instructions for use, side effects, contact details of complaints officer, etc.) may be put on a sheet of paper inserted inside the package or tagged to it. Too much information in an unreadable format can hardly be used by the consumers. Information that cannot be easily read by the consumer while choosing products and services is as good as no information. It serves no purpose even if it is provided.

Exempting Fast Food and Meals at Restaurants and Outlets

There is also a need to take a closer look at the exemptions granted under Packaged Commodities Rule 34(d) for packages, containing fast food items packed or served by restaurants/hotels and the like. While the consumers continue to pay higher prices for French Fries, Pizzas and Burgers, and other items like vegetables, *dals* etc., the quantities offered are reduced or accompaniments available earlier are downsized or removed without correspondingly reducing the prices. In buying french fries for example, the consumer has to depend upon the 'mood' of the person serving him at the fast food outlet; there is simply no weight definition as to what constitutes a regular, or small pack and what constitutes a large helping. This happens even though the pictures in the restaurants show a serving including the peripherals. In view of the increasing popularity and consumption of fast foods, there is a need to regulate the marketers here too. It is not too difficult to prescribe sizes, or portions of helpings as is done in many other countries.

The Impact of Language in the Legislation

The Andhra Pradesh Legal Metrology Department recently caught big companies like Titan, Reliance Communications, Videocon, Samsung Electronics, and Madhura Coats violating the provisions of the Weights and Measures Act, 1976. Videocon Industries, for example, failed to mention the name and address of the manufacturer, the date of packing and the sale price was smudged. Titan Industries did not mention the sale price and the details of the manufacturer. Samsung Electronics did not mention the date of packing. Reliance communications did not disclose details regarding customer care as well as those of the manufacturer. Madhura Coats also defaulted on mentioning the details of Consumer care officer.

When the Legal Metrology Department of Andhra Pradesh came down heavily on these companies and seized their products, the companies went in appeal to the Andhra Pradesh High Court and challenged some of the provisions of Standards of Weights and Measures Act and Rules. The legal representatives of the companies emphasized that the notification under Section 1(3)(d) did not cover the companies products. According to them, this clause of the Standards of Weights and Measures Act, 1976 lays down that the Act "shall come into force on such date (the specified date was 20th September, 1977) as the Central Government may, by notification, appoint, and different dates may be appointed for different areas...(and) classes of goods." The applicability of the Act and Rules to sale and distribution of goods cannot be brought under the purview of the Act and Rules unless specific notifications regarding a particular class of goods and area are issued.

The Andhra Pradesh Legal Metrology Department, however, has not let the matter rest and has approached the Ministry of Consumer Affairs to issue a separate notification to plug the loopholes. A letter from the Andhra Pradesh Controller of Legal Metrology Tej Deep Kaur Menon, IPS to the Central Government in September 2007 has set the ball rolling and it remains to be seen if this initiative will bring in a more comprehensive legislation to protect the consumers' interest.

A Way-Out...

Under Section 23(4), the manufacturer/packer is required to indicate by not less than two advertisements in one or more newspapers and also by circulation of notices to the dealers and to the Director in the Central Government and Controllers of Legal Metrology in the States and Union Territories, the revised prices of packages on account of changes in taxes payable. A similar declaration may be made mandatory for the manufacturers/packers in case of variations in the quantity as well. The provisions should be applicable to all products that are sold in packages irrespective of size or nature of institution purchasing them.

Thus, the Department of Consumer Affairs, Government of India, should come out clearly with a policy directive on standardizing quantities in packages in exercise of its right under Section 39(5) of The Standards of Weights and Measures Act, 1976. It cannot be a mute spectator to the silent exploitation of the consumers. Further, it must initiate steps to amend the rules to delete the rule that allows non-standard packages to prevent such occurrences in the future in the interests of the consumers. The rules are in the nature of subsidiary legislation and the Ministry is competent to make the necessary amendments. An easier solution would be to revoke the amendments made in this respect and restore the pre-amendment position in the wider interests of the consumers.

The Department of Consumer Affairs, Government of India has recently set up an Inter Ministerial Group (IMG) which has taken up some of these issues and invited comments of the stakeholders. The last date was January 31, 2009. The authors have also communicated their observations on the issues raised. It is expected that a decision will soon be taken by the Department keeping in mind the interest of the consumers.

While efforts are being made at the governmental level, the consumers must also take reasonable and proactive measures to protect their interests. They must understand that the choice of making purchases and spending money on the brands is with them because it is they who have to spend their money. In purchasing products that are packaged only in standard sizes, they can be successful in dissuading manufacturers and packers in adopting unethical practices in packaging.

Appendix

Price quantity Comparisons for Various Brands of Biscuits

Brand Name	*Price (₹)*	*Weight*	*Date of Manufacturing/ Packing*
Sunfeast-Snacky-Salted Biscuit With Chilli Flakes	8	75 g	June 08
Sunfeast-Marie Light	13	711 g	August 08
Britania-Nutri Choice Digestive Biscuits	38	250 g	2-9-2008
Britania-Nutri Choice Digestive Biscuits	15	100 g	5-9-2008
Britania-Nutri Choice Cream Cracker	10	100 g	30-7-2008
Britania-Nice Time	10	86 g	6-8-2008
Britania-50-50	7	71 g	20-3-2008
Britania-Good Day Rich Cashew	12	92 g	23-8-2008
Britania-Good Day Rich Pista Badam	15	92 g	18-8-2008
Britania-Good Day Rich Rich Butter	10	92 g	20-8-2008
Britania-Good Day Choco Chip	15	75	31-8-2008
Britania-Good Day Choco Nut	15	100 g	23-8-2008
Britania-Classic Cookes	15	75 g	21-6-2008
Britania-Pure Magic	15	100 g	13-8-2008
Britania-Treat Jim Jam	14	100 g	30-8-2008
Britania-Good Day Rich Butter	21	207 g	21-9-2008
Britania-Good Day Rich Cashew	17	207 g	14-9-2008
Britania-Good Day Rich Pista Badam	28	207 g	13-9-2008
Britania-Masti Treat Orange	18	164 g	2-9-2008
Britania-Treat Jim Jam	24	200 g	8-8-2008
Britania-Tiger Glucose Biscuits	10	210 g	4-9-2008
Britania-Time Pass Salted	10	114 g	28-8-2008
Britania-Vita Marie Gold	14	140 g	2-9-2008
Britania-Marie Gold	13	176 g	3-9-2008
Parle-Hide and Seek Milano	15	65 g	June 08
Parle-Krack Jack	7	75 g	September 08
Parle-Hide and Seek Choco Chip Cookies	15	100 g	August 08
Parle-Parle-G	4	100 g	August 08
Parle-Monaco	20	240 g	September 08
Parle-Milk Shakti	10	150 g	August 08
Parle-Monaco	7	75 g	September 08
PriyaGold-Snacks Zig-Zag	5	70 g	June 08

(Contd.)

(*Contd.*)

Brand Name	Price (₹)	Weight	Date of Manufacturing/ Packing
PriyaGold-Kids Cream Choco Vanilla	10	150 g	July 08
PriyaGold-CNC	10	120	August 08
PriyaGold-Coconut Crunch	30	350 g	August 08
PriyaGold-Marie Lite	30	350 g	August C8
Premium-Pickwick Wafers Orange Flavour	48	200	March 08
Premium-Pickwick Wafers Choco Flavour	48	200	March 08
Premium-Pickwick Wafers Pineapple Flavour	48	200	March 08
Premium-Pickwick Wafers Strawberry Flavour	48	200	March 08
Premium-Pickwick Wafers Pticks (Strawberry/Choco)	90	300	July 08

Source: Survey conducted during October 2008.

NOTES

1. *Hindustan Times*, April 8, 2008, New Delhi.
2. Baby food, weaning food, biscuits, bread including brown bread but excluding bun, uncanned packages of butter and margarine, cereals and pulses, coffee, tea, materials which may be constituted or reconstituted as beverages, edible oils, vanaspati, ghee, butter oil, milk powder, non-soapy detergents powder, rice powdered, flour, atta, rawa and suji, salt, soaps (laundry soap, non-soapy detergent cakes/bars; toilet soap) including all kinds of bath soap (cakes); aerated soft drinks and non-alcoholic beverages, mineral water and drinking water, cement in bags and paint, varnish etc.
3. N.B. Grant, "Maximum retail price — For whose benefit?" *Financial Express*, April 15, 1999.
4. Local taxes in the country mean the following taxes: Central Sales Tax - by the Union Government; State Sales Tax - by the State; Entry Tax - by the state; Octroi - by the municipal or gram panchayat authority and Luxury Tax - by the state.

REFERENCES

Anonymous, *Labels with More Weight, Choice* (0009-496X); June, p. 16, 1/2 p. 2008.

Buhl, Timo, Kampmann, Hubert, Martinez, Jose, and Fuchs, Thomas (2008) "The European Labelling Law for Foodstuffs Contains Life-Threatening Exemptions for Food-Allergic Consumers", *International*

Archives of Allergy and Immunology; Vol. 146, Issue 4, pp. 334-337, 2008.

Consumer Protection Act, 1986.

Food Safety and Standards Act, 2006.

Nachay, Karen, "FDA Posts Food Labelling Guide", *Food Technology*; Vol. 62, Issue 6, p. 18, 2008.

Rigby, P.M. and Tommis, Y. (2008) "Improving Food Purchasing Choices through Increased Understanding of Food Labels, Using Itemized Till Receipts to Measure these Changes", *Journal of Human Nutrition and Dietetics*; August, Vol. 21, Issue 4, pp. 400-401.

Standards of Weights and Measures (Packaged Commodities) Rules, 1977.

Standards of Weights and Measures Act, 1976.

13
Grievance Redressal Mechanism: A Study of Insurance Sector

Sheetal Kapoor

Introduction

The objective of liberalization of the insurance sector was to enhance consumer awareness of various products and to provide world-class policy servicing with cost effectiveness and full justice in case of dispute. There is no doubt that well-informed customers are an asset for any industry.

The insured is always exposed to many kinds of risks such as, failure of the product to meet its forecast or perceived performance or the promises made by the agent about the product and its benefits, delay in services or not attending to the customer's request/queries/objections. Further, there can be expectations based on perception of the Insured and rejection of the claims/delay in settlement of claims. Insurance is a matter of solicitation. The individual has considerably less knowledge about the product and therefore, the individuals, rely heavily on the Insurer/Agent/ Adviser or its intermediary for guidance and support. It has been observed that the proposal papers are generally completed by Agents but the Insured/Claimant has to face its implications as adequate information is not provided. Medical Reports/Agents Reports are filled in a routine manner. Keeping in view this, it requires a regulated market with proper control to buy a product in a truly competitive market with the confidence that there is a regulatory system that will provide an environment of trust and even if something goes wrong. The individual can approach an independent body to get his grievance redressed. This is the level of confidence that needs to be built into the system.

This paper highlights the grievance redressal mechanism that is available to the consumers which includes, CGC (Consumer Grievance Cell) at IRDA, Ombudsman (Quasi-Judicial forum), In-house-Internal Grievance Redressal Mechanism and Consumer Forums (District, State and National Commission and Civil Courts). The paper discusses the merits of using the various grievance redressal tools for speedy handling of consumer complaints and suggests remedies to strengthen the redressal mechanism.

The Grievance Redressal Mechanism available to customers in the Indian Insurance Industry are as follows:

1. In-house-Internal Grievance Redressal Mechanism
2. Consumer Grievance Cell at IRDA (CGC)
3. Ombudsman
4. Consumer Forums (District, State and National Commission)
5. Civil Courts

Internal Grievance Redressal Mechanism

Generally every Insurance Company has a call centre which clarifies most of the queries of the customers over the phone. A customer relationship team caters to all the grievances of the customers. An independent Claims Review Committee, generally having a retired judge as a member, ensures equity and justice.

Consumer Grievance Cell at IRDA (CGC)

Insurance Regulatory Development Authority (IRDA) came into existence by an Act of Parliament in December 1999 and a subsequent notification in April 2000. Its mission is to protect the interest of holders of insurance policies, to regulate, promote and ensure orderly growth of the insurance industry. The powers and functions of the authority mentioned under Section 14(1)(b) of the IRDA Act, 1999, includes protection of the interest of the Policyholders in matters concerning assigning of policy, nomination by policyholders, insurable interest, settlement of Insurance Claims, surrender value of the policy and other terms and conditions of the Contracts of Insurance. To address the consumer complaints the IRDA constituted the CGC in November 2002. The Cell receives complaints from the insurance customers and forwards them to companies concerned for early resolution. The customers are required to first approach the Grievance/Customer Complaints Cell of the concerned insurer. If they do not receive any response from the insurer within a reasonable period or are dissatisfied with the response, they can approach the CGC. It plays a facilitative role by taking up such complaints with respective insurers. It also handles complaints relating to:

1. Delay/non-response regarding policies and claims.
2. Where complaints require adjudication, the policyholder has to approach quasi-judicial or judicial channel, i.e. ombudsman, consumer forum or civil court.

Cases of delay/non-response in matters relating to policies and claims are taken up by the CGC with the insurers, for speedy disposal.

Claims/Policy Contracts in Dispute

Complaints relating to these are analyzed and forwarded to the insurers for examination. If required, their attention is called to specific issues for examination/re-examination. The IRDA does not carry out any adjudication. Complaints against Non-life insurance companies can be e-mailed at nonlifecomplaints@irdaonline.org and complaints against life insurance companies at lifecomplaints@irdaonline.org. The Grievance Cell of the IRDA receives complaints from policyholders, insurance intermediaries and from other sources against different Life Insurance companies. On receipt of the complaints the cell functions in *two* ways:

(a) facilitates an early resolution of the complaint by the insurer through direct interaction with the policyholder, and

(b) analyses the complaints based on duration of disposal and functional area.

Nature of Complaints Received – Life Insurers

As on March 31, 2007, there were 299 complaints pending with the CGC for want of resolution by life insurance companies. During the year 2007-08, the Authority had received 2057 complaints, out of which, 651 related to LIC and 1406 to the private sector insurers. 57 per cent of the total complaints received against life insurers by the IRDA during the year 2007-08 were resolved by the former. While the private life insurers resolved 78 per cent of the complaints registered, LIC had resolved only 19 per cent of the complaints filed against them with the Authority. Table 13.1 shows the number of complaints received by the CGC related to life insurers.

Table 13.1. Status of Grievances Related to Life Insurers

Insurer	*Outstanding as on 31-3-2007*	*Grievance Reported during 2007-08*	*Total No. of complaints as on 31-3-08*	*Resolved during the year 2007-08*	*Outstanding as on 31-3-2008*
LIC	197	651	848	163 (19.22%)	685
Private	102	1406	1508	1176 (77.98%)	332
Total	**299**	**2057**	**2356**	**1339 (56.83%)**	**1017**

Source: IRDA Annual Report, 2007-08.

Nature of Complaints Received – Non-Life Insurers

As on March 31, 2007, there were 623 complaints pending with the general insurance companies for resolution. During 2007-08, 2229 complaints were received out of which 1339 pertained to public sector companies and the remaining 90 were against private sector companies. Of the total grievances of 2852, 69 per cent of the grievances were resolved in the current year. 63 per cent of the complaints were resolved by the public sector companies whereas the private sector insurers resolved 81 per cent.

Table 13.2: Status of Grievances Related to Non-Life Insurers

Status of Grievances-Non Life Insurers									
Insurer	*Outstanding as on 31-3-2007*	*Grievances Reported during 2007-08*	*Total No. of Complaints as on 31-3-08*	*Resolved during 2007-08*	*Outstanding as on 31-3-2008*	*Break-up of outstanding grievances according to nature*			
						(i)	*(ii)*	*(iii)*	*(iv)*
Public	517	1339	1856	1174 (63.25)	682	226	299	132	25
Private	106	890	996	812 (80.52)	194	108	47	33	6
Total	623	2229	2852	1976 (69-28)	876	334 (38.13	346 (39.50)	165 (18.84)	31 (3.54)

Note: Figures in bracket are percentage to the respective totals.

Source: IRDA Annual Report, 2007-08.

As on March 31, 2008, 876 complaints were pending for resolution with the insurers out of which 682 were with public sector companies and the remaining 194 with the private sector. Of the total pending grievances, 38.13 per cent are policy related issues, 39.50 per cent to non-settlement/delay in settlement of claims, 18.84 per cent to repudiation/partial settlement of claim and the remaining for other reasons.

Insurance Ombudsman

'Ombudsman' is a Swedish word, meaning 'legal representative'. Worldwide it stands for an official appointed by the government to investigate individuals' complaints against public authorities[1]. Ombudsman was initially started in Sweden in 1809 and adopted in many countries thereafter, e.g. Finland, Denmark, Norway, New Zealand, Mauritius, Guyana and United Kingdom.

The Ombudsman Scheme in the Financial Sector was initially introduced in the Banking Sector with RBI Notification in 1995, subsequently amended in 2002. The Government of India introduced the Insurance Ombudsman Scheme in the Insurance Sector through a notification of "Redressal of Public Grievance Rules, 1998" (RPG Rules) under Section 114 of the Insurance Act, 1938. At that time, IRDA had not come into existence. Insurance Ombudsman handles complaints of aggrieved insured persons. This institution is of great importance and relevance for the protection of interests of policyholders and also in building their confidence in the system. The institution has helped to generate and sustain the faith and confidence amongst the consumers and insurers.

Appointment of Insurance Ombudsman

The governing body of Insurance Council issues orders of appointment of the Insurance Ombudsman on the recommendations of the committee comprising Chairman, IRDA, Chairman, LIC, Chairman, GIC and a representative of the Central Government. Insurance Council comprises members of the Life Insurance Council and General Insurance Council formed under Section 40-C of the Insurance Act, 1938. The governing body of Insurance Council consists of representatives of insurance companies. Ombudsmen are drawn from Insurance, Industry, Civil Services and Judicial Services. An Insurance Ombudsman is appointed for a term of three years or till the incumbent attains the age of sixty-five years, whichever is earlier. Re-appointment is not permitted.

Territorial Jurisdiction and Powers of Ombudsman

The governing body has appointed twelve Ombudsman across the country, allotting them different geographical areas as their areas of jurisdiction. The Ombudsman may hold sittings at various places within their area of jurisdiction in order to expedite disposal of complaints. The offices of the twelve Insurance Ombudsmans are located at (1) Bhopal, (2) Bhubaneswar, (3) Cochin, (4) Guwahati, (5) Chandigarh, (6) New Delhi, (7) Chennai, (8) Kolkata, (9) Ahmedabad, (10) Lucknow, (11) Mumbai, (12) Hyderabad. The areas of jurisdiction of each Ombudsman has been mentioned in the list of Ombudsmen. The Insurance Ombudsman has *two* types of functions to perform:

(1) Conciliation
(2) Award making

The Insurance Ombudsman is empowered to receive and consider complaints in respect of personal lines of insurance from any person who has any grievance against an insurer. The complaint may relate to any grievance against the insurer, i.e. (a) any partial or total repudiation of claims by the insurance companies, (b) dispute with regard to the premium paid or payable in terms of the Policy, (c) dispute on the legal construction of the Policy wordings in case such dispute relates to claims, (d) delay in settlement of claims, and (e) non-issuance of any insurance document to the customers after receipt of premium. Ombudsman's powers are restricted to insurance contracts of value not exceeding ₹ 20 lakh. The insurance companies are required to honour the awards passed by an Insurance Ombudsman within three months.

Manner of Lodging the Complaint

The complaint by an aggrieved person has to be in writing, and addressed to the Insurance Ombudsman of the jurisdiction under which the office of the insurer falls. The complaint can also be lodged through the legal heirs of the insured. Before lodging a complaint:

(i) the complainant should have made a representation to the insurer named in the complaint and the insurer either should have rejected the complaint or the complainant have not received any reply within a period of one month after the concerned insurer has received his complaint or he is not satisfied with the reply of the insurer.

(ii) The complaint is not made later than one year after the insurer had replied.

(iii) The same complaint on the subject should not be pending with before any court, consumer forum or an arbitrator.

Recommendations of the Ombudsman

When a complaint is settled through the mediation of the Ombudsman, he shall make the recommendations which he thinks fair in the circumstances of the case. Such a recommendation shall be made not later than one month and copies of the same should be sent to complainant and the insurance company concerned. If the complainant accepts the recommendations, he will send a communication in writing within 15 days of the date of receipt of accepting the settlement.

Award

The Ombudsman shall pass an award within a period of three months from the receipt of the complaint. The awards are binding upon the insurance companies. If the policyholder is not satisfied with the award of the Ombudsman he can approach other venues like Consumer Forums and Courts of Law for redressal of his grievances. As per the policyholder's protection regulations, every insurer shall inform the policyholder along with the policy document in respect of the Insurance Ombudsman in whose jurisdiction his office falls for the purpose of grievances redressal arising, if any, subsequently.

Steady increase in the number of complaints received by various Ombudsmen shows that the policyholders are reposing their confidence in the institution of Insurance Ombudsman. During 2007-08, 10865 complaints were lodged with the Ombudsmen against the insurers both life and non-life. Of these, 5565 were against life insurers and remaining 5300 were against the non-life insurers. As on April 1, 2007, there were 1947 complaints pending with the Ombudsmen for disposal. Of these, 603 complaints were pending against the life insurers and the remaining were against the non-life insurers. As such, complaints outstanding with the Ombudsmen for disposal as on April 1, 2008 were 1419; of which 390 were in the case of life insurers and 1344 were against non-life insurers.

The Consumer Protection Act, 1986

The most important milestone in the consumer movement in the country has been the enactment of the Consumer Protection Act, 1986. The Act has set in motion a revolution in the field of consumer rights, that perhaps cannot be paralleled anywhere else in the World. The Act applies to all goods and services unless specially exempted by the Central Government, in all sectors whether Private, Public or Co-operative[2].

'Service' as defined under the Consumer Protection Act

The expression service has been defined in the Consumer Protection Act[3] as service of any description which is made available to the potential user and includes but not limited to, the provision of facilities in connection with banking, financing, insurance, transport, processing, supply of electrical or other energy, board or lodging or both, housing construction, entertainment, amusement or purveying of news or other information, but does not include the rendering of any service free of charge or under a contract of personal service. The definition of service, as stated above, may be divided in three parts: (i) inclusive, (ii) illustrative, and (iii) exclusionary. The deficiency in service is one of the grounds for filing complaint under the Act and at present majority of the complaints before these adjudicatory bodies relate to the deficiency in service of various service providers. The term 'deficiency' has also been defined in Section 2(1)(g) of the Act. It means any fault, imperfection, shortcoming or inadequacy in the quality, nature and manner of performance which is required to be maintained by or under law for the time being in force or has been undertaken to be performed by a person in pursuance of a contract or otherwise in relation to any service.

Nature of Complaints Received by the Consumer Courts

Consumer Courts in their various judgments have directed the insurance companies:

- To give the policyholders complete information pertaining to the policy.
- Not to exploit the ignorance of consumers to deny the legitimate claim.

It is the fundamental principle of 'insurance' that utmost good faith must be observed by the contracting parties. After the completion of the contract, no material alteration can be made in its terms except by mutual consent. The insured cannot claim anything more than what is covered by the insurance policy. If the contract is vague, the benefit should be given to the insured.

Table 13.3: Disposal of complaints by Insurance Ombudsman

	Particular	No. of Complaints as on 31.3.07	From 1.4.07 to 31.3.08	Total	Disposed	Recom-mendation	Awards	With-drawal/ settlement	Non-Acceptance	Dismissal	Not Entertain-able	complaints Out-standing
		Disposal of Complaints by Ombudsman 2007-08				*No. of Complaints disposed of by way of*						
Life	Public	491	4414	4905	4581	111	751	612	112	371	2624	324
	Private	112	1151	1263	1197	12	216	110	2	110	747	66
	Total	**603**	**5565**	**6168**	**5778 *(93.68)**	**123 (2.13**	**967 (16.74)**	**722 (12.50)**	**114 (1.97)**	**481 (8.32)**	**3371 (56.34)**	**390 (6.75)**
Non-Life	Public	1147	4294	5441	4603	206	1457	496	65	541	1838	838
	Private	197	1006	1203	1012	23	240	101	20	134	494	191
	Total	**1344**	**5300**	**6644**	**5615 *(84.51**	**229 (4.08)**	**1697 (30.22)**	**597 (10.63)**	**85 (1.51)**	**675 12.02)**	**2332 (41.53)**	**1029 (18.33)**
Combined		1947	10865	12812	11393 *(88.92)	352 (3.09)	2664 (23.38)	1319 (11.58)	199 (1.75)	1156 (10.15)	5703 (50.06)	1419 (12.46)

Note: AUC, ECGC are included in the Public Sector
* represents percentages to the respective complaints disposed.

Source: IRDA Annual Report, 2007-08.

Insurance works on customer's trust and service. Some of the instances of deficiency in insurance sector are:

Ambiguous Terms of Policy

Three double benefit insurance policies in a total sum of ₹ 1,50,000 taken by respondent's husband covering his life. As the scooter which he was driving suddenly slipped and he died in this accident. Insurance company paid the insured amount of ₹ 1,50,000 to the respondent but failed to pay the double accident benefit. National Consumer Dispute Redressal Commission held that if the insurance policy is capable of two interpretations, interest of justice would be served if it is interpreted for the benefit of the assured as it would serve the purpose and object of getting insurance coverage[4]. Thus, the insurance company could not escape its liability to pay the accident benefits.

Motor Accident

Mr. Narayan Singh bought a Maruti car from the original owner on May 31, 1995. Unfortunately within just five days of its purchase, the car met with an accident. The original owner from whom he had purchased the car had insured it for ₹ 1,40,000 which was valid till August 2, 1995. However, the insurance company refused to indemnify the loss on the ground that the insurance policy had not been transferred to the new owner[5].

On the basis of facts, the apex consumer court said that the insurance company ought not to have rejected the claim on the ground that the vehicle was not transferred in favour of the complainant. Even, under Section 157 of the Motor Vehicle Act, a transfer application is to be made within a period of 14 days and those 14 days had not lapsed in the above case. The Commission said that it was highly improper and unjustified on the part of the insurance company to reject the claim of the vehicle owner. The Commission directed the company to pay a punitive damage of ₹ 1 lakh, in addition to paying the consumer, ₹ 1,40,000 along with interest at the rate of 12 per cent per annum calculated six months from the date of the accident.

Both Insurer and Insured must disclose all Facts

The insured must disclose all the material facts about the things to be insured. Insurance contract is a contract of utmost good faith. This principle is applicable to both insured and insurer[6].

Delay in Settling Claims

Undue delay in payment of insurance claims amounts to deficiency in service[7]. Abnormal delay by insurer in appointment of surveyor and settlement of claims of losses was also held 'deficiency of service'[8].

Repudiation of Insurance Policy

The insured should be careful in furnishing information while buying an insurance policy. According to a ruling given by the Supreme Court on 20th November, 2007, the apex court dismissed a petition filed by the claimants seeking recovery of the amount of insurance on the death of the insured. The insured had undergone an operation but in application form for taking policy he had not mentioned the same. It was found by the court that if a fraudulent act is discovered the policy can be repudiated[9].

Medical Insurance and Pre-existing Diseases

Insurance is a contract upon speculation. It is a contract of utmost good faith—*uberrima fides*. The person who desires to take an insurance policy must disclose to the underwriter all the material facts as the insurer knows nothing and the insured knows everything. The special facts lie commonly in the knowledge of the insured and the insurer trusts the insured's representations.

Understanding Pre-existing Illness

- Pre-existing illness is an important term in the medical insurance.
- It refers to the illness that is present or experienced before the insurance policy is undertaken.

- This could be a disease or illness suffered before the policy.
- Normal medical insurance policies do not allow coverage for expenses arising out of such pre-existing illness.
- A move to ensure that there is some way to tackle this area is under discussion.
- One option is to have a separate policy that would cover such pre-existing illness.
- Or an existing policy will cover the illness after making the necessary disclosures.
- In such cases the premium to be paid increases.
- As a policyholder, one should make a full and proper disclosure of any such illness.

An insurer who issued a mediclaim insurance policy was not permitted to escape liability to pay the expenses of bypass surgery by saying that there was a ten-year history of chest pain, which was not disclosed in the proposal form. In case of mediclaim insurance policy it is highly relevant to understand the term pre-existing illness. Concealment or misrepresentation of material facts is fatal to the contract. Fraud invalidates the insurance and deprives the party from all his rights arising out of the contract. But once the insurance policy has been taken after disclosure of all the material facts then the insurance company cannot later on repudiate the claim on the grounds that the disease was pre-existing and the insured had concealed the facts at the time of taking Mediclaim Policy. The whole idea behind this is to ensure that there are no problems when it comes to claiming a payout on the policy.

Redressal Mechanism under CPA

The Act provides for a three-tier quasi-judicial body established at three levels, District, State and National. At present there are 35 State Commissions, one in each State/UT and 621 district fora besides the National Commission. The pecuniary jurisdiction of the District Forum is up to ₹ 20 lakh, and that of the State Commissions is above ₹ 20 lakh and below ₹ 1 crore and claims involving more than ₹ 1 crore are to be filled directly before the National Commission.

Table 13.4: Redressal Agencies and Jurisdiction

	Redressal Agency	*Establishing Authority*	*Area of Jurisdiction*	*Compensation Claim*
1.	District Forum	State Government	District	Not exceeding ₹ 20 lakh
2.	State Commission	State Government	State	Exceeding ₹ 20 lakh but less than ₹ 1 crore
3.	National Commission	Central Government	Country	Exceeding ₹ 1 crore

During the last two decades the consumer redressal agencies at the district, state and the central level have resolved numerous complaints related to insurance under the 'deficiency of service'.

Consumer Guidance and Education

There is a dire need for sustained consumer education programmes and various initiatives to inform the consumers about how to seek redressal and also to ensure high-level service from insurance companies for higher customer satisfaction. Ombudsman is a free, fair and fast method of seeking redressal and there are no fees required for seeking grievance redressal under this method. The need of the hour is Consumer care for versatility and more independent professional force to help in making choice amongst wide ranging products and a common service standard for all. Non-transparency and lack of empathy towards the policyholder on the part of the insurer have been the main irritant factor coupled with vague policy conditions. Ignorance of the rules and conditions of the policy contract on the part of the insured public is another major factor for grievances. The policy terms and conditions are neither explicit nor quoted in a simple language. The policy conditions should invariably be given to the policyholder along with educative material on "why the claim is denied", "free look period"—how it helps you with most Frequently Asked Questions (FAQ). In case of complaints, the full address of the Grievance Officer and thereafter the address of the Ombudsman of that area should also be mentioned. The basis of repudiation needs to be elaborated in order to minimize the complaints.

The role and responsibility of the distribution channel is to be highlighted by the insurer through pamphlets and other means, so that the insured can understand the consequences of handing over cash/cheque to the Agent and also what care is required to be taken when the Agent completes the proposal form and delay in submission of various documents by the insured to the insurer. In mediclaim policy the exclusion imposed on the policy should clearly state its consequences. The medical report forms are well designed to elicit vital information but they do not serve the desired purpose, whereas the insured feels that once he was declared fit by the medical examiner there is no reason to deny the claims at a future date. Thus, in a contract of insurance, there is a requirement of *uberrima fides,* i.e. good faith on the part of the assured and the contract is likely to be construed *conta proferentem,* i.e. against the insurance company in case of any ambiguity or doubt. The insurance sector is now open to both private and public entities. Therefore, it is hoped that through healthy competition the insurance sector would meet the requirements of the consumer.

NOTES

1. Consumer Network (Vol. 14, No. 2, June 2007) pp. 28-29.
2. CPA Section 1(4).
3. *Ibid.* Section 2(1)(o) .
4. 2008 CTJ 450 (CP) (NCDRC).
5. *Sri Narayan Singh* v. *New India Assurance Company,* RP No. 556, 2002.
6. *United India Assurance Co.* v. *MKJ Corporation,* (1997) 5 CTJ 649 (SC).
7. *Ajmer Singh Cotton and General Mills* v. *United India Assurance Co.,* (1993) CTJ 469 (NCDRC).
8. *Delkon India Pvt. Ltd.* v. *Oriental Insurance Co.* (1993).
9. "Incorrect Information Can Lead to Repudiation of Insurance Policy", *Consumer Protection and Trade Practices Journal,* p. 19.

14

Consumer Participation in Electricity Regulation

Y.G Muralidharan

Introduction

During the past two decades many developed as well as developing countries have embarked on electricity sector reforms. These reforms have taken place within the backdrop of a wider paradigm shift from state ownership and centralized organization of infrastructure industries to private ownership, public regulation, and market-oriented structures. Governments have recognized the need for reassessment of the performance of infrastructure sectors hitherto in the exclusive domain of monopoly service providers. The objectives of these reforms have been to achieve economic efficiency and lower prices for business and consumers.

Even as the waves of programmes for the deregulation of public utilities were being undertaken, governments have also begun to explore the need to make utilities more accountable to the consumers. There is a growing recognition that the decades of annual reporting to Parliament and Legislatures, and internal complaints handling supervised by government departments, has been inadequate. Though the initial focus of economic reforms was dominated by the need to establish competitive markets and appropriate regulatory systems, governments soon realized the need for adequate consumer protection and effective processes for consultation with, and involvement of consumers in the regulatory system.

The transformation of the electricity industry from a regulated monopoly to an industry where it is expected that the free play of market forces will play a greater regulatory role, has emphasized the need for consumer participation and involvement in the power sector. In order that the transition of the sector to a competitive market be successful, it is important to ensure the participation of consumers.

Legal Background

In India, consumer participation in electricity regulation is of a recent origin. Despite the fact that consumers had opportunities for involving actively in electricity issues, there was hardly any efforts made. The Electricity Act, 1910 provided for constitution of an Advisory Board consisting of a Chairman and not less than two other members. The State Governments were given the powers to determine the number of such members, their duties, role etc. Yet consumers were never treated as one of the stakeholders. It was only in 1998 when the Electricity Regulatory Commission Act was enacted that some space was provided for consumer participation in the power sector regulation. Section 14 of the Act says that the 'Central Commission may, by notification, establish with effect from such date as it may specify in such notification, a Committee to be known as the Central Advisory Committee.' Further, it provided that the Committee shall consist of not more than 31 members to represent the interests of commerce, industry, transport, agriculture, labour, consumers, Non-Governmental Organizations and academic and research bodies in the energy sector.

Very soon some of the States moved ahead with unbundling the power sector with the aid of State Electricity Reforms Act. Orissa was the first state to move in that direction. This was followed by states like Andhra Pradesh, Karnataka, Delhi, Rajasthan and Maharashtra (not in that order). Yet none of these with the exception of Karnataka did institutionalize consumer participation. Perhaps for the first time in the country the Karnataka Electricity Reforms Act (KERA), 1999 introduced the concept of Consumer Advocacy as prevalent in UK, USA and other countries. Section 8 of KERA says that the Commission shall have a senior officer to represent the common interest of the consumers in all matters, hearings and proceedings before the Commission. Provided, that such appointment of the senior officer to represent the interests shall be in addition to, and not in derogation in any manner of the other rights of the individual consumers and also of the representations by consumer for a organization before the Commission, as may be recognized by the Commission in the regulations or otherwise.

The Electricity Reforms Act of almost all States gave other opportunities for consumers to intervene. Tariff setting, the most contentious issue in power sector was made the function of the Commission. As a result, consumers got an opportunity to participate. Commissions were under obligation to determine tariff only after conducting a public hearing and giving all consumers an opportunity to express their views. Further, the Commissions were to fix tariff keeping the interest of consumers in view.

The Commissions were also empowered to recognize consumers and consumer groups as affected parties and were allowed to appear before the Commission in any matter relating to electricity brought before the Commission. Apart from rate making (tariff setting) rule making is another area where consumer participation has been allowed. The electricity regulatory commissions cannot frame rules and regulations without a public debate. The draft rules are to be issued to the public, put on the website and widely disseminated through the media. Commissions have to invite comments, suggestions and objections before finalizing the regulations. Some of the proactive Commissions have also arranged public hearings to elicit the opinion of the consumers and other stakeholders.

The enactment of the Electricity Act, 2003 has given ample opportunities for consumer participation. Besides, it has widened the rights of the consumers in terms of quality of power supply. The Electricity Act, 2003 has created a three-tier consumer grievance redressal machinery thereby putting consumers in an advantageous position. The Act has made it mandatory for the Commissions to specify the Standards of Performance relating to supply of electricity and other related services. A system of payment of compensation in case of failure of the distribution licensee to meet the standards is another encouraging development.

The National Electricity Policy announced by the Central

Government has recognized the role of consumers. Para 14 of the policy states that both the State Governments and the Regulatory Commissions take necessary steps for greater involvement of consumers in the regulatory process. Recently, the Chairman of the Central Electricity Regulatory Commission has addressed letters to all the State Commissions about the need for consumer involvement in electricity regulation. The CERC has even suggested setting up a separate Consumer Advocacy Cell within the State Commission to strengthen consumer participation. Apart from KERC, the Assam Electricity Regulatory Commission has established a Consumer Advocacy Cell within the Commission.

Obstacles to Consumers Participation

Despite the above, consumer participation in electricity reforms has not been successful. The reasons are not far to see. Firstly, there are not enough consumer advocacy groups which can articulate issues related to electricity. Power sector is a highly technical issue that needs knowledge, expertise and the capacity to argue before the Commission. Consumer groups should not only be able to argue for their cause but also be able to act as a countervailing force on the electricity companies and the regulatory commissions. Consumer participation can be effective only when they are able to independently collect and analyze technical and financial data. However, consumer groups lack this capacity. Secondly, consumers are not a unified constituency, but have several classes of consumers, often with conflicting interests. For example Industrial consumers are well organized and have considerable technical and financial resources to represent their concerns before the regulators. On the other hand, agricultural consumers have considerable political influence to affect policy decisions. It is only the domestic and poor consumers who have no organized representation.

Despite several structural changes in the power sector brought about by the Reforms Act and the Electricity Act like establishment of regulatory commissions, consumer participation has not been given its due place. The regulatory commissions have not created a conducive atmosphere where consumers can participate effectively. A majority of the regulatory commissions have no mechanism for consumer involvement. However, almost all regulatory commissions have constituted the Commission Advisory Committee (CAC) under the Reforms Act. The functions of the CAC are to (a) advise the Commission on major questions of policy, (b) advise the Commission on matters of quality and continuity and extent of service and supply, and (c) ensure that stakeholders in the power sector have a formal mechanism to put their views before the Commission.

Experience in both India and other developed countries has shown that, in the early phases of deregulation and privatization, industry representatives have a far greater capacity than consumer representatives to undertake this task. The inherent weakness in this type of advisory committee is the assumption that all stakeholders have the knowledge and resources to represent their respective constituencies.

Consumer Participation – Best Practices

Despite obstacles, a few resourceful consumer organizations and other Non-Governmental Organisations have been able to make their presence felt in raising matters of importance to electricity consumers. For example, the Citizens' Organisation for Regulated Electricity (CORE), a wing of Lok Satta in Andhra Pradesh has been able to participate effectively. CORE has strong technical, commercial, managerial and legal expertise. Another notable organization is Prayas, based at Pune, Maharashtra. The Mumbai Grahak Panchayat and Akhil Bharat Grahak Panchayat are other groups involved in power sector reform process.

CUTS-FES Model

The Consumer Unity and Trust Society (CUTS) launched a project titled 'Consumer Involvement in Power Sector Reforms' three years ago and has been successful in the state of Rajasthan. Power sector reforms were introduced in Rajasthan in 2000. The broader objective of reforms were to curb operational inefficiencies, maintain judicious balance among interests of various stakeholders, ensuring commercial viability of the sector, improving the service delivery in terms of quality and quantity and so on. CUTS felt that there were not enough advocacy efforts from consumers and they were not aware of their rights and responsibilities. It was realized that there was a clear communication gap and a feeling of mistrust between the consumers and service providers, since no provision for multi-stakeholder dialogue was in existence.

In this background CUTS and FES joined hands and launched a programme called 'Involvement of Consumers in Power Sector Reforms in Rajasthan. The objectives in brief were to: (1) identify and create a network of grassroots consumers, mobilize them to get involved into the process, build their capacity to work as a watchdog to get their rights and responsibilities actually implemented, (2) build a common platform for these groups so that they could partner with each other and collectively improve the service, (3) build an efficient communication channel, and (4) protect consumers interest. After three years, the programme has been receiving overwhelming support not only from consumers but from the Government, service providers, media and regulators too. All the three distribution companies in Rajasthan issued a circular to its field offices for allowing a consumer to take along anyone but lawyer, while negotiating with Distpute Settlement Committee.

The Rajasthan State Electricity Regulatory Commission (RSERC) released guidelines to all licensees to resolve consumer complaints in time bound manner and report back on periodic basis. Recognising the efforts of CUTS and the entire network of consumer groups the RSERC nominated CUTS to the Commission's Advisory Committee. Informal committees called Vidyut Sudhar Samities have been formed. The Jodhpur and Ajmer Vidyut Vitaran Nigam Limited have agreed to involve registered consumer organizations in service delivery in rural areas.

CREAT-USAID Model

The Consumer Rights, Education and Awareness Trust (CREAT), based at Bangalore, launched the 'Public Understanding and Participation' (PUP) in power sector reform assisted by USAID. The programme was for a short duration of six months from December 2003 to May 2004. The objectives of PUP were similar to that of CUTS programme. Since Karnataka was already progressing with reform process, emphasis was given to educate stakeholders about the regulatory process, the rights and responsibilities of electricity consumers, regulations issued by the KERC and also how consumers can intervene before the Commission. As a result of this programme CREAT was able to consolidate a large number of stakeholders like consumer groups, Irrigation Pump Set owners associations and residential welfare associations. A network comprising 25-30 member organizations emerged as a result of PUP. This group has acquired expert knowledge in power sector issues, regulatory affairs and is able to participate effectively.

Consumer Grievances

Consumer participation in electricity reform cannot be complete without a reference to consumer grievance handling. Because complaint handling is part of consumer representation. Without helping consumers in solving their grievances, consumer participation cannot be successful. Besides, in Indian context consumer grievance handling has never been institutionalized in the electricity sector. Until recently no electricity board or utility had established a mechanism for complaint handling. The enactment of the Consumer Protection Act in 1986 brought some relief to the consumers. A large number of complaints were and are being filed in the Consumer Forums against electricity supply companies. The Electricity Act, 2003, without taking away the rights of the consumers of approaching the Forums under the CPA, mandates the electricity companies to establish an internal complaints redressal mechanism, a consumer grievance redressal forum and the Electricity Ombudsman. Yet consumer complaints handling could be used as an effective tool for consumer participation. One view is that complaints handling should be the job of the utility. The other view is that, the regulatory commission should take up the task of grievance handling. Both have their merits and demerits. There is also another school of thought according to which, complaints handling should be left to an independent body.

A report by consultants KPMG in Australia found that vesting the complaints handling function with an independent industry complaints handling scheme was likely to lead to an increase in consumer complaints by a factor of three. The report attributes this to a number of factors, including (1) increased consumer expectations of complaints handling mechanisms, (2) increased consumer awareness as a result of the news scheme's promotional activities, and (3) consumer perceptions of independence.

In the United States of America, the long-term private ownership of utilities has led to a settled process where complaints handling and resolution has been the responsibility of the Regulator. However, some governments, Regulators and consumer groups have expressed concern at the possible loss of regulatory neutrality, and the impression of consumer bias, where resolution of individual consumer grievances is a regulatory function.

In the UK, the initial solution was to transfer the complaints handling function to the Consumer Consultative Councils. However, this was widely seen as unsatisfactory as the Councils had no statutory power to make a determination in relation to a complaint and any enforcement action remained the responsibility of the Regulator. In Australia, Federal and State Governments have shown a preference for co-regulatory processes, and industry-funded structures, resulting in the establishment of industry-based schemes for electricity, gas water and telecommunications. In November 2000, the UK Parliament established the Gas and Electricity Consumer Council (Energywatch) by way of the Utilities Act, 2000. This is independent of the industry regulator, Ofgem, and the regulatory governing Authority. It replaced the former Gas Consumers' Council and several regulatory Regional Electricity Consumers.

Energywatch is government funded as approved by the Secretary of State. It operates in co-operation with the Ofgem and the regulatory Authority under a formal memorandum of understanding. The Secretary of State appoints a chairman and other members, for maximum terms of five years. The functions of Energywatch broadly comprise:

- Receiving and investigating consumer complaints.
- Obtaining and keeping under review information about consumer matters and the views of the consumers on such matters.
- Making proposals or providing advice and information about consumer matters and representing the views of consumers on such matters.

- Providing and where appropriate publishing information about consumer matters to energy matters.

Energywatch in an 'independent and assertive consumer champion committed to promoting informed consumers and to improving the service provided to all gas and electricity consumers.' Its aim are to: (a) champion the interests of all gas and electricity consumers, to enable them to set the agenda with energy companies and other key organizations and to be instrumental in developing an effective and competitive market and (b) understand and protect the needs of all gas and electricity consumers, particularly in relation to customer service, fuel poverty, safety and the disadvantaged.

In California, the California Public Utilities Commission (CPUC) has several advisory units, an enforcement division and a strategic planning group. The Office of Ratepayer Advocates (ORA) is an independent CPUC arm that represents consumers in CPUC proceedings and closely follows informal and formal complaints before CPUC to monitor patterns of individual consumer concerns. The CPUC Consumer Affairs Branch or its Public Adviser's Office, which assists the public in participating in the Commission proceedings, deals with customer complaints.

The Attorney General's Office in some States and Consumer Advocates Division of Regulatory Commissions in other States are acting as a representative of small commercial and domestic consumers, watchdog for continuity and quality of power supply including handling consumer complaints. In Commonwealth States, Consumer Advocates division of the Commission even file appeals before the Appellate Courts against the orders of the Regulatory Commissions according to the Report of Study tour by Prof. Manu Bhai Shah, CERC, Ahmdabad.

Consumer Advocacy: The Indian Experience

Unlike in other developed countries where the concept of Consumer Advocacy is in existence for many years, it is a new concept in India. Though Infrastructure Regulation stated in 1998, there is hardly any regulatory commission setting up a Consumer Advocacy wing with the exception of KERC and Assam Electricity Regulatory Commission (AERC). However, the Telecom

Regulatory Authority of India (TRAI) has initiated steps to recognize and interact with certain consumer advocacy groups. The KERC established the Office of Consumer Advocacy (OCA) in September 2001. A senior officer has been appointed to head the OCA. The objectives of OCA include the following:

1. Assist the Commission in review of policies, programmes, and regulations that govern consumer protection.
2. Advocate for appropriate credible, and equitable consumer protection rules and standards.
3. Advocate for specific performance standards for utilities.
4. Ensure standards for quality and reliability of service to customers are met.
5. Ensure that high quality education and information is made available to consumers.
6. Empower consumers with the tools they need to advocate for themselves.
7. Monitory compliance with consumer protection rules and standards.
8. Bring continued violations of consumer protection rules and standards to the attention of the Commission.

The OCA of KERC has identified *five* major areas of activities like Grievance Handling, Empowerment, Information, Representation and Monitoring Consumer Protection Rules and Standards. The KERC has established the Consumer Advocacy cell with the following objectives:

1. To represent consumers' interests in all matters relating to power sector before the Commission by getting feedback from consumer representatives.
2. To act as a source of information to consumers of electricity and provide them with the necessary guidance on various power related issues.
3. To conduct survey of performance standards of licensees for the benefit of consumers.
4. To ensure that all decisions and actions in the power sector in the state are not just consumer friendly but also environment friendly.

Recently, other electricity regulatory commissions like Kerala, Tamil Nadu, Assam, Uttar Pradesh, etc. have shown interest in involving consumer groups for promoting active involvement in the electricity regulatory process.

Consumer Participation: The Road Ahead

Consumer participation in power sector reform process is a challenge that needs to be addressed seriously. Stray cases like that of CUTS or CREAT needs to be replicated in all States. The electricity sector is moving towards the third step, i.e. Privatisation of the distribution system. Hence, consumer participation becomes more important and crucial. If a level playing field is to be created, a strong consumer advocacy system is to be in place. This requires a strong consumer group with funding, technical and legal expertise. Besides, the establishment of a consumer advocacy cell in the regulatory commissions should be made a legal mandate by amending the Electricity Act, 2003.

15
Endangered Consumers: A Case Study of Bank Lok Adalat in Delhi

Som Raj Choudhury and *Anu Sharma*

Introduction

It is no secret that India has introduced significant reforms in the economic sphere since 1991. Its economy entered a new phase as it opened its doors to be a part of globalised world. Since then Indian economy has witnessed rapid changes with foreign investment into various sectors of our economy. The policy of liberalization ushered in a new era for banking sector as well. This augured well for the growth of private players in the banking sector which was hitherto dominated by nationalized banks. These private banks got impetus for growth due to the emergence of consumerist middle class Indians, who were reaping the benefits of the open door economic policies. Following this, banks started rendering personalized services in the form of various kinds of loans (home loan, car loan, education loan, etc.) and credit card facilities.[1] This had an impact on the number and nature of disputes related to the banking sector. As per one estimate, some 38 lakh cheques bouncing cases are awaiting trial in various courts across the country.[2]

The Delhi Legal Services Authority (DLSA), in order to deal with the mounting case load related to the banking sector, has started organizing the *lok adalats* for settling cases related to personal loans, credit cards, and so on. The DLSA seeks to settle these cases at pre-litigation stage only. As per the official website of the DLSA, these *lok adalats* "provide an opportunity to the borrower to settle their liability with the bank by negotiation and thereby, it saves time, energy and money of the people as well as potential litigation is settled in its inception."[3] The paper attempts to demonstrate how the discourse around consumers of the banking services is constructed in such adalats. Critically analysing the so-called achievements of these adalats, the paper is based on a preliminary study based on participant observation in one such bank *lok adalat* organized by the DLSA in June 2009, in the Karkardooma Court situated in the east Delhi. Interviews were also conducted with the consumers who had come for this *adalat*, with bank representatives and lawyers. This was followed by a series of interviews with the employees of various private banks dealing with personal loans, credit cards and insurance.

The DLSA and Pre-litigation *Lok Adalats*

The pre-litigation bank *lok adalats* received overwhelming attention in 2009 when the DLSA organized one-day paperless mega *lok adalat* to dispose of cases related to one of the private banks (ICICI Bank).[4] The *adalat* was reported to be a huge success with 90 per cent of cases 'settled' within few hours. Though the Delhi District Courts' Annual Report, 2007 mentioned about the pre-litigation *lok adalats* and their performance, however, due to the success and widespread publicity of the mega digital *adalat*, these courts have come into the limelight. Now even public sector banks like Canara Bank and the State Bank of India have joined the bandwagon of these *adalats* to dispose of cases. The DLSA has come to acknowledge these *adalats* as a means to reduce the inflow of new cases in courts as well as an effective mechanism to dispense speedy justice. The project officer of the DLSA, while talking about one such *adalats*, maintained: The disposal rate was excellent with almost 90 per cent of the cases reaching settlement. The event was a step ahead towards the settlement of disputes at the pre-litigation stage to check the fresh inflow of cases in courts besides according speedy justice to all the parties involved.[5]

However, one should not be critical about the functioning of such *lok adalats*.[6] The issues which these *adalats* are dealing with are also related to the interests of the consumers. The main purpose of these *adalats* is to arrive at negotiations as certain 'unfair trade practices' and harassment never surface and hence remain unaddressed. Moreover, due to lack of awareness about Consumer Protection Act, 1986, most of the customers remain unaware that wrong has been done and that they can seek redress in the consumer forums. Keeping these issues in mind it is pertinent at this juncture to discuss and debate around access to justice, alternate dispute resolution, as it would help one understand the evolution of *lok adalats* and Consumer Protection Act, 1986.

Access to Justice and Alternate Dispute Resolution

Mario Cappelleti and Braynt Garth's work on the civil justice system, more popularly known as the Florence-Access-to-Justice-Project regarded the right to access to justice as "the most basic human right". They maintained that it simultaneously happened with the emergence of the welfare state as it was realized that the rights would be meaningless if there was no mechanism of their vindication. They identified three waves of access to justice reform. S. Muralidhar, explaining three waves, maintains that the first wave revolves around the provision of legal aid; while the main concern of the second wave is representation of "diffuse, collective interests"; and the third wave widens the scope to encompass different kinds of dispute processing mechanisms. The last wave incorporates the thrust of the first two waves also. Muralidhar holds that the aims of these three waves have been part of initiatives that have taken place to provide access to justice for all in India. Our Constitution guarantees right to legal aid (first wave); the emergence of Public Interest Litigation, Social Action Litigation corresponds to the second wave propounded by Cappelleti and Garth. And the establishment of *nyaya panchayats, lok adalats,* permanent *lok adalats,* consumer courts, matrimonial *lok adalats,* evening courts, and various tribunals may be perceived as broadening of dispute resolution institutions that characterize the third wave of access to justice programme.

The third wave of access to justice, however, may also be examined to explore the politics behind the alternate dispute resolution mechanisms. ADR mechanisms are often put forth as having "win-win" outcome.[7] Laura Nader notes that the move towards ADR started with the Pound Conference in St. Paid, Minnesota, 1976 and claims that ADR is portrayed as devoid of the formal procedures and rules, inexpensive and participatory, however, the revolution in civil justice system brought about by ADR movement is: less a legal innovation concerned with social inequalities of the 1960s and early 1970s than a movement away from justice towards harmony and efficiency models. The political concerns of the left and the right have converged to transform dispute resolution from the rule of law to the rule of coercion by economists and therapists. By manipulating multi-culturalism, a dispute resolution model appears to be unfractured by power differences and increasingly originating from multinational institutions.

Nader terms ADR as "coercive harmony" model and cautions that it has emerged as a very powerful mode of control. She feels that ADR "industry" treats plaintiffs as "patients" who require treatment and not courts, thus, policy was formulated to cure patients than empowering citizens.[8] She emphasizes that the aim of ADR is not to prevent the reasons of discords, what it seeks is to prevent the "expression" of it. She believes that with the advent of ADR the justice motive has been replaced with 'harmony' and it was exported abroad to facilitate smooth market transactions. Also holds that the ADR was exported worldwide by its incorporation into the Structural Adjustment Programmes, popularly known as SAP.[9] Both Nader and Mattei believe that this export of ADR was justified on the grounds of "imaginary litigation explosion". Nader substantiates: It began to look very much as if ADR were a pacification scheme, an attempt on the part of powerful interests in law and in economies to stem litigation by the masses, disguised by the rhetoric of an imaginary litigation explosion.

Nader's insight helps one to understand the worldwide move towards directing litigation by common plaintiffs to ADR mechanisms. This "imaginary litigation explosion" also serves to curtail "frivolous litigation". The 'myth' of litigation explosion[10] not only stimulated numerous writings in America but also affected the course of legal and judicial reforms in India. In this light, programmes related to 'access-to-justice' in India, can also be thought of as the part of the global nexus of the ADR 'industry'.

Access to Justice and India

Moog holds that there are two possible ways to improve access to justice: first includes reform of the formal justice system; while second includes the formulation of the alternatives to the formal justice system. And India, according to him, has been pretty active in creating alternatives to the formal justice system. He writes that, "attempts at state sponsored ADR have ranged from the less formal *nyaya panchayats, lok adalats,* and court conciliation, to more formal tribunals." The need for such ADR mechanisms has always been justified by lamenting huge judicial delay and backlog.[11]

However, there is a gap between the official discourses of judicial reform and the practice of such reforms. The difference is highlighted by Galanter and Krishnan's work on *lok adalats* in India. They have maintained that the *lok adalats* are a "new arrival" on the access to justice scenario in India and have called these *adalats* an illustration of "debased informalism" as they are "commended not by the virtues of the alternative process but by avoidance of the torments of the formal institutional process." They call them a "bypassing strategy" whereby instead of reforming the regular courts, alternative dispute resolution mechanisms are evolved. They further feel that with the advent of *lok adalats,* the state seems to have abandoned the attempts to supply remedies and protection to the people by the means of accessible and effective lower courts. They believe that the tilt towards the *lok adalats* and accompanying informalism has stratified the system of civil justice. The cases of "little people" are routed to the *lok adalats,* so that higher courts could take cases from the government and business sector easily. On the basis of the findings of their research they emphasized that the justice imparted by the *lok adalats* "falls seriously short of the aspirations of 'access to justice' proponents". They hold that new variants of these *adalats* would keep on evolving and new patterns would also emerge within the existing ones. The pre-litigation bank *lok adalats* can be examined in this light. Before proceeding further the analysis of how consumer forums are perceived and analysed in the existing literature is quite apt and relevant.

Consumer Protection Act, 1986

Consumer Protection Act, 1986 was formulated to give effective and speedy redress to the consumers of various goods and services. It is regarded as "benevolent social legislation" which provides "a cheap and speedy remedy to the aggrieved consumers by way of an alternative to the time consuming and expensive process of civil litigation."[12] Thus, for redressal one need not go to the civil court rather one can approach consumer forum as the Act contains provision for the establishment of three-tier quasi-judicial machinery for speedy redressal of the grievances of the consumers. In developed countries the "mechanisms of consumer redress are firmly established as an integral part of the larger tradition of civil rights."[13] But in India such an Act was required as the concept of consumer redress is relatively new in India. The Act lays down time limit for the disposal of cases. Moog has maintained that these forums have "filled a void by providing access to justice to some consumers" but even they suffer from limitations and reflect problems affecting civil courts.

Many studies have found out that consumer forums too are facing problems. Anderson has pointed out that the courts are essentially "reactive", i.e. the litigant has to take the first step to file the case and it is essentially one of the important reasons for the need to have rigorous efforts to spread legal education and consumer awareness.[14] One of the studies related to health sector and the CPA revealed the apparent links between the education one has and the consumer awareness. It brings to light the fact that people employed in the formal sector having fixed income are likely to make use of consumer forums for their problems whereas disadvantaged and "vulnerable sections of society" like Scheduled Castes, Scheduled Tribes and women are yet to gain benefit from such forums.

Another study has found out that the functioning of consumer forums is a major impediment to implementing the CPA effectively.[15] It has been pointed out by the survey of *Economic Times* that these forums would soon become "clogged" and "ineffective" as they would not be able to handle the pressure of increasing inflow of cases. In fact, Uttar Pradesh State Legal Services Authority organized a day long *lok adalat* to settle consumer cases pending in the consumer forums.[16] This particular *lok adalat* was perceived as a benevolent method of benefiting the litigants and the consumer forums which were overburdened with the problem of mounting arrears. Due to the delays it has been suggested that now these forums require their own ADR forums to tackle the problem of delay.[17] If this is the condition of consumer forums, then we may pause and ask how pre-litigation bank *lok adalats* are carrying on their agenda of curbing the fresh inflow to courts? And how are they dispensing justice?

Pre-litigation Bank *Lok Adalats*

The DLSA has started organizing bank *lok adalats* on the initiative of the private banks to settle the cases related to the Negotiable Instruments Act and credit cards. The interested bank identifies the potential cases and finalizes the list of the cases to be taken up to the DLSA. The latter sends the notices to the borrowers of the bank to appear before the *lok adalat*. The DLSA finalizes the day and place for the *adalat* while the concerned bank provides the technical assistance. Here the question arises that why the banks are coming out for settling cases by the means of such *adalats*? Why the authority which is responsible for educating people on legal matters and providing legal aid to poor and needy collaborating with banks? Let us first briefly discuss the field experience of such *adalats* as it will shed light on these questions.

Field Observations

The *lok adalat* which was attended by the author was organized on the second Sunday in the Karkardooma court complex. Near the entrance of the main court building a help desk was set up which was responsible for providing the litigants with the court numbers depending upon the summons. The second floor of the building was booked for organizing these *adalats*. It had five rooms, one of which was booked for matrimonial *lok adalat*. There was an open space between the rooms, where some chairs were placed. At the first look it seemed some sort of bargaining was going on. Later when the author entered room number two (as many people were sitting in that room) he realized that the bank officials were trying to break the unity of the people who had come well before the time and had resolved to present their problems before the presiding judge sahib. One by one the bank officials would enter the room and start calling the names from the causelist. Then they would ask the person to come out of the room to settle the case before the Metropolitan Magistrate (MM) comes. People who had come much earlier told them that they (bank officials) had already 'settled' four cases like that. It seemed the bank officials had used the setting of the court to tacitly threaten the customers to settle the cases.

In room two, most of the cases were related to the credit cards. An elderly widow was also sitting nervously. She had come from resettlement colony of Tilak Vihar. Her way ward son had been using the credit card of the bank. She claimed that he had run away from home long back and that she was not aware when he had applied for the credit card from the bank. She told that no bank official came for inquiry before issuing the card to him, however, since April this year she was continuously threatened by the bank. With anguish she told that the recovery agents of the bank had been visiting her at odd hours and threatening her of dire consequences. She had come to the court with one of her neighbours who was a graduate and could speak before the judge sahib as she had no money to offer. There were two other men who told that their young sons have been using credit card without their knowledge. All of them had decided to speak collectively about the faulty credit card policy of the bank before the MM. However, they received a set back when the MM entered the room, as he was stopped politely by one of the bank officials and was requested to conduct the *adalat* from his chamber. Thus, people were called individually for negotiation. The author was also stopped by the bank official.

Meanwhile, there was a rush before room number one, where people were sitting while awaiting for the court to begin, as the people were asked to vacate the courtroom. A peon was standing before the room latching one of the doors and calling the names of the individuals whose files were placed before the courts. In order to enter that room the author had to request one of the clerks sitting in the room number three. Thus, the subversion of the justice started right at the beginning of such *adalat*—an open courtroom was transformed into closed one with limited access to those whose cases were to be decided there. Moreover, when the authors entered the room they found that the bank manager was sitting in close proximity with the MM. A small table was placed where usually advocates and public prosecutors stand during the hearing of the cases. At the head of the table was sitting the MM and to his right was the manager with his laptop showing the former all the data related to the cases. To the manager's right, a lawyer representing the bank was sitting along with two other bank officials who were continuously reporting the manager about the cases which were going on in the chamber of another MM. On the opposite side of the table was placed a chair diagonal to that of MM's chair where customers/borrowers of the bank were asked to sit.

In this room some 30 cases were taken up. Out of which, at the end of the *lok adalat* (it lasted for one and half hours), 25 were declared "settled". Customers were called into the room by the peon standing outside the room. Though the presiding judge, himself remarked that it was an open court accessible to all yet the bank official instructed the peon to close the door. Though most of the customers (24 of 30 whose cases were on the list) had brought with them various documents (receipts and papers) related to their loan and credit cards. However, the MM did not look at these documents brought by the customers. He was relying on the data available in the laptop of the manager. How did he perceive the customers who were appearing before the court? A revealing remark by him said it all: *Itne bade aadmi hote to bank se paisa kyon lete*?

The aforesaid remark best exemplifies the attitude of the judge towards the customers of the bank. He was not ready to have a look at their documents as he had already assigned them their place in his eyes. From his angle they were unsuccessful people in their lives due to which they had to take help from the bank. And as a result of their failures they had troubled the bank as well. While talking to the authors later regarding the urgent need for organizing such *adalats* he cited his own example by telling them that he had not taken any financial assistance or loan from any bank. Recognizing that there are complications and unnecessary hassles with the banks, he called himself lucky to have a secured job which saves him from falling "into the trap". Yet he was indifferent towards the problems faced by the people who had come after receiving notice from the DLSA.

Amidst such a scenario, concerns raised by Grillo and Delagado and others seem pertinent. As Grillo illustrated that in the "family mediation" the notions of the mediator about the participation of the women control the entire set up, similarly here in these *adalats* the MM's perception of the customers availing loan and credit services from the bank as "failed people" made him biased against them. The bias and prejudice get accentuated with the informal setting. Delagao and others while studying the effects of ADR's informal structure maintained that the informal process increases the chances of biased treatment towards women, poor and racial minorities. The role of the presiding officer is very crucial in such setting as they play a key role in administering the negotiations and if their own perceptions and beliefs facilitate the interests of powerful players then in the name of access to justice, such forums serve to restrict access to justice.

The fears regarding unequal footing and power play became evident when in two similar cases the MM disposed of the matter differently. The customers in both the cases had made use of the credit card facility of the bank and both had claimed to repay the entire amount. However, the bank had put up their cases for the *lok adalat* hearing. One of the customers had hired a lawyer for the settlement of the case.[18] As his turn came, he entered into the room aggressively and started alleging the bank for harassing him. His lawyer showed the file containing the receipts of all the payments. The customer blamed the bank staff for unnecessary troubling him and told the judge that he had suffered huge financial loss as he had to appear before the court that day and urged to settle the matter for once and all so that he can concentrate on the expansion of his business. When the MM asked from the manager about the case, he kept silent. Upon this the judge tried to pacify the young customer and asked him to be patient as such mistakes are "likely to happen". Later when the customer left the room, the MM told the manager that they should be careful regarding such cases as the customer could have filed a civil suit for harassment.

In the second case, a man had come up with a 'settlement receipt' given to him by one of the employees of the bank after he had paid all the dues. Unlike the previous customer, this man worked for a courier agency and hailed from a humble background. When the MM asked him about the due amount, he tried to show his receipt and told that he was asked to pay ₹ 5,000 as final settlement which he did. The manager again looked lost but he kept staring at his laptop. When the MM looked at him for the answer, he told that though the man has paid the amount but in order to get No Objection Certificate (NOC) he was required to pay ₹ 5,000 more. At this the customer looked puzzled but before he could present his views, the MM interrupted the manager and asked him to fix the settlement at ₹ 3,000 and asked the man to pay the amount. The man paid the money, folded his hands before the MM, who assured him that the NOC would be delivered at his residence.

The difference in financial status and employment, I believe, made the difference in the outcome. The first customer had taken aggressive stand against the unreasonable behaviour of the bank while the second customer appeared before the court without any blame and aggression. His innocence was capitalized by the manager who asked for ₹ 5,000 for final settlement. When this man was interviewed, he maintained that he had already taken a vow, not to use credit card ever again as it had become difficult for him to even assess how much he had paid the bank. Though he was not clear why he was asked to pay more but he did so as the MM asked him. Of the 25 cases settled almost 20 customers accepted that they settled as they were asked by the presiding judge. However, almost everyone (24) lamented that they were not given the chance to speak. When all the cases were over the MM promptly asked the clerk to calculate the recovery amount so that he could assess the success or failure of the *adalat*. The authors could not get to know the recovery amount as they left for interviewing people who had appeared before the court.

Endangering Consumers: An Analysis

(i) DLSA's Interest

In this entire exercise of organizing *lok adalat* for "bank recovery cases" (as they are called by the staff of DLSA), the amount recovered possess enormous importance. It is highlighted in the media reports as well as in the annual report of the district judiciary. It seems that the amount recovered exemplifies the success of these *adalats*. As per the Annual Report of Delhi District Judiciary, 2007, in 168 sittings, these *adalats* had disposed of 2,570 cases and recovered ₹ 9,25,89,697. This 'numerical narrative' serves to explain the reason of the involvement of the DLSA in such cases. As on the basis of number of cases disposed of and the amount recovered, the DLSA advances its successful role in not only disposing of cases speedily but also recovering money which civil courts take years to realize. One of the public prosecutors also flagged this point. He maintained that ADR is backed by the state because of its disposal rate. It has become one of the important bureaucratic practices whereby the success is boasted in terms of rate of disposal and thus, inflow of grants and funds are ensured.[19] But what could be the reason for the "haves" to adopt the mechanism of these lok *adalats*?

(ii) Banks' Interests

The amount recovered is also important for the banks who participate in these *adalats*. Instead of going to civil courts, where delay is endemic and expenditure is high, resorting to these *adalats* is not only economical and ensure speedy disposal of cases but also maintain the power equation of the banks *vis-à-vis* the customers. As is evident from the comment of the bank manager himself: "They are bad debtors and in this setting we can recover the money quickly without spending much and without losing our credibility."

This reminds of Galanter's discussion of the APs (artificial persons), whereby talking about litigation pattern observed by the big organizations in United States of America, he asserts that organizations are likely to "bring more cases of the kinds that are easiest to win (such as collections, foreclosures, etc.) and organizations bring not only different cases but 'better' cases. As plaintiffs, they can avoid weak cases by forbearance to bring suit or by readily accepting a low settlement; as defendants, they can settle the more meritorious and attractive cases against them—perhaps before filing." Thus, by bringing their cases to these *adalats* under the aegis of the DLSA, the banks are not only recovering money but also effectively closing avenues for unaware customers regarding the redress against the unfair practices pursued by the banks.

The Consumer Education and Research Centre (CERC) study brought to the light that the consumers of the banking sector complained about "unfair and one-sided contract terms, undisclosed fees, usurious service charges and unclear interest rates, incorrect calculation of equated monthly instalments, restrictions on prepayment of loans, excessive securities/ guarantees, unethical recovery drives, low consumer awareness, misleading advertisements and gift offers, selective waiver of fees and ambiguous add on cards etc."

The interviews with the employees of the different private sector banks revealed that unethical practices are employed almost on the daily basis by these officials. On the condition of anonymity, an official of the leading private sector bank revealed that if a person comes with loan application, they study him for getting approval for insurance loan as well. And if they think that the person is going to turn their proposal down, they get the insurance papers signed by keeping them within the loan document. In his three years career with the bank, the official asserted only two people created problem when they received insurance papers. He held that most of the time when customers come up to us for inquiring about the insurance we make it a matter of bank policy and treat them with "*chai-paani*". Another employee added to this point by citing that even if the customer is adamant on returning the policy, he would yet pay 12 per cent of the insurance amount over and above the loan amount as 4 per cent is deducted as the employees commission and 8 per cent is the processing fees, so only 88 per cent is returned.

This technique is termed "bread and butter" by those employees whose main earnings come from the commission.[20] Though almost all the banks now have a customer grievance redressal cell/forum, but their performance is yet to be studied. One interviewee claimed that these cells are a means to buy time so that the bank can react before the customer. Another bank employee who deals with personal loans cautioned about terms and conditions of the policies. He held that not many consumers are aware that in case of the death of the person who had taken loan from the bank, family should inform the bank within 15 days. However, due to lack of information most of the people fail to do so. As a result, they are required to pay the penalty along with the amount of the loan. However, he maintained that, generally, they observe leniency in such cases. One of the reasons, according to him, is the shorter length of the loan document. Reminding the bulky loan documents, he said that those papers used to contain all the clauses clearly, however, due to the introduction of the shorter loan documents many terms and conditions remain unclear and unexplained. Hence, helps the banks. Unfortunately, it adds to the problems of the customers as they do not even get to know the true amount of charges levied by the banks. Another student of banking and consumer protection has pointed out that bank statement can no longer be understood by "checking debits and credits".

Conclusion

Though it is not an exhaustive study yet few preliminary observations can be made about such *adalats* in the light of arguments presented above. "Debased informalism" seems to be the chief characteristic of these *adalats* where the very structural setting seems to be titled towards the interests of the banks. The close proximity of the bank manager with the judge has a psychological effect on the customers. The unequal footing and weak position of the customer become explicit in this setting. In such a scenario the customers are not able to place their problems before the court and succumb to the settlement put forth by the MM. The manner in which the cases are handled and disposed of, raises crucial questions regarding the fairness of the entire process and its outcomes. If the chief reason guiding these *adalats* is to check the "fresh inflow of cases" to the courts then the very ground is faulty. Litigation explosion can never be the just reason to redirect cases to such forums where there are no hearings. The matter becomes more sensitive when it is related to the consumers. Despite having a consumer protection law promulgated especially to protect the consumers, we have not been able to address the prevalent inadequacies properly. The "bypassing strategy" seems to benefit the banks doubly as they are not only able to recover money but also successfully checking the nature of disputes. On the one hand, their unfair practices never get surfaced and on the other, they increase their credibility in the judicial circles by showing their eagerness to resort to such courts before going to regular courts. Resultantly crucial issues remain unaddressed, like that of accountability of their own grievance forum and the customer care. Thus, it is important that we do an "audit" of this means of disposing cases before we start relying on it.

As the banks and their services would expand further it is important to direct our efforts and energies towards educating common people about the CPA and their rights. It is important that the legal services authority also undertakes rigorous step to spread the legal education so that the people can be more confident in accessing courts for the legal remedies so that they no longer remain endangered but become empowered.

NOTES

1. As per one observer, the private banks are trying to attract customers, however, they want "young account holders" who do not shy from borrowing heavily for homes, cars, and other consumer durables. Mukherjee, 2008.
2. Law Commission of India (2008). *Two Hundred and Thirteen Reports on Fast Track Magisterial Courts for Dishonoured Cheque Cases*. New Delhi: Ministry of Law, Justice and Company Affairs, p. 10.
3. As per DLSA official website.www.dlsa.nic.in
4. Various newspapers reported the event and quoted the number of disposals. see "*Lok adalats* held for *credit card defaulters in Delhi*" available at ibnlive.in.com/news/lok-adalats-held-for.../84861-7.html;" ICICI Bank sponsors mega *lok adalat* for 1 lakh cheque bounce cases", available at wwww.indianexpress.com/icici-bank...lokadalats/419353 etc.
5. As quoted in "*Lok Adalats Caps Long-Pending Problems through Mediation*," available at http://www.expressindia.com/latest-news/lok-adalt-caps-longpending-problems-through-mediation/435013
6. As the limitations of the functioning *lok adalats* is succinctly pointed out by Marc Galanter and Jayanth K. Krishnan's work (2002, 2004).
7. As maintained by Justice Sabharwal (2006) and Justice Lokur (2003).
8. Sally E. Merry (1990) also pointed it out in her study of working class Americans that the interpersonal conflicts brought to the lower courts were thought of as belonging to the realm of mediation programme and were termed "garbage cases" by the court officials.
9. For instance the World Bank in *Initiatives in Legal and Judicial Reforms* (2004) stressed on the adherence to the rule of law for economic and social development. The Bank has emphasized on having clear and enforceable property rules. Other donor agencies too have fallen suit. See Messick (1999).
10. Apart from Galanter and Krishnan, Moog (1993) has also pointed out that in India rather than litigation explosion, implosion is happening whereby large number of cases are coming from those cases which are lying in courts.
11. Schackelford (2007) and Sinha (2008).
12. *S.K. Abduk Sarkar* v. *State of Orissa*, II 1991 CPJ 202, p. 205.
13. National Human Rights Commission. 2001. Regional Consultation on Public Health and Human Right, 10-11 April, Reports and Recommendations, p. 185.

14. Even though one can file PIL and courts can take up cases *suo motu* and registered consumer organizations can also file in complaints.
15. It has been found out that these forums face infrastructural difficulties, shortage of staff and technical difficulties, especially in cases of medical negligence.
16. TNN 4 February, 2002, Lucknow, webpage.
17. As cited in Moog (2002: 23).
18. This was the only customer who had come with the lawyer. During personal interaction he told us that he owned a garment factory.
19. Coutinho, Bisht and Raje (2000) highlighted the documentary practices of public health programme where "numerical narratives" were aimed at highlighting the ability of the state to deliver welfare services rather than "interaction between the health administration and people."
20. Interestingly, one of the employees remarked that after using this strategy for his own livelihood, he has become conscious of the paper work and he remains conscious if he is dealing with some other bank or telecom company for his personal use.

REFERENCES

Bhat, Ramesh. 1996. "Regulating the Private Health Care Sector: The Case of the Indian Consumer Protection Act", *Health Policy and Planning*, Oxford University Press, volume 11, number 3, pp. 265-79.

"Bread for the Poor, 2004: Access to Justice and the Rights of the Needy in India", *Hastings Law Journal*. Vol. 55, No. 4, pp. 789-833.

Coutinho, Lester, Suman Bisht and Gauri Raje. 2000. "Numerical Narratives and Documentary Practices: Vaccines, Targets and Reports of Immunisation Programme." *Economic and Political Weekly*, February 19-26, pp. 656-666.

Galanter, Marc and Jayanth K. Krishnan 2002. *"Debased Informalism: Lok Adalats and Legal Rights in Modern India"*, Paper presented at the First South Asian Regional Judicial Colloquium on Access to Justice, New Delhi, November 1-3.

Galanter, Marc. 2006. "Planet of the APs: Reflections on the Scale of Law and its Users", James McCormick Mitchell Lecture. *Buffalo Law Review*, 2005 volume 53, number 5, special edition, pp. 1369-1417.

Law Commission of India 2008. *Two Hundred and Thirteen Reports on Fast Track Magisterial Courts for Dishonoured Cheque Cases*, New Delhi: Ministry of Law, Justice and Company Affairs, p. 10.

Lokur, Madan B., (Judge, Delhi High Court) 2003. *Case Management and Court Management*, Available at www.lawcommissionofindia. nic.in/adr-conf/Justice_Lokur.pdf

Marshall, Pam. 1998. "Would ADR have Saved Romeo and Juliet?", *in Osgoode Hall Law Journal*, volume 36, number 4, pp. 771-805.

Mattei, Ugo. 2007. *"Access to Justice: A Renewed Global Issue?"*, in *Electronic Journal of Comparative Law*, volume 11.3, December, http://www.ejcl.org.

———2002. *"Democratization of Justice: The Indian Experiments with Consumer Forums"*, Centre for Research on Economic Development and Policy Reform, Working Paper No. 141.

Merry, Sally Engle. 1990. *Getting Justice and Getting Even: Legal Consciousness among Working-Class Americans*, Chicago: University of Chicago Press.

Messick, Richard E. 1999. "Judicial Reform and Economic Development: A Survey of the Issues," in *The World Bank Research Observer*, volume 14, number 1, February.

Moog, Robert. 1993. "Indian Litigiousness and the Litigation Explosion: Challenging the Legend", *Asian Survey*, Vol. 33, No. 12, pp. 1136-1150.

Muralidhar, S. 2003. *"Alternative Dispute Resolution, Conciliation, Mediation and Case Management"*, Special Address made at the International Conference on ADR, Conciliation, Mediation and Case Management organized by the Law Commission of India. May 3-4, New Delhi. Also avaialbale at www.ielrc.org/content/n0301.htm

——— 2004. *Law, Poverty and Legal Aid: Access to Criminal Justice*. New Delhi: Butterworths, Lexis Nexis. Mukherjee, Utsav, Banking Services and Consumer Laws (June 2008). Available at SSRN: http://ssrn.com/abstract=1143827

Nader, Laura. 2002. *The Life of the Law: Anthropological Projects*. Los Angeles: University of California Press.

Sabharwal, Y.K., (Former Chief Justice of India) 2006. *"Delayed Justice"*, Justice Sobhag Mal Memorial Jain Lecture, July. Available at www.supremecourtofindia.nic.in/news_links/Delayed Justice.pdf

Sarkar, J., S. Sarkar and S.K. Bhaumik (1998): "Does Ownership Always Matter? Evidence from the Indian Banking Industry", *Journal of Comparative Economics*, 26, 262-281.

Shackelford, Scott. J. 2007. *"In the Name of Efficiency: The Role of Permanent Lok Adalats in the Indian Justice System and Power Infrastructure"*, April 2007, Available at www.ssrn.com

Sinha, S.B. 2008. "ADR Vision 2025", in *Nyaya Kiran*. January-March, pp. 1-22.

16
Education as a Service under Consumer Protection Act

Ashok R. Patil

Introduction

Consumer exploitation is a common phenomenon in all the countries of the World. For the first time in a systematic way the consumer rights were recognised by United States when on 15th March, 1962, President, John F. Kennedy introduced the consumer rights in the Congress. Subsequently the United Nations General Assembly adopted the guidelines for consumer protection on 9th April, 1985. The guidelines provide a framework for Governments, particularly those of developing countries, to strengthen consumer protection policies and legislation. They also intended to encourage international co-operation in this field. The basic objectives of the Guidelines[1] are to assist countries in achieving or maintaining adequate protection for their population as consumers; to facilitate productions and distribution patterns responsive to the needs and desires of consumers; to encourage high levels of ethical conduct for those engaged in the production and distribution of goods and services to consumers; to assist countries in curbing abusive business practices by all enterprises at the national and international levels which adversely affect consumers; to facilitate the development of independent consumer groups; to further international co-operation in the field of consumer protection; to encourage the development of market conditions which provide consumers with greater choice at lower prices; and to promote Sustainable Development.

In India, the need for consumer protection is paramount in view of the fact that there is an ever-increasing population and an increasing demand for goods and services. Consumer exploitation is more due to lack of education, poverty, illiteracy, lack of information, traditional outlook of Indians to suffer in silence and ignorance of their legal rights against the remedy available in such cases. It was, therefore, necessary that a forum be created where a consumer dissatisfied with the goods supplied or services rendered may ventilate his grievance and, to devise a machinery to protect him adequately. As a result, a new law in the form of the Consumer Protection Act, 1986 (COPRA) was enacted with this end in view and also to fulfil the guidelines of the United Nations.

The COPRA, 1986 was made operative in two stages. Chapter I, II and IV came into force on April 15, 1987[2] and Chapter III came into force on July 1, 1987.[3] The Act states that the provisions of this Act shall be in addition to and not in derogation of the provisions of any other law for the time being in force.[4] The Consumer Protection Rules, 1987 were framed by the Central Government and came into force on April 15, 1987. The Act has been amended three times, i.e. in 1991, 1993 and 2002. The National Consumer Disputes Reddressal Commission framed the Consumer Protection Regulations in 2005.[5]

Education: Need and Importance

Education is "continual growth of personality, steady development of character, and the qualitative improvement of life. A trained mind has the capacity to draw spiritual nourishment from every experience, be it defeat or victory, sorrow or joy. Education is training the mind and not stuffing the brain."[6] Therefore, the service of education, rendered by educational institutions like schools, colleges and universities is one of the most valuable services in the human society. Education is national wealth essential for the nation's progress and prosperity. Due to expanding opportunities educational services have become a costly affair and most of the educational institutions are doing unreasonable profit oriented business by collecting huge money for various activities including conducting examinations, valuations, revaluations, re-totalling, infrastructural facilities and also funds for institution's future developmental purpose, etc. without providing qualitative service to the students. This amounts to exploitation of the students. Various judgments have been delivered by the National Commission regarding education as a service. But there is some amount of confusion and divergence in the decisions of the National Commission on examination issue. In some cases, it has been held that Examination Boards do not come within the purview of the Act while in some other cases, the Commission has held that though holding of examinations is a statutory function, issue of mark-sheets and certificates etc., is an administrative function, and therefore, the Examination Boards are amenable to the jurisdiction of consumer fora if there is negligence amounting to deficiency in service, in such consequential administrative functions. Therefore, the object of this paper is to clarify the present legal position as regards educational institutions and student community about, whether a student is a "consumer" and educational institutions are providing "service" as defined under COPRA by case analysis. For better understanding of the provisions related to service under the COPRA and the decisions of the Consumer Fora and Supreme Court, it is necessary to know the following important definitions as defined under Section 2 of the COPRA.

The "consumer" in service sector means, 'any person who hires or avails of any services for a consideration which has been paid or promised or partly paid and partly promised, or under any system of deferred payment and includes any beneficiary of such services other than the person who hires or avails of the services for consideration paid or promised, or partly paid and partly promised, or under any system of deferred payment, when such services are availed of with the approval of the first mentioned person but does not include a person who avails of such services for any commercial purposes;'[7] and "comn ercial purpose" does not include use by a person of goods bought and used by him and services availed by him exclusively for the purposes of earning his livelihood by means of self-employment.[8] According to this definition 'consumer' is a person who hires or avails of any services for a consideration. However, the following category of service-availors will not be consumers: (i) persons who avail any service for any commercial purpose; (ii) persons who avail any free service; and (iii) persons who avail any service under any contract of service. A consumer is entitled to file a complaint under the

COPRA, if there is any deficiency in service provided or rendered by the service-provider.

The "service" means service of 'any description which is made available to potential users and includes, but not limited to, the provision of facilities in connection with banking, financing insurance, transport, processing, supply of electrical or other energy, board or lodging or both, housing construction, entertainment, amusement or the purveying of news or other information, but does not include the rendering of any service free of charge or under a contract of personal service.'[9] It is not exhaustive definition. Therefore, the educational service provided by the institutions for consideration is covered under this definition. Further "deficiency" means 'any fault, imperfection, shortcoming or inadequacy in the quality, nature and manner of performance which is required to be maintained by or under any law for the time being in force or has been undertaken to be performed by a person in pursuance of a contract or otherwise in relation to any service.'[10] For deficiency in service of educational institutions, the student as a consumer is having a right to file a complaint against the educational institutions because student is getting educational service for consideration.

Educational Services may be classified into Statutory Services and Non-Statutory Services. Let us analyse whether these services are covered under COPRA or not in the context of cases decided by the Supreme Court and the National Commission.

Non-Statutory Service under Educational Services

Non-statutory services are those which are administrative in nature and provided by the educational institutions to the students other than examination services and falls within the ambit of 'Service' as defined under COPRA. Giving admissions to the students in a school/college/institution/university by recovering fees and in such cases if there is any dispute with regard to the validity of such admission or illegality, irregularity committed by such institution in giving admissions, it would be covered under the COPRA. This is on the basis of contract between the parties, i.e. students and the institution, and is based on the consideration (fees) for rendering education. To understand the liability of the educational institutions under COPRA one of the decided cases have been discussed below.

(i) Admissions without Following Merit List

In *M. Ravindranath* v. *Principal, Mercy College, Palakkad*[11] case, the complainant Ms. Deepa Ravi had applied to the Mercy College (Opposite Party - OP) for admission in B.Sc. Course, i.e. Maths as her first preference. She was called for interview and the Principal informed her that the seats in Maths main had been filled. The Principal assured Deepa that her chance stood as no.1 in case, any vacancy occurred or seats increased and offered her admission in Chemistry main which was her second choice. Accordingly, Deepa took admission to Chemistry course. Afterwards OP provided seats to 5 students in Maths superseding the merit list in which Deepa stood first. The father of Deepa met principal and requested a seat for Maths but the Principal refused. So he was compelled to withdraw his daughter from the college and got her admitted in another college for Maths course. The Principal also refunded the fees paid to Chemistry course.

Hence, a complaint was filed before the District Forum (DF). The DF came to the conclusion that there was deficiency in service on the part of the Principal and awarded ₹ 18,000 as compensation and refund of ₹ 250. The Principal filed appeal before State Commission of Kerala. The State Commission held that the matter did not fall within the purview of the COPRA. If the Principal wrongly admitted the students overlooking the claim of the complainant, that was not a matter which could be agitated before a Consumer Forum. The State Commission set aside the order of the DF. Deepa filed Revision before the National Commission (NC). The NC held that OP had committed deficiency in service under COPRA and it set aside the order of the State Commission and restored that of the DF.

(ii) Fake Certificate

In *Naresh Jaggi* v. *R.R. Gupta*[12] case, the appellant had been running a college and the complainant's daughter Ms. Bindu was admitted to BA and paid ₹ 16,000. Later on the petitioner informed the respondent that due to a strike of the employees, the Magadh University had decided not to hold the examination and passed a resolution that all the candidates who got admission, will be declared as passed. The respondent on becoming suspicious, having come across some rumours, sent a letter by registered post to the University to ascertain about the genuineness of the certificates issued. Although the letter was received by the University but no response was sent by it. Thereafter, on personally visiting the concerned officers of the University, the respondent was not told that no such certificates were ever issued by the University nor was there any strike in the University. Hence, the complainant alleging deficiency in service on the part of the University filed a complaint before the District Forum. The District Forum allowed the complaint and directed the opposite party to refund the fees with 18 per cent interest and ₹ 5,000 as compensation. The same was upheld by the State Commission. The National Commission held that both the orders were *ex parte* because the opposite party sent a written version and had not participated in the proceedings. The opposite party voluntarily lost the opportunity to defend before both the forums and said that the State Commission Order was well reasoned so it declined to interfere is the revision.

(iii) Correspondence Course

In *Sai Correspondence College* v. *Harikrishna D.*[13] case, the complainant desired of taking a degree in B.Ed. and contacted the petitioner who was engaged in the business of providing correspondence courses. For the year 1996, the complainant could not get admission in Annamalai University as they debarred all the external candidates. The complainant asked for refund of money deposited by him and when this was not forthcoming a complaint came to be filed before the DF, who after hearing the parties, allowed the complaint and directed the petitioner to refund ₹ 43,000 along with interest cost of ₹ 1,000. An appeal was filed in the State Commission and the National Commission which was dismissed by upholding the decision of the District Forum.

(iv) Liability for Administrative Negligence in Examination Process

In the *President, Board of Secondary Education, Orissa* v. *D. Suvankar*[14] case under writ petition, the respondent appeared at the High School Certificate Examination, 2004, conducted by the appellant

Board. The appellant Board issued erroneous marks card to the student (respondent). Hence, the student filed a writ petition before the Orissa High Court and got an award of ₹ 20,000 from the Board for its negligence. Then the Board filed an appeal before the Supreme Court of India. In this case the Hon'ble Supreme Court observed that:

Award of marks by an examiner is to be fair, and considering the fact that revaluation is not permissible under the Statute, the Examiner has to be careful, cautious and has a duty to ensure that the answers are properly evaluated. No element of chance or luck should be introduced. An examination is a stepping-stone on career advancement of a student. Absence of a provision for revaluation cannot be a shield for the Examiner to arbitrarily evaluate the answer script. That would be against the very concept for which revaluation is impermissible.

It has to be ensured that the Examiners who make the valuation on answer papers are really equipped for the job. The paramount consideration in such cases is the ability of the examiner. The Board has bounden duty to select such persons as Examiners who have the capacity and capability to make valuation and they should really be equipped for the job. Otherwise the very purpose of evaluation of answer papers would be frustrated. Nothing should be left to show even an apprehension about lack of fair assessment. It is true that valuation of two persons cannot be equal on golden scales but wide variation would affect credibility of the system of valuation. If for the same answer one candidate gets higher marks than another that would be arbitrary. As indicated above, the scope for interference in matters of valuation of answer papers is very limited. For compelling reasons and apparent infirmity in valuation, the Court steps in. Care should be taken to see that the examiners who have been appointed for a particular subject, belong to the same faculty. It would be a mockery of the system of valuation if a teacher belonging to the Arts stream is asked to evaluate answer papers of Science stream. It may be that a teacher had Physics, Chemistry or Biology at the intermediate level, but at Graduation stage he had a special paper in Zoology. To ask such a teacher to evaluate Botany paper would not be proper.

Similarly, in the case of a teacher having Mathematics in Intermediate level while he took his higher studies in Physics or Chemistry, or Botany at the Graduation level, evaluation of answer paper in Mathematics by him would not be proper. May be that he has working knowledge in the subject. But the valuation should be done by an Examiner who is well equipped in the subject. That would rule out the chance of variation in proper valuation. Board authorities should ensure the anomalous situations as pointed out above do not occur. Additional steps should be taken for assessing the capacity of a teacher before he is appointed as an Examiner. For this purpose the Board may constitute a Body of Experts to interview the persons who intend to be appointed as Examiners. This process is certainly time-consuming but it would further the ends for which the examinations are held. The Chief Examiner is supposed to act as safety valve in the matter of proper assessment.

Ultimately, it is the Board which has to ensure that the correct marks sheet is issued to the candidates since candidates who appear at the High School Certificate are of tender age. Therefore, it is imperative on the part of the Board to ensure that errorless marks sheet is issued to each candidate. The plea of the computer firm that considering the large number of candidates the mistake is not serious has no substance. The computer entries are made to ensure accuracy and to do away with defects, which arise from manually recording of marks, and to ensure accuracy. The Assistant Examiner and the Scrutiniser appear to have taken their jobs casually unmindful of the consequences, which results from their negligence act. Therefore, the sum of ₹ 20,000 has to be paid to the respondent No.1 by the Board out of which it shall recover ₹ 15,000 from the computer firm. It appears that the Board has taken action against the Assistant Examiner and Scrutiniser for their negligence. While affirming action taken against them, we express our displeasure for their careless and negligent acts which have led to unnecessary litigation.

(v) Administrative Functions of Statutory Duties covered under COPRA

In a landmark judgment, *Lucknow Development Authority* v. *M.K. Gupta*[15], the Supreme Court held that a government or semi-government body or a local authority is as much amenable to the Act as any other private body rendering similar service. Truly speaking, it would be a service to the society if such bodies instead of claiming exclusion, subject themselves to the Act and let their acts and omissions be scrutinised as public accountability is necessary for healthy growth of society. Finally, the SC held that the Lucknow Development Authority being a Statutory Body is liable for its negligence while doing administrative functions. The SC has observed the following reasoning to its conclusion.

The services are discharged both by the statutory and the private bodies. In absence of any indication, express or implied there is no reason to hold that authorities created by the statute are beyond purview of the Act. When banks advance loan or accept deposit or provide facility of locker they undoubtedly render service. A state bank or nationalized bank renders as much service as a private bank. No distinction can be drawn in private and public transport or insurance companies. Even the supply of electricity or gas which throughout the country is being made, mainly, by statutory authorities is included in it. The legislative intention is thus clear to protect a consumer against services rendered even by statutory bodies. The test, therefore, is not if a person against whom complaint is made is a statutory body but whether the nature of the duty and function performed by it is service or even facility.

The theoretical concept that King can do no wrong has been abandoned in England itself and the State is now held responsible for tortuous act of its servants. The first Law Commission constituted after coming into force of the Constitution on the liability of the State in Tort, observed that the old distinction between sovereign and non-sovereign functions should no longer be invoked to determine liability of the State. Friedmann observed, "It is now increasingly necessary to abandon the lingering fiction of a legally indivisible State, and of a feudal conception of the Crown, and to substitute for it the principle of legal liability where the State, either directly or through incorporated public authorities, engages in activities of a commercial, industrial or managerial character. The proper test is not an impracticable distinction between governmental and non-governmental function, but the nature and form of the activity in question."

Even *M/s. Kasturi Lal Ralia Ram Jam* v. *State of Uttar Pradesh,*[16] did not provide any immunity for tortuous acts of public servants committed in discharge of statutory function if it was not referable to sovereign power. Since house construction or for that matter any service hired by a consumer or facility availed by him is not a sovereign function of the State, the ratio of Kasturi Lal could not stand in the way of the Commission awarding compensation. We respectfully agree with Mathew, J., in *Shyam Sunder* v. *State of Rajasthan*,[17] that it is not necessary, 'to consider whether there is any rational dividing line between the so-called sovereign and proprietary and commercial functions for determining the liability of the State'. In any case, the law has always maintained that the public authorities who are entrusted with statutory function cannot act negligently. As far back as 1878 the law was succinctly explained in *Geddis* v. *Proprietors of Bann Reservoir*[18] "I take it, without citing cases, that it is now thoroughly well established that no action will lie for doing that which the Legislature has authorised, if it be done without negligence, although it does occasion damage to anyone; but an action does lie for doing what the Legislature has authorised, if it be done negligently."

Further Court held that under our Constitution sovereignty vests in the people. Every limb of the constitutional machinery is obliged to be people oriented. No functionary in exercise of statutory power can claim immunity, except to the extent protected by the Statute itself. Public authorities acting in violation of constitutional or statutory provisions oppressively are accountable for their behaviour before authorities created under the Statute like the Commission or the Courts entrusted with responsibility of maintaining the rule of law.

Statutory Duty under Educational Services

Recently, the Supreme Court held that the examination Service of Board (Educational Institutions) is considered as a Statutory Service and it did not fall within the ambit of 'Service' as defined in the COPRA.[19] But, in its earlier decision the Supreme Court held that examination was a statutory duty, however, administrative failure in issuing correct mark-sheet and certificate in time is part of service and to this extent under the garb of non-sovereign statutory duty, the Board can neither take shelter nor avoid liability for negligence of examiner, and chief examiner for failure to issue correct mark-sheet in time.[20]

(i) Earlier Position: Administrative Nature of Statutory Services covered under COPRA

In *Deputy Registrar (Colleges) and another* v. *Ruchika Jain and others*[21] case, the National Commission held that the performance of the statutory duties by a University or a College in laying down criteria/rules/regulations for conducting examinations, eligibility criteria for permitting the student to appear in the examination or declaration of the results of a student who appeared in the examination and such other activities, cannot be considered to be hiring of service for fees. Those are statutory functions not depending upon the contract between the parties. The services which are to be rendered on the basis of the statutory provisions by the University/educational institution cannot be construed as rendering of service for consideration in the form of fees.

Further, the Commission held that giving admissions to the students in a school/college/institution/university by recovering fees and in such cases if there is any dispute with regard to the validity of such admission or illegality, irregularity committed by such institution in giving admissions, such dispute would be covered under the COPRA. This is on the basis of contract between the parties, i.e. students and the institution, and is based on the consideration (fees) for rendering education.

(ii) Present Position: All Examination Services not covered under COPRA

Earlier to *Bihar School Examination Board* v. *Suresh Prasad Sinha*[22] case there was some confusion and divergence in the decisions of the National Commission on the issue that whether a statutory School Examination Board comes within the purview of the COPRA. In some cases, it has been held that Examination Boards do not come within the purview of the Act. In some other cases, the Commission has held that though holding of examinations is a statutory function, issue of mark-sheets and certificates etc., is an administrative function, and therefore, the Examination Boards are amenable to the jurisdiction of consumer fora if there is negligence amounting to deficiency in service, in such consequential administrative functions. This confusion is clarified by this recent decision.

The facts of this case are that the complaint was filed by the respondent, Suresh Prasad Sinha on behalf of his minor son Rajesh Kumar. In the said complaint it was mentioned that Rajesh Kumar appeared in the Bihar Secondary School Examination (Board) in 1998. Rajesh Kumar and another student Sunil Kumar Singh were allotted the same Roll No. 496. Hence, the Centre Superintendent allotted to Rajesh Kumar Roll No. 496A and this was communicated to the Board Office at Patna. The result of Rajesh Kumar was not published in spite of several letters written by him and hence he had to re-appear in the Board Examination the following year, and thus he had to suffer a loss of one year allegedly due to the fault of the Bihar School Examination Board. The result of Roll No. 496A was not declared and it is alleged that this was because Rajesh Kumar had been given another Roll number. The Board took one of the contentions that the complainant is not a consumer within the meaning of Section 2(1)(d) of the Act. The District Forum, State Commission and National Commission decided in favour of the complainant. Hence, the Board filed this Appeal before the Supreme Court.

The Board is a statutory authority established under the Bihar School Examination Board Act, 1952. The function of the Board is to conduct school examinations. This statutory function involves holding periodical examinations, evaluating the answer scripts, declaring the results and issuing certificates. The process of holding examinations, evaluating answer scripts, declaring results and issuing certificates are different stages of a single statutory non-commercial function. It is not possible to divide this function as partly statutory and partly administrative. When the Examination Board conducts an examination in discharge of its statutory function, it does not offer its "services" to any candidate. Nor does a student who participates in the examination conducted by the Board, hires or avails of any service from the Board for a consideration. On the other hand, a candidate who participates in the examination conducted by the Board, is a person who has undergone a course of study and who requests the Board to test him as to whether he has imbibed sufficient knowledge to be fit to be declared as having successfully completed the said course of education; and if so, determine his position or rank or competence *vis-à-vis* other examinees. The process is not, therefore, availment of a service by a student, but participation in a general examination conducted by the Board to ascertain whether he is eligible and fit to be considered as having successfully completed the secondary education course. The examination fee paid by the student is not the consideration for availment of any service, but the charge paid for the privilege of participation in the examination.

Further, it was held that the object of the COPRA is to cover in its net, services offered or rendered for a consideration. Any service rendered for a consideration is presumed to be a commercial activity in its broadest sense (including professional activity or quasi-commercial activity). But the Act does not intended to cover discharge of a statutory function of examining whether a candidate is fit to be declared as having successfully completed a course by passing the examination. The fact that in the course of conduct of the examination, or evaluation of answer-scripts, or furnishing of mark-sheets or certificates, there may be some negligence, omission or deficiency, does not convert the Board into a service-provider for a consideration, nor convert the examinee into a consumer who can make a complaint under the Act. We are clearly of the view that the Board is not a 'service provider' and a student who takes an examination is not a 'consumer' and consequently, complaint under the Act will not be maintainable against the Board.

The Supreme Court has not followed the precedent, i.e. in *Lucknow Development Authority* v. *M.K. Gupta*[23] case on the ground that the facts in hand are different from the precedent. The facts in Lucknow Development Authority were that even after the payment of the entire amount by the respondent for the flat which was allotted to him, possession was not given to him and the work of constructing the flat was still incomplete, although the time for handing over the possession had expired. In these circumstances, the National Consumer Commission ordered possession of the flat to be handed over without delay after completing the construction work and it further directed payment of 12 per cent simple interest on the deposit made by the respondent. The question that was considered was whether any act or omission by the Development Authority relating to housing activity such as delay in delivery of possession of the houses to the allottees, non-completion of the flat within the stipulated time or defective or faulty construction etc. will come within the purview of the Act. The submission before this Court in that case was that Statutory

Development Authorities do not come within the purview of the Act. While negativing the said contention, the Court observed that the activities which are not otherwise commercial, but professional or service oriented in nature will come within the purview of the definition of 'service' in Section 2(1)(o) of the Act. But the said observation is of no relevance. The Board is not carrying on any commercial, professional or service-oriented activity. No 'benefit' is conferred nor any 'facility' provided by the Board for any consideration. Therefore, the said decision is inapplicable.

The Supreme Court further referred to many cases[24] through which it has held that the courts should guard against the danger of mechanical application of an observation without ascertaining the facts and context in which it was made. For the reasons mentioned above, the Supreme Court is of the view that the Bihar School Examination Board is not rendering any 'service' as defined under the Consumer Protection Act, 1986. The appeal is allowed. The impugned orders of the Consumer Fora are set aside. But in this case the Supreme Court has not given reasons for its deviation from all observations made in Lucknow Development Authority case.

Conclusion

By looking into the decisions of the Supreme Court, educational service are divided into two categories, i.e. statutory service and non-statutory service. Statutory service is a service like laying down criteria/rules/regulations for conducting examinations, eligibility criteria for permitting the student to appear in the examination or declaration of the results, issuing marks card of a student who appeared in the examination and such other activities, cannot be considered to be hiring of service for fees.[25]

Further in another case, the National Commission held that giving admissions to the students in a school/college/institution/ university by recovering fees and in such cases (Non-Statutory Duty) if there is any dispute with regard to the validity of such admission or illegality, irregularity committed by such institution in giving admissions, such dispute would be covered under the COPRA.[26]

But, young students are very sensitive minds and any exploitation of them results in harm to their minds and automatically deviates them from the moral values of good human being. Therefore, parents, teachers and State have to take diligent care of their education, so that in future they should become good human beings. According to the Supreme Court, 'Education' means "the systematic instruction, schooling or training given to the young in preparation for the work of life. It also connotes the whole course of scholastic instruction which a person has received.... What education connotes is the process of training and developing the knowledge, skill, mind and character of students by formal schooling."[27] "Education plays a cardinal role in transforming a society into a civilised nation. It accelerates the progress of the country in every sphere of national activity. No section of the citizens can be ignored or left behind because it would hamper the progress of the country as a whole. It is the duty of the State to do all it could, to educate every section of citizens who need a helping hand in marching ahead along with others."[28]

The provisions of the COPRA have to be construed in favour of the consumer to achieve the purpose of enactment as it is a social benefit oriented legislation. The primary duty of the court while constructing the provisions of such an Act is to adopt a constructive approach subject to that it should not do violence to the language of the provisions and is not contrary to attempt objective of the enactment.[29] Accordingly, the SC and the National Commission have given landmark judgments like in *Indian Medical Association* v. *V.P. Shantha*[30] case the Supreme Court held that service rendered at a Government or private hospital/health centre/ dispensary where services are rendered on payment of charges and also rendered free of charge to other persons availing such services would fall within the ambit of the expression 'service' as defined in Section 2(1) (o) of the Act irrespective of the fact that service is rendered free of charge to persons who do not pay for such service. Free service would also be "service" and the recipient a "consumer" under the Act. *In Vijay Prakash Goyal (Dr.)* v. *Network Ltd.*[31] case the National Commission held that if goods are purchased for commercial purpose and these goods develops defects during the warranty period, then the purchaser was still a consumer under the COPRA.

When private undertakings are taken over by the government or corporations are created to discharge what is otherwise State's function, one of the inherent objectives of such social welfare measures is to provide better, efficient and cheaper services to the people. Any attempt, therefore, to exclude services offered by statutory or official bodies to the common man would be against the provisions of the COPRA and the spirit behind it. Therefore, the reasoning in Lucknow Development Authority's case[32] is sound in interpreting the provisions of COPRA.

NOTES

1. United Nations, General Assembly, Consumer Protection Resolution No. 39/248 dated 09-04-1985. Department of International Economic and Social Affairs, New York (1986), para 1.
2. *Vide* Notification No. S.O.390 (E), dated 15th April, 1987, published in the *Gazette of India*, 1987, Extra., Pt. II, Sec.3 (ii).
3. *Vide* Notification No. S.O.568 (E), dated 10th June, 1987, published in the *Gazette of India*, 1987, Extra., Pt. II, Sec.3 (ii).
4. Consumer Protection Act, 1986: Sec. 4.
5. W.e.f. 31st May, 2005.
6. See *"Eternal Values for A Changing Society" in Education for Human Excellence,* Vol. III published by Bharatiya Vidya Bhavan, Bombay, at p. 19.
7. *Supra* note 4, Sec. 2(1)(d)(ii).
8. *Id*, Sec. 2(1)(d): explanation.
9. *Id*, Sec. 2(1)(o).
10. *Id*, Sec. 2(1)(g).
11. 2002 (3) CPJ 0158 NC.
12. 2003 CPJ 0056 NC.
13. 2004 (4) CPJ 0003 NC.
14. MANU/SC/4882/2006: 2006 INDLAW SC 757.
15. AIR 1994 SCW 97: 1993 (3) CPJ 7 SC.
16. AIR 1965 SC 1039.
17. (1974) 1 SCC 690: AIR 1974 SC 890.
18. (1878) 3 App Gas 430.
19. *Bihar School Examination Board* v. *Suresh Prasad Sinha,* MANU/SC/1605/2009.
20. *Supra* note 15.
21. 2006 (3) CPR 18 (NC): 2006 (1) CPJ 343 NC.
22. *Supra* note 19.
23. *Supra* note 15.
24. In *C.I.T.* v. *Sun Engg. Works (P) Ltd.* MANU/SC/0707/1992: 1992(4) SCC 363, para 39; *Government of Karnataka and Ors.* v. *Gowramma and Ors.* AIR 2008 SC 863; *State of Orissa* v. *Sudhansu Sekhar Misra and*

Ors. MANU/SC/0047/1967; AIR 1968 SC 647 and *Union of India and Ors.* v. *Dhanwanti Devi and Ors.* MANU/SC/1272/1996: 1996 (6) SCC 44; In *Quinn* v. *Leathem* (1901) AC 495 (H.L.); In *Sarva Shramik Sanghatana (K.V.), Mumbai* v. *State of Maharashtra and Ors.* MANU/SC/8144/2007: AIR 2008 SC 946; In *Bhavnagar University* v. *Palitana Sugar Mills Pvt. Ltd.* MANU/SC/1092/2002: (2003) 2 SCC 111, para 59; *Bharat Petroleum Corporation Ltd. and Anr.* v. *N.R. Vairamani and Anr.*, AIR 2004 SC 4778.

25. *Supra* note 19.
26. 2006 (3) CPR 18 (NC): 2006 (1) CPJ 343 NC.
27. *The Sole Trustee, Lok Shikshana Trust* v. *C.I.T.* (1976) 1SCC 254: AIR 1976 SC 10: 1976 Tax LR 1.
28. Quadri, J. in *T.M.A. Pai Foundation* v. *State of Karnataka,* 2002 AIR SCW 4957: AIR 2003 SC 355: (2002) 8 SCC 481. See also *India-Vision 2020* published by Planning Commission of India, it is stated (at p. 250).
29. AIR 1994 SCW 97: 1993 (3) CPJ 7 SC [also see *Regional Director, Employees' State Insurance Corporation* v. *Highland Coffee Works of P. F. X. Saldanha and Sons,* (1991) 3 SCC 617: (1991 AIR SCW 2821); C. I. T., *Andhra Pradesh* v. *M/s. Taj Mahal Hotel, Secunderabad* (1971) 3 SCC 550: (AIR 1972 SC 168); and *State of Bombay* v. *Hospital Mazdoor Sabha,* AIR 1960 SC 610].
30. AIR 1996 SC 550: 1995 AIR SCW 4463.
31. 2005 (4) CPJ 0206 NC.
32. MANU/SC/0178/1994: 1994 (1) SCC 243; see also *Ghaziabad Development Authority* v. *Balbir Singh,* AIR 2004 SC 2141.

17
Consumer Protection and Electricity Services: A Case Study of Delhi

Eqbal Hussain

Introduction

India is the world's sixth largest energy consumer, consuming about 3 per cent of the world's total energy per year. India's electricity sector faces problems of capacity, poor reliability, and frequent blackouts. The anticipated electricity shortage is estimated at between 11 and 18 per cent. To combat many of these problems and improve the situation, the Indian Government set up the Central Electricity Regulatory Commission or the CERC in 1998 under the Electricity Regulatory Commissions Act, 1998. This Act also served to create SERCs (State Electricity Regulatory Commissions) in states all across the country. The first regulatory body was, however, established by the Orissa Government back in 1996 even before the CERC or the SERCs were set up. Reforms in the Indian power sector originated officially in September 1991. Due to power reforms many states have unbundled their generation, transmission, and distribution into separate corporations while some like Orissa and Delhi have gone as far as privatizing distribution.

The main purpose of the CERC is to establish tariffs and related issues. It regulates electricity tariffs and transmission up to the boundaries of any of the states. CERC has two types of jurisdiction; one is regulatory and the other is adjudicatory. The Commission has since passed orders on availability-based tariff and has brought out terms and conditions for determination of such tariffs. It regulates tariff of generating companies which are owned or controlled by the Central Government or by companies that are neither owned nor controlled by the government if they have a plan for the generation and sale of electricity in more than one state. CERC has also finalized the Indian Electricity Grid Code.

Apart from the above, the Central Regulator also regulates inter-state transmission of energy including tariff of the transmission utilities. Its main function is also to arbitrate or adjudicate upon disputes involving the generating companies and transmission utilities in matters relating to tariffs. The SERCs function at the state level would determine the tariff for electricity wholesale bulk, grid or retail. They determine the tariff payable for use by the transmission facilities to regulate power purchase and procurement process of transmission utilities and distribution utilities. They aim to promote competition and efficiency at the state level. Apart from the CERC, 21 States have constituted State Electricity Regulatory Commissions.

The objectives of the new legislation were to consolidate the laws relating to the generation, transmission, distribution, trading and use of electricity and generally for taking measures conducive to development of electricity industry, promoting competition therein, protecting interest of consumers and supply of electricity to all areas, rationalization of electricity tariff, ensuring transparent policies regarding subsidies, promotion of efficient and environmentally benign policies, constitution of Central Electricity Authority, Regulatory Commissions and establishment of Appellate Tribunal and for matters connected therewith or incidental thereto.[1]

Background and Salient Features of the Act

Power is today a basic human need. It is the critical infrastructure on which modern economic activity is fully dependent. Only 55 per cent households in India have access to electricity. Most of those who have access do not get uninterrupted reliable supply. The industry in India has among the highest tariffs in the world and is not assured of the quality of supply. In this era of globalization, it is essential that electricity of good quality is provided at reasonable rates for economic activity so that competitiveness increases. Being internationally competitive is now essential for achieving the vision of 8 per cent GDP growth per annum, employment generation and poverty alleviation.

In recent years the financial health of SEBs has been deteriorating. There is a big gap between unit cost of supply and revenue and the annual losses of SEBs have been increasing and have reached unsustainable levels (over ₹ 33,000 crore). In the last two Plan periods, barely half of the capacity addition planned was achieved. The optimistic expectations from the IPPs have not been fulfilled and in retrospect it appears that the approach of inviting investments on the basis of government guarantees was perhaps not the best way. The energy as well as peaking shortages across the country is a matter of concern and the situation would have been worse but for the slowdown in manufacturing sector.

The Hon'ble Prime Minister and Chief Ministers had set before the nation the goal of electrifying all villages by 2007 and all households by 2012. Access is yet to be provided to about 80,000 villages. Uninterrupted and reliable supply of electricity for 24 hours a day needs to become a reality for the whole country including rural areas. Enough generating capacity need to be created to outgrow the situation of energy and peaking shortages and make the country free of power cuts with some spare generating capacity so that the system is also reliable. The sector is to be made financially healthy so that the State Government finances are not burdened by the losses of this sector. The sector should be able to attract funds from the capital markets without government support. The consumer is paramount and he should be served well with good quality electricity at reasonable rates.

It is in this context that the Electricity Act, 2003 seeks to bring about a qualitative transformation of the electricity sector through a new paradigm. The Act seeks to create liberal framework of development for the power sector by distancing Government from regulation. It replaces the three existing legislations, namely Indian Electricity Act, 1910, the Electricity (Supply) Act, 1948 and the Electricity Regulatory Commissions Act, 1998. The objectives of the Act are to consolidate the laws relating to generation, transmission, distribution, trading and use of electricity and generally for taking measures conducive to development of electricity industry, promoting competition therein, protecting interest of consumers and supply of electricity to all areas, rationalization of electricity tariff, ensuring transparent policies regarding subsidies, promotion of efficient and environmentally benign policies, constitution of Central Electricity Authority, Regulatory Commissions and establishment of Appellate Tribunals.

The Electricity Act, 2003

The Electricity Bill, 2001 was introduced in the Lok Sabha on 30th August, 2001 and was subsequently referred to the Standing Committee on Energy for examination and report. The Standing Committee submitted its report on 19th December, 2002. Based on the recommendations of the Standing Committee on Energy, the Government of India moved certain amendments. The Electricity Bill, 2001 along with these amendments, was passed by the Lok Sabha on 9th April, 2003. The Electricity Bill, 2003 as passed by both Houses of the Parliament received Presidents assent on 26th May, 2003 and was notified in the Gazette of India on 2nd June, 2003. The provisions of the Act except Section 121 were brought into force with effect from 10th June, 2003. The Act strikes a balance which takes into account the complex ground realities of the power sector in India with its intractable problems. The salient features of the Act are:

(I) The Central Government to prepare a National Electricity Policy in consultation with State Governments. (Section 3)

(II) Thrust to complete the rural electrification and provide for management of rural distribution by Panchayats, Cooperative Societies, non-Governmental Organizations, franchisees etc. (Sections 4, 5 and 6)

(III) Provision for licence free generation and distribution in the rural areas. (Section 14)

(IV) Generation being delicensed and captive generation being freely permitted. Hydro projects would, however, need clearance from the Central Electricity Authority. (Sections 7, 8 and 9)

(V) Transmission Utility at the Central as well as State level, to be a Government company with responsibility for planned and coordinated development of transmission network. (Sections 38 and 39)

(VI) Provision for private licensees in transmission and entry in distribution through an independent network. (Section 14)

(VII) Open access in transmission from the outset. (Sections 38-40)

(VIII) Open access in distribution to be introduced in phases with surcharge for current level of cross subsidy to be gradually phased out along with cross subsidies and obligation to supply. SERCs to frame regulations within one year regarding phasing of open access. (Section 42)

(IX) Distribution licensees would be free to undertake generation and generating companies would be free to take up distribution businesses. (Sections 7, 12)

(X) The State Electricity Regulatory Commission is a mandatory requirement. (Section 82)

(XI) Provision for payment of subsidy through budget. (Section 65)

(XII) Trading, a distinct activity is being recognized with the safeguard of the Regulatory Commissions being authorized to fix ceilings on trading margins, if necessary. (Sections 12, 79 and 86)

(XIII) Provision for reorganization or continuance of SEBs. (Sections 131 and 172)

(XIV) Metering of all electricity supplied made mandatory. (Section 55)

(XV) An Appellate Tribunal to hear appeals against the decision of the CERC and SERCs. (Section 111)

(XVI) Provisions relating to theft of electricity made more stringent. (Sections 135-150)

Provisions safeguarding consumer interests. (Sections 57-59, 166) Ombudsman scheme (Section 42) for consumers grievance redressal.

The Delhi Electricity Regulatory Commission (DERC) and its Functions

The Delhi Electricity Regulatory Commission was constituted by the Government of NCT of Delhi *vide* Notification No. F.11(28)/98-EB/341 dated 3-3-1999 for discharging of the following functions:

1. to determine the tariff for electricity, wholesale bulk, grid or retail, as the case may be, in the manner provided in Section 29 of the Electricity Regulatory Commission Act, 1998;
2. to determine the tariff payable for the use of the transmission facilities in the manner provided in Section 29 of the Electricity Regulatory Commission Act, 1998;
3. to regulate power purchase and procurement process of the transmission utilities and distribution utilities including the price at which the power shall be procured from the generating companies, generating stations or from other sources for transmission, sale, distribution and supply in the National Capital Territory of Delhi; and
4. to promote competition, efficiency and economy in the activities of the electricity industry to achieve the objects and purposes of the Central Electricity Regulatory Commission Act, 1998.

Subsequently the Government of NCT of Delhi notified the Delhi Electricity Reforms Act, 2000 deemed to be in force from 3rd day of November, 2000. The Delhi Electricity Reforms Act provides that the Commission established and constituted under Section 17 of the Electricity Regulatory Commissions Act, 1998 shall be the first Commission for the purposes of this Act also. Under this Act the following functions have been assigned to the Commission:

1. to determine the tariff for electricity, wholesale bulk, grid or retail, as the case may be;
2. to determine the tariff payable for the use of the transmission facilities;
3. to regulate power purchase and procurement process of the licensees and transmission utilities including the price at which the power shall be procured from the generating companies, generating stations or from other sources for transmission, sale, distribution and supply in the National Capital Territory of Delhi;
4. to promote competition, efficiency and economy in the activities of the electricity industry to achieve the objects and purposes of this Act;

5. to aid and advise the Government in matters concerning electricity generation, transmission, distribution and supply in the National Capital Territory of Delhi;
6. to regulate the operation of the power system within the National Capital Territory of Delhi;
7. to set standards for the electricity industry in the National Capital Territory of Delhi including standards related to quality, continuity and reliability of service;
8. to promote competitiveness and make avenues for participation of private sector in the electricity industry in the National Capital Territory of Delhi and also to ensure a fair deal to the customers;
9. to regulate the working of the licensees and other persons authorized or permitted to engage in the electricity industry in the Territory of Delhi and to promote their working in an efficient, economical and equitable manner;
10. to aid and advise the Government in the formulation of its power policy;
11. to collect and publish data and forecasts on the demand for, and use of, electricity in the National Capital Territory of Delhi and to require the licensees to collect and publish such data;
12. to regulate the assets, properties and interest in properties concerned or related to the electricity industry in the National Capital Territory of Delhi including the conditions governing entry into and exit from the electricity industry in such manner as to safeguard the public interest;
13. to issue licences for transmission, bulk supply, distribution or supply of electricity and determine the conditions to be included in the licences;
14. to require licensees to formulate prospective plans and schemes in coordination with others for the promotion of generation, transmission, distribution, supply and utilization of electricity, quality of service and to devise proper power purchase and procurement process;
15. to adjudicate upon the disputes and differences between the licensees and/or transmission utilities and to refer the matter for arbitration; and
16. to aid and advise the Government on any other matter referred to the Commission by the Government[2].

Forum for Redressal of Grievances of the Consumers

On 11th March, 2004, Delhi Electricity Regulatory Commission notified the Delhi Electricity Regulatory Commission (Guidelines for establishment of Forum for redressal of grievances of Consumer and Ombudsman) Regulations, 2003. The salient features of the Forum for redressal of grievances of the consumers are as below:

1. with these regulations, DERC prescribed a Forum and Ombudsman;
2. the constitution of the Forum for redressal of grievances of the consumer shall be established by every distribution licensee;
3. The Forum shall consist of not more than three members;
4. the age, qualifications, and experience of the members have been prescribed in these regulations;
5. in these regulations, DERC has specified that for the purpose of appointment of members, the licensee shall invite applications through public advertisement. The members of the Forum would have a tenure of three years;
6. licensee shall appoint one of his officers as full time secretary to the Forum and shall also provide the required supporting staff;
7. the Forum shall be independent of the licensee;
8. the Forum shall for removal of members, other conditions of appointment and jurisdiction of the Forum has been prescribed; and
9. grievance filing procedure and grievance handling procedure has been prescribed.

Other relevant clauses concerning order of the forum and monitoring of the consumer grievances by the Forum has been prescribed[3].

Complaint Handling Procedure

Delhi Electricity Regulatory Commission has approved the 'Complaint Handling Procedure' relating to distribution and retail supply of electricity in Delhi. The salient features are:

1. Nature of complaints;
2. Where to lodge complaints:— The contact telephone numbers where consumers can lodge their complaints as also the name and contact telephone number of the Assitant Engineer concerned, who can be approached in case of delay in the redressal of complaints would be notified as under:
   - by display/dissemination of the above information on separate hand-outs attached to the electricity bills from time to time,
   - by display of the above information at the bill collection centres, and
   - by display on the company's website;
3. No current/failure of power supply;
4. Voltage complaints;
5. Scheduled outages/load shedding;
6. Metering problems;
7. Billing problems;
8. Periodic inspection by the next higher authority; and
9. Petition before DERC for grievance redressal.

It is the obligation on the licensee to respond to a consumer's complaint in a timely and effective manner. In case a consumer is not satisfied, he may go to the DERC in accordance with Commission's Grievance Handling Procedure[4].

Deficiency in Services in Respect of Supply of Electricity

The consumers can approach to the Redressal Forums established under the Consumer Protection Act, 1986 for deficiency in services in respect of supply of electricity such as disconnection of electricity, disconnection without notice, discontinuance of supply to consumer neglecting to pay charges, theft of electricity, excess billings, billing on average basis, electrical inspector, recovery of arrears, fluctuation of voltage, etc.

Jurisdiction of Consumer Forum

This question first arose before the Haryana State Commission in the case of *Haryana State Electricity Board* v. *Dinesh Kumar*[5].

Upholding the decision of the District Forum that the complainant had a *locus standi* to file the complaint and the Forum had jurisdiction to entertain it, the Commission observed that the supply of electrical energy is hiring of service and not sale of goods. The Commission observed as follows:

> "The supply of electrical energy has in express terms been included in the definition of 'service' I clause (o)... when the statute expressly labels the same as 'service' then it is obviously difficult and, indeed, impossible, to label it as a 'sale of goods' instead by an interpretative exercise. It is a well known principle of construction that the special overrides the general. Even if generally under other statutes, the supply of electrical energy may tantamount to sale of goods, still when the Act specially places the same within the definition of 'service', the same would have an overriding effect. General consideration under other provision would, thus, be to little relevance. Therefore, on the larger principle, it has to be held that even though ordinarily or under statute the supply of electrical energy may come within the ambit of "sale of goods", yet for the special purpose of the Act, it would be excluded therefrom. If the Act has classified the same as a 'service', then mandate of legislature must be given its full effect."

Elaborating the point further, the Commission added that "Again, on the larger scheme of the Act, it deserves notice that the same draws a clear distinction between a consumer who purchases goods for consideration and who hires any service for the same. Whilst a person purchasing the goods for a commercial purpose is ousted from the definition of a 'consumer', a person who hires services for consideration even for commercial purposes, remains, squarely within its ambit. The definition of a 'defect' pertaining to goods in clause (f) of sub-section (1) of Section 2 of the Act is distinct and different from a 'deficiency' in service which is defined in clause (g) thereof. Both a defect in goods and a deficiency in service will give a cause of action to a consumer, but different considerations would necessarily apply because of the aforesaid definitions. Barring exceptional cases of composite nature, where to a sale of goods a further after-sales service may be annexed, the defect in goods and deficiency in services are things apart. Supply of electrical energy, therefore, cannot possibly be both 'sale of goods' or 'hiring of services'. It has to be either. When the Parliament in its wisdom has expressly placed the supply of electrical energy squarely within the definition of 'service' in clause (o) then by no interpretative casuistry can this subject be taken out of the definition in clause (o) and thrust or inserted in clause (i). In essence when the Act labels the supply of electrical energy as a 'service' one cannot possibly read it as a 'sale of goods' by a strained process of interpretation. Holding so would not only be doing violence to the language of this statute, but would be contrary to all sound cannons of construction."

It follows from this judgment that the consumers of electrical energy who hires the service even for commercial purpose are entitled to such redress by invoking the provisions of this Act. However, in a recent case the jurisdiction of Consumer Forum, to deal with electricity cases, was raised before the Supreme Court after commencement of the Electricity Act, 2003. In case of *Accounts Officer, Jharkhand State Electricity Board and Anr.* v. *Anwar Ali*[6] the basic grievance of the respondent was that the electricity supply was disconnected without notice. Compensation of ₹ 50,000 was awarded along with 12 per cent interest per annum by the District Forum and upheld by the State Commission. The National Commission took the view that since notice was given after disconnection, the action was clearly unsustainable. It was submitted before the Supreme Court that whether the consumer of the electricity can be covered under the provisions of the Consumer Protection Act, 1986. The question which arose for determination and which was not decided was whether the beneficial consumer jurisdiction extended to determination of tortuous acts and liability arising therefrom by the Consumer Forum. In this connection, it was urged on behalf of the Nigam that assessment of the duty for unauthorized use of electricity, tampering of meters, distribution of meters and calibration of electric current were matters of technical nature which cannot be decided by the Consumer Forum. It was urged that under the Electricity Act, 2003 the jurisdiction of the civil court was excluded. In this connection reliance was placed on Section 145[7] of the Act, 2003 under which the jurisdiction of the civil court to entertain suits in respect of matters falling under Section 126 was expressly barred. The Apex Court held that since the National Commission had not addressed the question as to whether consumer of electricity was covered by the Consumer Protection Act, 1986 the impugned order was set aside and remitted to the National Commission to a positive finding on the aspect.

Cases relating to Supply of Electricity in Delhi

Some of the cases relating to the electricity which came before the consumer courts in Delhi are discussed hereafter.

Disconnection of Electricity

In the case of *Y.N. Gupta* v. *D.E.S.U.*[8], three bills for three electric connections in the house of the complainant were delivered by the DESU on 25.3.1990. The last date for payment was 28.3.1990, the total amount of the bills being a whopping ₹ 1,06,566. The current demand was ₹ 3,110. The amount of previous arrears was ₹ 1,03,456. The period to which the arrears related was not mentioned in the bills. On the next working day the complainant requested the Executive Engineer for details of the arrears and the period to which they relate. Instead of furnishing the requisite information, the electricity connection was disconnected on 26.3.1990 without assigning any reason or serving any notice on him. The supply was, however, restored on 28.03.1990 on the intervention of the General Manager.

The complainant submitted that he had paid the entire amount due from him for electricity consumption till 6.10.1988, after which the bills of 25.3.1990 was received by him. Luckily for him the DESU discovered during the proceedings before the State Commission that the meters installed were defective as they showed the consumption in five digits instead of four digits. The bills were accordingly revised and the amount due came only to ₹ 13,649 for the period 21.10.1988 to December 1990, as against ₹ 1,06,566 and ₹ 50,583 from December 1988 to September 1990 on the basis of actual recording in September 1990. In the meantime, the DESU further discovered that the charges for consumption of another 10,000 units of energy for the period 1.1.1986 to 6.12.1988 were not included in the bills due to oversight. The complainant was also asked to pay late fee, though according to him, bills were paid by him before the due date.

The State Commission held that:

1. DESU had been negligent in preparing bills of the complainant. As a result, he suffered unnecessary harassment and that it acted irresponsibly in raising the bills of more than ₹ 50,00, that the amount due from him for a much longer period was only ₹ 13,600. It did not rectify the bills in spite of request from the complainant,
2. The action of the officials of DESU in disconnecting the electric supply was *mala fide* and was taken to harass him as a result of which he must suffered mental torture,
3. DESU was not entitled to charge late fee from the complainant and the same was liable to be returned,
4. The complainant was liable to pay charges for 10,000 units of energy because it was a genuine mistake on the part of the officials and was detected only when the metres were minutely examined.

Against the claim for damages for harassment and mental torture amounting to ₹ 1.44 lakh, the State Commission allowed only ₹ 7000 as exemplary damages. Not fully satisfied with decision of the State Commission, the complainant, *inter alia,* contended before the National Commission that the State Commission erred in:

1. allowing the claim of DESU for 10,000 units of energy stated to have remained unbilled through oversight; and
2. awarding grossly inadequate compensation to him.

Allowing his appeal, The National Commission held the following deficiencies in service to have been established:

1. there was deficiency in service as the bill for electrical consumption were not prepared and served at the appointed time in accordance with the billing cycle and thereafter harassing the consumer with heavy arrears bill (the bill for the period from 21.12.1988 to 25.3.1990 was raised on 25.3.1990);

2. there was deficiency in service in revising the bills without actual meter reading;
3. there was deficiency in service to have raised the arrears bill without details of the period to which the arrears pertained;
4. there was deficiency in service to have served the bills to the consumer on Sunday, the 25th of March, 1990, and expect him to pay a sum of ₹ 1,06,566 by 28th March, 1990; We cannot understand as to how the respondent DESU expects consumer to find funds of such magnitude at short notice even if the bill is correct;
5. For the meters belonging to DESU, the meter rent has been claimed in the bills. It is, therefore, the responsibility of the DESU to maintain them in good condition. A mere scrutiny of the meter readings would have shown that the bills reflected consumption in five digits instead of four. Evidently, the bills were prepared most casually and indifferently and even elementary care was not exercised to see that the meters were malfunctioning. This constitutes deficiency in service as it inevitably leads to wrong billing against the consumer;
6. charging of late fee wrongfully, however, small it might be, also constitute deficiency in service towards the consumers; and
7. above all, the disconnection of power supply was arbitrary, high-handed and, as observed by the State Commission, *mala fide* with a view to harass the consumer.

The Commission expressed its distress over the manner in which the complainant and the members of his family were tortured by DESU by arbitrarily and *malafidely* disconnecting supply of power. It enhanced the compensation from ₹ 7,000 awarded by the State Commission to ₹ 30,000 and also awarded ₹ 5,000 as costs. The claim of DESU for 10,000 units of electricity for the period 1986 to 1988 was also disallowed.

The Delhi State Commission has also held in *Vikas and Co.* v. *Delhi Electric Supply Undertaking*[9] and *Mahinder Pal Jain* v. *D.E.S.U.*[10] that disconnection of supply of electricity of appellant was illegal because no notice under Section 24 of the Indian Electricity Act was served prior to disconnection.

Electrical Inspector

In *H.D.Shourie* v. *Delhi Municipal Corporation*[11], the Delhi High Court has pointed out the illegalities committed by the respondents in dealing with the matter. The case was never referred to the Electrical Inspector for adjudication. The respondents took a unilateral decision and that also without notice to the petitioner and behind his back that the meter was defective. They themselves estimated the quantity of electricity consumed during the period and that also without notice to the petitioner. Another alleged illegality committed was that the bill sent by them was for a period in excess of six months which was contrary to the provision of Section 26(6) of the Indian Electricity Act, 1910. In view of the fact that the mandatory provisions of Section 26(6) of the Act were not complied, the court quashed the demand raised by the respondents and left it to them to revise the bill only after complying with the provisions of Section 26(6).

In *Y.N. Gupta's* case[12], the National Commission held that the Electricity Board was required to refer the dispute of defective metre to the Electrical Inspector which was not done in the instant case. The opposite party cannot assume the statutory powers and functions of the Electrical Inspector. The action of the opposite party, the Commission observed, is not sustainable in law.

Recovery of Arrears

Sub-section (1) of Section 26 of the Indian Electricity Act, 1910 provides that in the absence of an agreement to the contrary, the amount of energy supplied to a consumer or the electrical quantity contained therein shall be ascertained by a correct meter, and the licensee shall, if required by the consumer, cause the consumer to be supplied with such a meter. Ordinarily, if not invariably, the meter is supplied by the licensee and it is he who is responsible to maintain it and keep it correct (Sub-section 3). But what if the meter goes wrong or is burnt or otherwise ceases to function? Sub-section (6) of this section takes care of such contingency. It provides that, in that case, the matter shall be decided upon the application of either party by an Electricity Inspector, and where the meter has, in the opinion of such Inspector ceased to be correct, such Inspector shall estimate the amount of the energy supplied to the consumer or the electrical energy contained therein during such time, not exceeding six months, as the meter shall not, in the opinion of such Inspector, have been correct....

In *Shourie's case*[13], the Delhi High Court has held as follows:

> "... the maximum period for which a bill can be raised in respect of a defective meter is six months and no more. Therefore, even if a meter has been defective for, say a period of five years, the revised charge can be for a period not exceeding six months. The reason for this is obvious. It is the duty and obligation of the licensees to maintain and check the meter. If there is a default committed in this behalf by the licensee and defective meter is not replaced, then it is obvious that the consumer should not be unduly penalized at a later point of time and a large bill raised. The provision for a bill not to exceed six months would possibly ensure better checking and maintenance by the licensee."

The same view was reiterated in another case by the same High Court in the case of *Major Zorawer Singh* v. *Municipal Corporation of Delhi*[14]. Following these two decisions, the Delhi State Commission also held in *Northern India Tiles Corporation* v. *D.E.S.U.*[15], that the opposite party cannot charge the amount of arrears, if any, for a period of more than six months.

Fluctuation of Voltage

People file actions against the electricity supply agencies for compensation due to sudden high voltage surge causing damage to their electrical equipments. In all such cases the consumer has to prove before the Redressal Agencies that:

(a) he suffered loss or injury by the action of the other party;
(b) such loss or damage was due to the negligence of the opposite party;
(c) there was deficiency in service rendered to him by the opposite party.

The case for compensation will not even take off the ground

unless all these ingredients are proved.[16] In the case of *New Delhi Municipal Corporation (Committee)* v. *S.P. Singh*[17], the Delhi State Commission held that the alleged voltage was not caused due to the negligence of any of the respondents. In this case the V.C.R. of the complainant was damaged due to the allegedly too high voltage supply of electricity caused by the negligence of N.D.M.C. or C.P.W.D. The District Forum allowed the claim of ₹ 900 of the complainant against the N.D.M.C. On facts the State Commission held in appeal that there was no negligence either on the part of the N.D.M.C. or on the part of C.P.W.D. which was impleaded as a party by the State Commission. The order of the District Forum was accordingly set aside.

The suppliers of electricity are expected to exhibit due fair play and care. In *P.H. Sehgal Gaggal* v. *Delhi Vidyut Board*[18], an inspection of the complainant's premises had been carried out by the opposite party during which they claimed to have found that the connected load of electricity was more than the sanctioned load and the half seals in the meter were tempered. On this the complainants were made to pay the FAE bill. The complainant stated that the board had neither provided them any show cause notice nor given them any opportunity to personal hearing. Moreover, the previous consumption pattern was also not considered. Only on the threat of disconnection and lodging of FIR, they were forced to deposit the said amount of FAE bill and therefore, they filed a complaint in the District Forum.

The Forum held that in this case no presumption of theft could be raised by the opposite party simply on the basis of tampered half seals. If the connected load was more than the sanctioned load, it could be due to overloading and not necessarily due to theft. Moreover, no evidence was available that the meter was defective as contended by the board. In view of this, the board was held liable for deficiency in service and was directed to quash the FAE bill and refund the amount deposited by the complainant with interest. Compensation was also awarded in favour of the complainant. The State and the National Commissions upheld the decision of the District Forum.

It is, therefore, concluded from the above discussion that the electricity department in Delhi has developed its internal mechanism to settle the dispute of its consumers. Under the Electricity Regulatory Commissions Act, 1998 one of the functions assigned to the Commission is to adjudicate upon the disputes and differences between the licensees and/or transmission utilities and to refer the matter for arbitration. Accordingly on March 11, 2004, Delhi Electricity Regulatory Commission notified the Delhi Electricity Regulatory Commission (Guidelines for establishment of Forum for redressal of grievances of consumer and Ombudsman) Regulations, 2003 and the Commission has approved the 'Complaint Handling Procedure' relating to distribution and retail supply of electricity in Delhi.

However, the consumers have also approached the Consumer Forums for redressal of their grievances. In one of the cases though it is from Haryana, the court has specifically laid down that the issues related to electricity is covered under the Consumer Protection Act, 1986 and held that when the Parliament in its wisdom has expressly placed the supply of electrical energy squarely within the definition of 'service' in Clause (o) then by no interpretative casuistry can this subject be taken out of the definition in Clause (o).[19] The issues came for the adjudication before the various Consumer Courts of Delhi are related to the disconnection of electricity, electrical inspector, recovery of arrears, fluctuation of voltage etc.

Conclusion

To combat the electricity problems and improve the situation, the Indian Government set up the Central Electricity Regulatory Commission or the CERC in 1998 under the Electricity Regulatory Commissions Act, 1998. The main purpose of the CERC is to establish tariffs and related issues. It regulates electricity tariffs and transmission up to the boundaries of any of the states. CERC has two types of jurisdiction; one is regulatory and the other is adjudicatory. The Electricity Act, 2003 regulates the electricity issues and seeks to bring about a qualitative transformation of the electricity sector through a new paradigm. This Act seeks to create liberal framework of development for the power sector by distancing Government from regulation. It replaces the three existing legislations, namely Indian Electricity Act, 1910, the Electricity (Supply) Act, 1948 and the Electricity Regulatory Commissions Act, 1998. The study indicates that the Department of Power, Government of NCT of Delhi has developed its own mechanism to redress the consumer grievances. For example, it advertised in *Times of India,* dated 29.6.2008 ensuring to bring more convenience for electricity consumers to settle pending disputes. Through this process around 21,000 cases were settled under Amnesty Scheme, 3898 meters were replaced, 9718 new meters were installed in JJ cluster, 7429 cases of theft/DAE amounting to ₹ 21.45 crore were settled.

In a landmark decision the Apex Court expressed that the question of assessment of the duty for unauthorized use of electricity, tampering of meters, distribution of meters and calibration of electric current were matters of technical nature which cannot be decided by the Consumer Forum where it was urged that under the Electricity Act, 2003 the jurisdiction of the civil court was excluded. In this connection reliance was placed on Section 145 of the Act, 2003 under which the jurisdiction of the civil court to entertain suits in respect of matters falling under Section 126 was expressly barred. The Apex Court held that since the National Commission had not addressed the question as to whether consumer of electricity was covered by the Consumer Protection Act, 1986 the impugned order was set aside and remitted to the National Commission to a positive finding on the aspect.

NOTES

1. Available at http://www.corecentre.org/guest/focus/linkdetails.asp?ID=power2_focus.
2. Available at http://www.dercind.org/AboutUS/FunctionsDERC/FunctionDERC.html
3. (2007) 4 Comp LJ, 62.
4. *Ibid.*
5. II (1991) CPJ 38.
6. Appeal (Civil) 4734 of 2007 dated 9.10.2007.
7. Section 145, The Electricity Act, 2003: No civil court shall have jurisdiction to entertain any suit or proceeding in respect of any matter which an Assessing Officer referred to Section 126 or an appellate authority referred to in Section 127 or the adjudicating officer appointed under this Act is empowered by or under this Act to determine and injunction shall be granted by any court or other authority in respect of any action taken or to be taken in pursuance of any power conferred by or under this Act.
8. I (1993) CPJ 27 (NC).

9. III (1997) CJP 119.
10. II (1998) CPJ 574.
11. AIR 1987 Del. 219.
12. *Supra* n.8
13. *Supra* n.11.
14. 1991 RLR 312.
15. I (1994) CPJ 255.
16. Vats, R.M (2002), " *Law Relating to Electricity with Special Reference to Consumer Protection*", Universal Law Publishing Co. Pvt. Ltd., New Delhi, p. 73.
17. (1991) CPJ 560.
18. 2002(1) CPJ (NC).
19. *Supra* n. 7.

18
Fake Products Menace: A Case Study

D.Y. Chacharkar

Introduction

Like any other asset, brands are prone to various forms of attack. Counterfeiting, duplication, alteration, misuse, tampering or diversions are some of the various known and repeated forms of brand attack prevalent all over the world. When brand attack occurs, brand owners lose their revenue and market share that are legitimately theirs. More importantly, their reputation and image of the company suffer huge damage. Almost everyone in the value chain is affected when a brand is attacked. Imitation as a menace is a global phenomenon. Companies will never win the war against imitation on their own. At best they will keep imitators on the run. In order to ebb the rising tide of imitation, industry needs to work in tandem with the government and create consumer awareness.

The fact that duplicate products, look-alikes and spell-alikes exist cheek by jowl with genuine products on the same shelf, are less costly and earn the retailer higher profits was always known. What was not known and is still not corroborated is the extent of revenue loss it heralds, both for the companies and for the Government. In many cases, companies have been forced to employ investigative agencies to spot the offenders. Imitation deceives the consumer. It thus, tarnishes the image of a genuine manufacturer, as its brand is a promise of quality and value. The Brand—a company's most valuable asset—can be destroyed when a trademark is imposed on counterfeit products of inferior quality.

When a brand loses value, legitimate business loses sales and this can pose a long-term threat to profitability.

"The Economist" defines imitation as, "something that is forged, copied or imitated without the perpetrator having the right to do it, and with the purpose of deceiving or defrauding." Such rights are legally enshrined in patents (linked with inventions), copyright (which covers literary, musical and artistic works and software), trademarks (which include words, pictures and symbols), industrial designs and other forms of intellectual-property protection.

Imitation is also described as, "A deliberate attempt to deceive consumers by copying and marketing goods bearing well-known trademarks, generally together with packaging and product configuration, so that they look like they are made by a reputable manufacturer when they, are in fact, inferior copies." We usually think of designer purses, watches and scarves when we think of imitated merchandise. That is not the whole story, imitated come in many shapes and sizes. Imitation can be grouped into four broad categories, according to the quality of the product and the level of deception. They could be cheap replicas, fakes, look-alikes, spell-alikes, reproductions or knockoffs. They range from the cheap look-alike Rolex, bought knowingly by several happy customers, to the sub-standard brakes in an unsuspecting driver's car. Common imitated products include auto parts, airplane parts, apparel, cosmetics, sunglasses, computer software, fragrances, children toys, medicines, health, liquor, beauty aids, food products and more.

Imitation Hazards

The repercussions and dangers of imitation are widespread. The imitated products are potentially hazardous. The acts of imitation can and do create severe public health risks and safety hazards, besides economic harm. There is an ample evidence of people being injured or made seriously ill—and in some cases dying—after consuming or using a fake product. The repercussions and dangers of imitation on different stakeholders are as mentioned below:

- *Consumer:* Gets less value, feels cheated and could even risk his life by consuming spurious goods.

- *Brand Owner*: Loses profits, brand value and customers.
- *Government*: Loses tax revenue and incurs additional expenditure on enforcement due to the pressure to raid counterfeiters.
- *Society:* The resultant deterioration of culture, breeds dishonest behaviour.

However, the main hidden cost to society comes in the form of the damage to local and particularly national economies caused by trade in imitations. Local economies are damaged by the loss of sale of genuine products that could be made by legal traders and national economies lose million of dollars in unpaid taxes and excise revenue. The AC Nielsen study estimates the Indian Government loss on account of tax evasions by unauthorized manufacturers to be around ₹ 15,000 crore.

The sale of imitated products has far reaching effects. It is no longer a victimless crime that only affects the large corporations. Unwary consumers have suffered, a few have died and in many cases the profits from counterfeiting support anti-social activities like trafficking and terrorism. Imitation of goods is plain bad business.

Imitations: International Scenario

The international scenario too is not very different. It has been estimated that growing faster than the economy, the global counterfeiting represents from 8 to 10 per cent of the world trade, or approximately $600 billion annually. Briefly,

- 10 per cent of all cosmetics and toiletries worldwide are counterfeit.
- An estimated 11.5 per cent of the European toy market's annual revenue is lost to counterfeiting.
- Consumer electronics counterfeits are estimated as high as 15 per cent of trade.
- The global piracy rate for IT and software is estimated at 40 per cent, amounting to losses of nearly $13 billion.
- The losses to U.S. business due to counterfeiting are estimated at $200 billion/year.
- Of the counterfeit drugs seized each year, 43 per cent

contain no active ingredient; 24 per cent are of poor quality; 21 per cent offer a low content of active ingredient; 7 per cent contain the wrong ingredient; and 5 per cent have the wrong package.

- Counterfeit goods manufactured in some of large manufacturing countries are estimated to exceed US$25 billion annually, with the figure growing each year. Alarmingly, many of the counterfeit goods produced in such countries are now being exported worldwide, impacting revenues and profits not only for local companies, but also on their markets internationally.

Imitations: Indian Scenario

Fake brands flood India. India has 60 'Nike's, 65 'Rolex's and 217 'Intel's. An industry chamber said such is the impact of counterfeiting and piracy that over 400 companies begin with the word 'Reliance'. An ORG retail audit revealed that for every 100 strips of genuine Action 500, there were 54 look-alikes. Vicks Vaporub and inhaler had about 20 clones. The tide in India is turning against counterfeiters and infringers. Until now they were undeterred, given the inability of genuine branded product manufacturers to cause them financial damage, and the slow judicial redress. All this is now changing as a result of progressive judicial pronouncements and legislative amendments. And with numerous judgments given against the counterfeiters by Hon. Supreme Court of India and various High Courts it can be easily concluded that India is waging a war against the people who are into the business of counterfeit.

The practice of imitation is illegal. India does have laws for protecting Intellectual Property. However, in practice, protection is weak. Fighting imitation requires clear rules on enforcement and trained police, judges and customs officials. It also requires the inclination and the authority to check and seize the suspected imitations. It thus, requires the willingness to put imitations in the dock and out of the business as the penalties for imitations is light compared with, for instance dealing in illicit drugs. The need of the hour is an imposition of stiff penalties, even criminal, if required.

Worldwide companies are increasingly trying to load their vulnerable products with anti-imitation features. Some of these are borrowed from pioneering security features developed for use on currency. They are clearly visible and are intended to help consumers distinguish fakes from genuine goods. Companies could also use covert features, primarily to help them trace their products through the supply chain and to distinguish genuine articles from fakes, especially if they need to take recourse to legal measures. At best they will keep imitators on the run. In order to ebb the rising tide of imitation, the industry needs to work in tandem with the government and create consumer awareness. The enforcement agencies also appear to be getting proactive, considering that the Nielsen study estimates the Government's loss on account of tax evasions.

Imitations: Rural India Scenario

"A rural consumer is brand loyal and this also makes it easy to sell look-alike". Marketing And Research Team (MART) has undertaken an impressionistic survey to access the impact of fakes on the rural market. Their research, that covers villages in eastern and western Uttar Pradesh, kasbas around Bhopal and the fake products market in Delhi that services many of the rural areas, shows that the phenomenon is rampant and much more intense than in the cities. For instance, according to the MART report, in the traditional village haats, the main selling locales of rural India, the researchers found that the absence of original branded FMCG products was 100 per cent.

A consequence of the wake up call has been that 50 manufacturers; legal experts and research company AC Nielsen came together to set up a Brand Protection Committee under the aegis of the Federation of Indian Chambers of Commerce and Industry (FICCI). Its members consist of prominent players such as Proctor and Gamble, Hindustan Lever Ltd., Colgate, Marico, GlaxosmithKline, Coca-Cola, Pepsico, Gillette, Britannia, etc. The idea is to curtail fake products in the country and to this end work with the industry, consumer associations, government vigilance wings and trade associations.

Strategic Inputs of the Committee

- Focus on enforcement and application of laws;
- Publicising the negative economic impact of fake products;

- Taking direct action against illegal manufacturers, traders, wholesalers and retailers; and
- And enhancing communication among the stakeholders.

To increase information on the subject a Website, fake-busters.com was also launched. The Website provides information of companies and their crusade against counterfeits, including details of raids conducted and fake products seized. Besides, it carries a legal section which details existing laws on the subject and the legal remedies available. MART study in this context suggests that it is the demand-supply gap that is fuelling the problem in this sector. Distributors appointed by companies stick to the villages closest to their town, while tiny shops and *paanwallas* are serviced by mobile distributors on cycles who stock counterfeit products. Besides, in particular seasons the manufacturing of fake products rises and reaches the retailers much before the genuine brand.

For instance, during summer, fakes abound in cold drinks and talcum powder, while in winter it's cold cream and Vaseline. Another interesting observation is that FMCG counterfeit products only come in the smallest size of packaging. In the rural segment and slums where fake products thrive, the consumers' low purchasing power makes sachets, 25g and 30g packs popular. And it is in the case of these small packs that consumers are duped more easily as the quantity is not large enough for the buyer to discern its quality. Especially, in sachets of *pan masala*, shampoos, hair oils, tooth pastes, detergents and so on. Unaware and illiterate consumers are purchasing mostly imitated brands, as rural areas are huge markets for imitated brands. One such survey was conducted in the petty shops in the rural areas to find out the fake chocolates that are available. The list of Fake Chocolates/Toffees available in rural areas is as follows:

Sl. No.	*Original Brand*	*Imitated Brand*
1.	Dairy Milk	Daily Milk
2.	Kit Kat	Kir Kat
3.	Coffee Bite	Coffee Toffee
4.	Mango Bite	Mango Ripe and Mango Bits
5.	Aasai	Aasha
6.	Polo	Rolo
7.	Vicks	Vibex

The rural consumers by looking into the advertisements of leading chocolate companies unknowingly purchase the fake chocolate brands because of their impulses.

Companies War against Imitations

DABUR

The company in its war against counterfeits of its popular brand is finding way outs. Amla Hair Oil has been facing an increase in counterfeits for the past year-and-a-half and the company is trying to work a way out of it. The company has replaced its glass bottle with a pet bottle. Dabur finds that a subtle difference in packaging such as a gold foil stamping on the label or introducing holograms is not enough for home product consumers, specially the less educated who find it difficult to make out the difference between a genuine and a fake.

COCA-COLA

The leading soft drink brand Coca-Cola too is in the process of exploring changes in its packaging. The company has incorporated certain features that made their bottles tamper-proof. Apparently, this has been tested successfully in the world market.

PEPSI

Pepsi's experience has been similar. It has had to deal with copycat drinks called Dipsy, Tipsy, Sipsi, Toss Up, Dream Cola, 1UP, Lahar, and so on. The problem peaks in summer, when the consumption of colas and juices zoom. It is easy for the manufacturers to set up shop with a bucket, plenty of sugar, artificial flavours, dangerous colours and soda. And of course, these fakes piggyback on the success of the original. Though Pepsi and Coke have dropped prices substantially to make their products the flavour of the masses, spurious products still score because of poor consumer awareness. And fake product manufacturers reap windfalls because there are barely any input costs, no safety standards involved, excise or taxes paid. According to PepsiCo India officials, the Trade and Merchandise Marks Act and Copyright Act and

Indian Penal Code (IPC) authorise companies to protect their marks and properties. PepsiCo has market intelligence efforts and resources in place to survey suspect locations and identify the manufacturers/distributors of spurious goods.

PROCTER AND GAMBLE

P&G had got 55 injunctions against as many manufacturers. In fact, after one of the massive raids in Madhya Pradesh for Vicks, the company used the services of an elephant to destroy the counterfeit catch. P&G's Health care division sales were impacted up to 15 per cent.

Laws Governing Imitations

Following are the laws under which legal action can be taken against manufacturers and sellers of fake products:

(i) Indian Penal Code, 1860,
(ii) Drugs and Cosmetics Act, 1940,
(iii) Prevention of Food Adulteration Act, 1954,
(iv) Consumer Protection Act, 1986,
(v) Bureau of Indian Standards Act, 1986, and
(vi) Trademarks Act, 1999.

Survey on Imitations: Some Important Findings

Exploration on menace of imitation and to get first hand information about the issue, a survey was conducted in Amravati, Maharashtra State. The survey focused on presence of imitated brands and role of intermediaries in pushing imitated brands. The survey covered 100 retailers in different parts of the city. Retailers know where to buy imitated brands from, and the outlets where counterfeits are sold may look different across the region, but they operate in the same way. It is observed that retailers earn at least twice the margin on imitated brands that they do on the genuine product. The aim of the end seller is to sell it to consumers as genuine and, at the same price as the genuine product. It's about risk and reward, and currently there is little risk, but huge reward with very little risk of prosecution. The facts revealed in the survey are depicted in the following table.

Table 18.1: Retailers Margin in Limited Brands

Product Category	*Brand Name*	*Size (gm)/ml*	*Printed Price (in ₹)*	*Retailers Purchase Price (in ₹)*	*Retail Selling Price (in ₹)*	*Profit (in ₹)*	*Retail Margin*
Original	Dove (Soap)	300	35.00	33.40	35.00	1.60	4.79%
Imitated	Doue (Soap)	300	35.00	25.00	35.00	10.00	40.00%
Original	Sweet Heart (Fragrance)	60 ml	120.00	105.00	120.00	15.00	14.28%
Imitated	Sweet Heart (Fragrance)	100 ml	#	80.00	130.00	50.00	62.50%
Original	Park Avenue (Perfume)	50 ml	105.00	95.00	105.00	10.00	10.52%
Imitated	Park Avenue (Perfume)	150 ml	#	80.00	150.00	70.00	87.50%
Original	Axe (Body	150 ml	120.00	110.00	120.00	10.00	9.09%
Imitated	Spray)	200 ml	#	45.00	100.00	55.00	122.22%

Price labels stick on the product.

Majority of the respondents (retailers) knew about the brand imitations. Most of the sampled retailers possessed imitated brands. Almost 82 per cent of the respondents agreed that they possess imitated brands. Few questions were also included in the questionnaire to know from retailers how buyers respond towards imitated brands. They opined that almost 30 per cent are fully aware about the availability of the imitated brands in the market. 64 per cent of the retailers said that customers partially know about it and 6 per cent of the respondents said they were completely unaware about it. It is also important to know whether customers notice about the imitations while buying. 46 per cent of the retailers opined that majority of the customers are able to make out that they are buying imitated brands, while 48 per cent of the retailers opined that 48 per cent of the buyers know about it and 6 per cent of the retailers said that no customer is able to notice imitated brands.

Further in this context the researcher attempted to inquire as to what make customers to buy the imitated brands. Almost 40 per cent of the retailers said that imitated products suit the customers pocket,

24 per cent said it is a cheaper alternative. It is important to note here that almost 20 per cent of the retailers said that customers purchased imitated brand unknowingly, 10 per cent said customers are in a state of confusion at the time of buying, 3 per cent said mostly unaware customers buy it and 5 per cent said customers do not notice that they are buying imitated brands. So from the responses given by the retailers it can be safely stated that retailers are playing key role in pushing imitated brands. In the second section of the questionnaire the researcher unearthed the reasons behind it. It was observed that the important reason is that the retailers are getting greater margin of profit on imitated brands than the original ones. Further, in this context the researcher made an inquiry about the percentage sale of imitated brands out of the total sale. 50 per cent of the retailers said this percentage is 0-25 per cent, 35 per cent said it was between 25-50 per cent, and 14 per cent said it was 50-75 per cent.

Retailers hold moral responsibility to give truthful information to the customers about products they sell. It was inquired whether retailers are disclosing the information or not. It revealed that 34 per cent of them answered this question affirmatively. Other section of retailers who said no (15 %), never (14%), and sometimes (37%) are not doing their job honestly and are culprits. It means majority of the retailers are not doing their role of educating customers. The customer is not aware of the *mala fide* intentions of the retailers. The blind faith on the retailers many times compels the customers to buy the goods they have not asked for. Going further it was inquired if the retailers had preference to select between original and imitated brands what they will prefer. The preferences of customers were also ascertained. It was revealed that 56 per cent of the retailers select original brand, 30 per cent go for imitated brands, 14 per cent prefer product/s which suits their pocket if customers have choice.

All this clearly indicates that both the customers and the retailers are equally responsible for promotion of imitated brands. However, the retailer's role in this is very prominent and holds more responsibility. Hence, to put check on it, the retailer is an important intermediary to be focused on. Simply for higher profit margin they put exchequer in the form of taxes and health of the customers at stake. It also leads to generation of black money in the economy. Considering these important observations and findings the suggestions for different segments in trade and businesses are as follows:

What needs to be done by the Marketers?

1. Marketers should think on increasing retailers margin, Marketers should reduce the expenses on advertisements to increase retailers margin.
2. FMCG companies should focus on counterfeits mostly in small size packaging, where consumers are duped easily.
3. Innovative packaging is an important solution for putting a check on imitations.
4. Marketers should take all legal protection, particularly as regards design and packaging registration in order to protect their brands.
5. Regular comprehensive trade visits by marketing and sales department to the bottom end of the trade to seek co-operation will help build trust.
6. Awareness and education is a key in this context. Build awareness and work with dealers and consumer groups, educating their members, as well help lobby on manufacturer's behalf.
7. Marketers should make sure that the label looks distinct and consistent so that consumers can tell the difference between a genuine and a fake one, publicise it for wider publicity and invest more on brand protection.

What can the Government do?

1. Best practices and laws in the region to be adopted.
2. Adding more teeth to rules/laws on enforcement against imitations.
3. Train police, judges, and custom officials for enforcement against imitations.
4. Issue of absence of safety standards should be taken up on priority.

What should the Consumers do?

"Together we can" consumers can follow, come together and realize some prudence and caution on their part. This can go a long way in countering the menace. Some basic and simple measures that can be adopted by consumers across the country are—

1. Customer should buy products that they need from a reputed shop or establishment.
2. Consumers while buying products should check the labels of all the products thoroughly. If one observes poorly printed labels, absence of the label or lack of details of the product, faulty sealing and differences in the colour of the packing, the product should be rejected.
3. Should always look for the batch number, manufacturing date, expiry date, manufacturing licence number, manufacturer's name/address etc. on the pack.
4. Go for patch tests wherever required. For cosmetics, skin and beauty products it is necessary to look out for any extraneous matter in liquid preparations, lumps in creams or ointments and always check the labels and read the list of ingredients carefully.
5. Make it a habit of asking for a bill/receipt or cash memo for all products that you purchase. It is especially useful if and when you need to show proof of your purchase.
6. Destroy empty packs, bottles and containers of used or leftover medicines to avoid recycling or refilling because it may lead to reuse.
7. Complaint or report to the company if suspected that the original product is being duplicated or imitated. Try and ensure that company lodges complaint either with the local police or the necessary authorities in the state.
8. Always check hologram on the product. If you are aware of any particular mark, logo or hologram the product is supposed to have, please ensure it is present before you buy the product.

REFERENCES

Anjali Doshi, "Digest this, 5 per cent of Food items you buy are fake", *Hindustan Times* (Mumbai) September 29, 2005.

G.K. Kapoor, *Defective Goods and Deficiency of Service*, published by Indian Institute of Public Administration, New Delhi, 2005.

"Indian Rural Market", *Indian Journal of Marketing,* Volume: XXXII, Number: 10, October 2002.

"Intellectual Property Management in India, New Challenges and Opportunities Ahead", Vol. 6, No. I, Published by Director General, Council of Scientific and Industrial Research, New Delhi, 2007.

Rucha Biju Chitrodia, "Fake Brands dent co image", *The Times of India,* Nagpur, September 28, 2007.

Ruchi Trehan and Harmandeep Singh, "A Comparative Study on Urban and Rural Consumer Behaviour", *Indian Journal of Marketing,* Volume XXXIII, Number 7, July 2003.

S.A. Chunawalla, *Compendium of BRAND MANAGEMENT,* Himalaya Publishing House, First Edition, Mumbai, 2004.

S.S. Singh, *Consumer Protection in India, Some Reflection,* published by Indian Institute of Public Administration, New Delhi, 2005.

Shanthi Nachiappan, "Challenges in Teaching Business Ethics: Spurious Products in Rural Markets", *Indian Journal of Marketing,* Volume: XXXIII, Number: 9, September 2003.

Sheetal Kapoor, Dr., *Consumer and the Market,* published by Indian Institute of Public Administration, New Delhi, 2005.

www.consumercare.co.in

www.fakebusters.com

19

Role of VCOs in Consumer Protection: A Case Study of GOACAN

Renji George Amballoor and *Anu George*

Introduction

Many a times, the established formal government machinery characterized by bureaucratic and administrative hazards fails to reach out and empower the ordinary consumer. During the early Twentieth century 'market economy' propelled by 'globalization' along with the 'information economy' was considered as a panacea for all the socio-economic ills before the humanity. People's participation through voluntary civil society organizations emerged as the viable alternatives for globalization. Voluntary civil society organizations have been a powerful bludgeon for coalescing the energies of different stakeholders and social capital for the benefit of citizens.

The consumer redressal forums at the district and state level established under CPA, 1986 in all states were flooded with complaints. The redressal mechanism failed to dispense instant justice to the aggrieved consumers because of the inordinate delay in settlement of cases, cumbersome procedures, inadequate work-force, and non-execution of orders, statutory limitations and other constraints. Hence, as a panacea, the concept of Alternate Dispute Resolution (ADR) using the voluntary civil society organizations gained currency in the consumer protection map of India. Voluntary civil society organizations working on consumer issues should encourage the affected consumers to use the mechanism of Alternate Dispute Resolution. This in turn will reduce the burden on consumer courts and makes its operation more efficient.

In 1991 many citizens were facing problems relating to domestic LPG connection in Goa. The customers witnessed irregularities in getting a new connection and the malpractices in getting re-fill cylinders. Gas companies failed to provide every customer their book which contained details on booking and delivery of refill cylinder. They initially, as individuals approached Mr. Roland Martins, who along with 'Goa Resource Dese'[1] had made a number of interventions to stop socio-cultural illegalities in tourism sector. Previously he was also a part of the students' movement which pressurised the State Government to give half ticket concession to all students. This image of an activist in Roland Martins attracted the aggrieved LPG consumers of Mapusa. The LPG related problems of the aggrieved consumers of Mapusa were solved with the intervention of Mr. Roland. With this success they formed 'Consumer Guidance Forum' in collaboration with Department of Civil Supplies, Government of Goa for building consumer awareness and for interventions.

The news regarding solving of LPG problem in Mapusa spread to other coastal talukas. There was a spurt of aggrieved consumers from Saligao, Tivim, Aldona requesting a solution for their LPG related problems. The angry consumers of each region were told to hold village level meetings and elect their respective conveners. Before the first meeting, a few volunteers were identified from the region, who in turn mail postcards about the meeting to prospective consumers of the region. Once the first meeting is scheduled, the subsequent meetings take place on the same day of every month. Complaints received in between two consecutive meetings are not dealt independently. It will be referred to the local group formed for the issue. The formation of consumer cells witnessed an amoebic expansion during the period 1991-2000 fuelled by LPG related problems.

On April 22, 2002, on the occasion of World Earth Day, the Goa Civic and Consumer Action Network (GOACAN) was formed. It was an initiative in activism launched in 2002 by the Goa Dese Resource Centre to consolidate its positive experience from 1998 in forming village level cells, samitis and forums to deal with the Civic and Consumer issues plaguing the common man in his respective village. The name GOACAN also means that the people of the village forum can bring about changes through collective bargaining.

All the consumer cells were named as the civic and consumer association (for example, Saligao Civic and Consumer Forum). These forums act as voluntary civil society groups. In 2009, there are 14 forums in North, 5 in Central and 17 in South Goa. Out of the total 35 forums, 25 are systematic and functional village based civic and consumer forums covering 6 talukas of Tiswadi, Bardez, Salcete, Quepem, Pernem and Mormugao. The forums are financially independent. They accept voluntary contributions from those present for the forum meeting every month. There is no hard and fast rule regarding the contributions. The forums do not have any formal or informal organizational structure. It only elects a member as the convener for its meetings. The volunteers of the forum ensure adequate participation for the meetings. Every meeting is attended and guided by Mr. Martins and his team. Some forums give a part of their collections to GOACAN. The village forums and GOACAN are financially self-sufficient. GOACAN raises its resources by co-ordinating awareness campaigns for various agencies and government departments.

Once a consumer complaint is received, a letter is drafted and filed with the concerned department. The follow-up is carriedout by the forum and Mr. Martins. While filing complaints, they also collect citizen's charter and other relevant brochures concerning the department. They also hold interactions with the officials of the departments. The matter is also taken up with *adalats*, ombudsman, etc. pertaining to the department. The GOACAN and its village forums are not registered under any registration law in force. However, they are registered with the Department of Civil Supplies, Government of Goa. On the other hand, 13 of the registered NGOs in the consumer protection map of Goa have disappeared in a short span.

In coastal places like Benaulim, Calangute and Majorda, the forums are known as Residents and Consumer Forums. It was felt that the consumers in these tourism belts can affirm their rights as consumers only if they could assert their rights as a resident of the said locality. From 2002 onwards, GOACAN with its local network, organized a series of workshops and campaigns throughout the villages of Goa on consumer affairs, social action, environment, children and women, etc. GOACAN was based on the philosophy that if the villagers' awareness of their civic rights can be expanded, automatically their rights as consumers can be easily protected and ensured. Since 2007, GOACAN has become a separate entity independent of Goa Resource Dese Centre. GOACAN runs the following campaigns for ensuring the various rights of stake-holders including that of consumers.

Civic and Consumer Literacy

In this campaign information is provided about the rights of the consumer as enshrined in the Consumer Protection Act, 1986, the functioning of the State Commissions and District Consumer Redressal Forums and Consumer Conciliation Committee. The campaign also covers use of Citizen Charters in Government Departments, complaint redressal by private and public service providers, use of helplines, participation in *adalats,* open houses etc.

Making Democracy Work

The citizens are encouraged to participate in the Village Gram Sabhas, attend the fortnightly Panchayat meetings and the bi-monthly Municipal Council Meetings. Citizens are also encouraged to scrutinize the minutes of meetings, verify the budget expenditure and examine the audit reports as a step to curb corruption and to demand transparency and accountability in governance. Besides, citizens are also encouraged to volunteer on the various committees at the Panchayat and Municipal level. The campaign also focuses on advocacy work with Members of the Village Panchayat, Zilla Panchayat, Municipal Council, Legislative Assembly and Parliament.

Road Safety and Traffic Management

This campaign focuses on regular interaction between the Consumer Forums and the Directorate of Transport and Traffic Police through the sub-committees of the District Consumer Protection Council. It promotes the preparation of Road Safety and Traffic Management Plans at the neighbourhood, institution, all village panchayat and municipal levels. It creates awareness on the rules of the road, unsafe driving practices, need for Road Safety Patrols (RSP) in schools and the role of the PWD in Road Engineering. It also advocates that Public Transport must be "Comfortable, Affordable and Safe".

Waste Management

The campaign on waste management for environmental protection and sustainable consumption seeks to involve the consumer as a principal stakeholder by focusing on the consumption patterns and waste disposal practices. The campaign highlights the provisions of the Goa Non-Biodegradable Garbage Control Act, 1996 (Goa Act 5 of 1997), Municipal Solid Waste Management Rules, which provide for the principles of reduce, reuse and recycle, segregation at source and polluter pays besides methods to manage medical and toxic waste. The campaign also promotes methods such as home/garden composting, vermi-composting and use of effective microbes.

Right to Information

In this campaign, awareness is created about the Right to Information Act, 2005 (RTI) on how to use RTI by making necessary applications to the different authorities that can be approached for the same. The campaign through its "Drive against Bribes using RTI" guides citizens to use RTI instead of paying bribes to get their work done in case of pending applications with the concerned Government Departments. Citizens are also encouraged to approach and file complaints with the Vigilance Department and the Directorate of Public Grievances for matters concerning Government of Goa and the Anti-Corruption Cell of the CBI for Central Government agencies.

Legal and Human Rights Education

In this campaign awareness is created about the importance of Civil Liberties and Democratic Rights. Information is disseminated about the UN Charter of Human Rights, Fundamental Rights and Directive Principles as enshrined in the Constitution of India and various bodies such the National Human Rights Commission, State

Police Complaint Authority, National Commission for Women etc. Information is also disseminated about the judicial system and the use of various Courts.

The success of GOACAN has prompted them to form the 'Young Civic and Consumer Movement' in 2006. Under this movement they have initiated the task of setting up consumer cells in schools, higher secondary schools and degree colleges. The objective is to build awareness about the Consumer Protection Act, 1986 among students. Further consumer cells have to identify violations in their catchment areas, guide the consumer in grievance redressal and then act as pressure groups in ensuring civic and consumer rights. Today YCCM has a wide presence in schools and colleges of Goa. The GOACAN is not just concerned with consumer rights as defined in the narrow sense. It believes that in a globalized market driven paradigm, only participatory grassroots democracy can be a panacea for the ills of citizens and consumers. Building awareness about and ensuring the civic right of the consumer is the first priority of GOACAN. It is complemented by the guarantee of consumer rights. In some places, the village forums were told to enjoy their rights as a resident of the region and then take-up matters relating to consumer rights.

The village forums are also encouraged to discuss social issues relating to their locality and to take up necessary remedial measures. In villages of Nuvem, Ria and Navelim, GOACAN has used its network to group the farmers to redress their grievances. Similarly by 2010 they propose to have village based forums of the females and ST population in every village of Goa. According to Dre'ze and Sen, 'building up of capabilities[2] of citizens' will 'broaden their entitlements' and facilitate the expansion of 'substantive freedom'[3] and 'social opportunities' leading to their empowerment. Sen in his book *'Development as Freedom'* argues for the removal of 'unfreedom'[4] for the empowerment of citizens.

GOACAN is able to get bigger and sustain itself because it has first identified the civic interests of the consumer. The village forums also become a venue for discussing social issues and village level problems. Such informal discussions bind the villages together, create a feeling of oneness and empower them to fight against injustice and for their rights. This model of empowerment has made GOACAN very successful in protecting and promoting consumer interest. The problem with existing models of voluntary organizations in consumer protection is that they are concerned only with matters relating to consumer protection. GOACAN has a very broad definition of a consumer. This enables them to formulate and implement plans and programmes to keep the members of village forums occupied with one issue or the other. There is a positive correlation between the number of issues taken up and the degree of bargaining power to fight lapses, to put the system in order and to make the functioning of government departments user-friendly.

This model of GOACAN can be successfully replicated elsewhere in the country because it is based on grassroots planning and participation. The revenue model is also simple for easy adoption and does not involve complicated financial process. Further, this model is adopting a holistic view of the consumer. The model aims at empowering consumer in civic rights and thereby strengthens their consumer rights. According to Mr. Roland Martins, the GOACAN has witnessed tremendous growth for the period 1999-2008. At the same time, risk is arising due to the over-dependency of village forums on him for guidance, strength, motivation and sustainability. Further, about 10 of the village forums have become ineffective.

NOTES

1. The Goa Resource Dese Centre is an activist collective set up in 1988 and based in Mapusa. It works on various issues to popularize sustainable social development and enable democracy to function at the grassroots level through people's participation.
2. Expansion of capabilities empowers a person to lead the kind of lives they value and have reasons to value it.
3. Substantive freedom includes elementary capabilities like being able to avoid such deprivations as starvation, undernourishment, escapable morbidity and premature mortality, as well as the freedom that are associated with being literate and numerate, enjoying political participation and uncensored speech and so on.
4. Sources of unfreedom include poverty, tyranny, poor economic and social opportunities, intolerance, over-activity of repressive state.

REFERENCES

Avtar Singh, *Law of Consumer Protection,* Lucknow, Eastern Book Company, 2006.

Chaudhary, R.N.P., *Consumer Protection Law,* New Delhi: Deep & Deep Publications, 2005.

Dre'ze Jean & Sen, Amartya, *Development as Freedom,* New Delhi: Oxford University Press, 1999.

Dre'ze Jean & Sen, Amartya, *India Development: Selected Regional Perspectives,* New Delhi: Oxford University Press, 1999.

Dre'ze Jean & Sen, Amartya, *India—Economic Development and Social Opportunity,* New Delhi: Oxford University Press, 1998.

20
Consumer Rights Awareness among Women: A Case Study of Navi Mumbai

Durga Surekha and *Swati Kulkarni*

Introduction

Women constitute nearly 50 per cent of India's population. Given the socio-economic profile of the country they remain the most neglected and exploited class. This is mainly because they lack education as well as economic and political empowerment. The situation is still worse in the rural areas. A number of programmes have been initiated to empower the women but still a lot needs to be done. Women as consumers are exploited in the market economy. They are the ones who manage the affairs of the homes but have very little awareness about the products and services they purchase and use. Lack of awareness makes them an easy target for exploitation. If women are educated it would enable them to exercise their consumer rights and help them in seeking redressal of their grievances.

Even in larger cities the level of awareness is low and women continue to be silent sufferers. They are so busy that they are unable to understand the various forms of exploitation that they undergo daily at the market place. This paper attempts to reveal the level of awareness and concern about consumer rights among women who are educated and live in a well developed locality in Navi Mumbai.

Navi Mumbai formerly known as New Bombay is a city on the west coast of the Indian state of Maharashtra and was developed in 1972 as a twin city of Mumbai. The length of the city is almost the same as that of Mumbai. The Vashi and Airoli bridges connect Navi Mumbai to Mumbai. Vashi and Nerul are the most costliest and developed areas of the region. Although away from the main city of Mumbai, most of the people lead a hard life due to extensive travelling with no time for themselves. Time is regarded as something very valuable and commuting everyday to the workplace by Mumbai's local trains is not an experience but is an ordeal. It is because of this time constraints they are always in a hurry leaving no time for their personal lives. Here most men are business minded and always look forward for opportunities to succeed faster. As a result, women play the major role as successful consumers and are aware of how to stretch a rupee by keeping the costs down.

The literacy level of women in this region is high and as per statistics majority of the Navi Mumbai population is young with 55 per cent in the age group of 15-44 years and 13 per cent aged 45-59 years. Based on the understanding a minor research has been conducted to study the consumer right's awareness among women in Navi Mumbai. The broad objective of the study to assess the awareness of the women consumers towards consumer rights, quality issues and standardisation measures, consumer redressal mechanism and their perception towards the effectiveness of consumer protection laws.

The age groups were fixed on the basis of a pilot study of fifty questionnaires at the rate of ten from the survey of the five malls of Navi Mumbai. On this basis the respondents were classified under two age groups of 25 to 35 years and 36 to 45 years. Primary research was conducted using questionnaires as a means of collecting information. The total sample comprised three hundred women consumers drawn from the 5 malls located in the residential areas of Vashi, Nerul, Belapur, Kharghar and Panvel, covering the entire belt of Navi Mumbai.

General Profile of the Respondents

The sample comprised 60 per cent females in the age group of 36-45 years and 40 per cent between 25-35 years. 55 per cent of the women were housewives while the rest were engaged in some profession that did not disturb their family chores. It was taken as a pass time. 90 per cent were educated to the level of graduation and post-graduation. 75 per cent of the consumers were residents of Navi Mumbai for more than 5 years.

General Awareness of the Consumers towards Rights

Ninety per cent of the respondents in the sample were aware of the Consumer Protection Act and consumer forum. 63.6 per cent of the respondents were familiar with right to safety, 75 per cent with right to quality, 53 per cent with right to choose from a variety of goods/services at competitive prices. 50 per cent with right to be heard and 60 per cent with right to seek redressal when deceived while 58 per cent were aware of right to consumer education. A negligible (10%) of the respondents in the sample were totally unaware of Consumer Protection Act or consumer forum although they were qualified to the level of graduation. With regard to the Prevention of Food Adulteration Act, 80 per cent of the respondents were familiar. 20 per cent of respondents were familiar with Sales of Good Act, 10 per cent knew about the Indian Medical Council (Professional Conduct, Etiquettes and Ethics) Regulations, 2002. 20 per cent of them were familiar with Electricity Act, 2003 and more than 75 per cent of the sample respondents knew about the "Bureau of Indian Standards". It was seen that awareness towards specific consumer Acts and Rules like Indian Medical Council Regulations, Electricity Act and Sales of Goods Act was very less whereas there was greater awareness of certain Acts due to their involvement in the buying process.

Awareness Quality Control and Standardisation Measures

Ninety per cent of the respondents in the sample looked for I.S.I. mark of every batch in production process, 86 per cent looked for Hallmark when they purchase gold articles. With regard to the purchases of the net quantities of the products like biscuits, cereals and pulses, coffee, tea, salt only 9 per cent of them look into it and are not interested since the products are not expensive. 32.4 per cent of the respondents were aware that the weight of the gas cylinder can be verified and 34 per cent of them knew that the delivery man of gas cylinder should carry a spring balance. Only 5 per cent of the respondents looked for the generic name and brand name of the medicine prescribed to a patient. Among the total respondents, 85 per cent did not feel deprived but 15 per cent felt deprived with the manner the consumers are provided with defective goods/inferior quality goods, matters related to packed sweets etc. The respondents reported that after sales service was not provided and the consumers were charged exorbitant price. Therefore, only 2 per cent of the respondents replaced the goods to get the defect removed while the rest ignored it.

Awareness about Rerdressal Mechanism

Eighty-two per cent of the sample respondents were aware that consumer disputes redressal forum is a Quasi-Judicial authority under the statute to redress consumer disputes. 10 per cent of them were aware that a complaint in the District Consumer Disputes Redressal Forum can be filed in triplicate on plain paper. None of them was aware that complaint can be filed within two years from the date of the cause of action. 2 per cent of the respondents knew about the nominal fees payable for the compensation claimed. 84 per cent were familiar with the relief the consumer may seek in form of the refund of money, 80 per cent with replacement of the goods, 75 per cent with removal of the defects or deficiencies, 50 per cent with compensation for loss or harassment or mental agony, 40 per cent with prohibition of marketing of goods hazardous for health or environment.

Consumer Laws: Effectiveness

Eighty-nine per cent of the respondents reported that laws enacted for the consumers are ineffective since the process involved is complicated and not within the reach. The common myth is that, the costs involved are more and there is delay in the administration of justice.

Summary and Findings

- Only 10 per cent of the sample respondents lacked awareness towards Consumer Protection Act and consumer forum while 90 per cent were aware.
- Awareness towards different consumer Acts is poor.
- Basic motivation to approach consumer courts among women was lacking due to time and economic constraints.

- Knowledge of the laws and the ways to approach consumer courts are inadequate.
- Lot of disinterest was seen among the sample respondents with regard to redressal of complaints in consumer courts.
- Women lacked interest in knowing more on redressal mechanism since the issue of consumer exploitation is the last subject for consideration in their busy schedules.
- Though familiar with Consumer Protection Act, it does not affect them much in terms of monetary constraints as they value time more than fighting for the cause.

Suggestions

1. More awareness should be created by displaying ways to approach consumer court at shopping malls.
2. Media has recently started educating the consumers; however, the frequency and reach should be higher by organizing sessions in residential areas to educate consumers.
3. Access to redressal agencies should be made even simpler with more consumer courts being set up especially in cities like Mumbai.
4. Awareness needs to be created among people about their responsibilities as citizens, to voice their rights and to be concerned about it since they cannot afford to ignore it. The lethargic attitude should be removed.
5. Set up open forums to interact with people and create more awareness amongst them about the need for consumer education.
6. Consumers should be encouraged to approach forums with their complaints by giving wide publicity.
7. Consumer education should be incorporated at the school level itself and the students should be given a mandatory project on consumer studies.
8. Research studies on issues of consumer protection should be conducted at frequent intervals in different parts of the country.
9. The local channels of television should play tele serials that bring consumer awakening and imparts consumer education.
10. Marketers should also be better informed on consumer redressal issues.

11. Pamphlets regarding consumer awareness should be distributed in the localities to educate the consumers.

Conclusion

This study addressed an important issue of consumer awareness towards consumer rights among women of Navi Mumbai. The findings provide cautious pessimism that they are not developing the values to fight consumer exploitation. There is need for a major change in attitude on how they conceive of not being cheated nor deceived. Although the Government of India is trying hard to incorporate the concern into our culture, a significant positive step of translating this concern into effective action is still lacking in a city like Navi Mumbai.

REFERENCES

Annual Administrative Report, 2003-04. Consumer Affairs Department, Government of West Bengal, Kolkata.

Consumer Handbook, Department of Consumer Affairs, Government of West Bengal, 2004.

Das, S.K., Caring for the Consumer—West Bengal Consumer's Guide. Department of Consumers Affairs, Government of West Bengal, 2003.

Gangopadhyay, D., Detail Maps of 141 Wards with Street Directory. D.P. Publication and Sales Concern, Kolkata, 2001.

Insight—the consumer magazine, Ahmedabad, Consumer Education & Research Society, 2002.

Kumar, R., *Consumer Protection and Trade Practices Journal,* Jago Grahak Jago, 2002.

Kundu, B.K., *The Kolkata Statistical Handbook,* Bureau of Applied Economics and Statistics, Government of West Bengal, 2003.

Loulfi, M.F., *Women, Gender and Work,* Rawat Publications, Jaipur and New Delhi, 2002.

Mamoria, C.B. *Social Problems,* Kitab Mahal Publications, 1961.

Miles, S., *Consumerism as a Way of Life,* Saga Publications, London, 1984.

Murthi, S.K., *Consumer and Law Redressal of Grievances,* Vinod Law Publications, Lucknow, 2001.

Reddy, G.B., *Law of Consumer Protection,* Gogia Law Publication, Delhi, 2004.

21
Media Literacy and the Consumers: A Critical Study

Mayuri Tiwari and *Varun Thomas*

Introduction

The global market that has risen through the years has brought the world forward through free trade and commercialization. Giving consumers the freedom to choose has encouraged innovation as well as convenience. Due to globalization and liberalization the boundaries have broken down and the world has transformed into a global village. Due to this, business has crossed the seas and borders and is not afraid to step into unfamiliar territory. This confidence of the businessmen also stems from the fact that the purchasing power of the consumers has gone up as a result any product can be passed on to the consumers if it is marketed well. It's an era of marketing and packaging. When we say that consumers are spoilt for choice, we should not ignore the fact that the world is in a state of information explosion. So much of information is being disseminated that the consumers find it difficult to sieve through information and separate it from misinformation. Advertisement is important so that the marketers can educate the consumers about the product but when it misleads the consumers then it becomes a problem.

The main concern of this paper relates to the question of the consumers being misleading by the media. Of course, the global market is a big achievement, but the global market is being manipulated to make the consumers buy goods that are not healthy or actually beneficial to them. Talking of the global market, we must talk about brands and the influence of brand names on a consumer's everyday life. Through intense and rapid commercialization brand names today act as status symbols. The most active consumers, the youth and also peer pressure has helped these brands to grow larger instead of mere goodwill and quality on which they survived earlier.

But it would of interest to enquire as to how these big brand names and businesses are roping in the consumers. This is mainly done through aggressive advertisement of the product. Advertising is one of the most successful methods of marketing and is being used very effectively to lure the consumers. Advertising like every coin has two sides, good and bad. The good side being that more and more consumers come to know about the new product and the bad side being advertisements usually end up exaggerating and the product does not live up to the expectations of the consumers. With the above concerns, there is a compelling need to educate the media and to enhance awareness among the consumers about their rights and obligations.

An analysis of a few commercial establishments, that have gained popularity in India within a very short period mainly due to heavy advertising and media influences shows how powerful the media has become in the present era. It also exposes as to how advertisement has changed the taste and preferences of the consumers even though fast food is considered to be unhealthy.

Fast Food Chains

Unhealthy, processed food has become much more accessible following India's integration with global food markets. Also through globalization numerous foreign based fast food establishments have opened their establishments in almost all the cities of the country including small towns. Statistics[1] show that 5 per cent of India's population is obese mainly because of eating junk food.

McDonalds began fast food business in 1940, when Dick and Mac McDonald brothers opened a restaurant in San Bernardino, California. Since then this chain of fast food establishment has grown over 31,000 outlets worldwide. It hit India in 1996 and since then has opened 170 outlets and estimates are that they would open 180-190 more restaurants by 2015.[2] With its coming to India, came the dawn of a new era of fast food. According to a news report[3] American fast food outlets must list the nutrition details of each item on the menu so that the consumer can make healthy choices. In India, this practice is not prevalent and none of the fast food chains list any nutritional details of the items on their menus. This disables the consumer from making a smarter and healthier choice when he goes out to eat.

The Kellogg's Revolution

The Kellogg Company was founded in 1906 when they started with toasted corn flakes as a nutritive supplement food. Since then the company survived through Second World War and after under spending its competition in marketing and product development the Kellogg's US market share hit an all time low in 1983. It was only in 1994 that Kellogg's entered the Indian Market. Since then the company has introduced all its cereal products which are sold abroad in the Indian Market. These products include cereals like Chocos, Froot Loops etc. which are extremely sugary and have the target buyer group as children. To attract children, the simplest strategy would be and is, to advertise a cereal like Chocos as chocolaty and sweet and what's more when the company promises a spanking new toy with the box of cereal. The parents don't seem to mind since their mindset is that the child is taking in milk anyway. Thus the marketing tactic is successful and the product sells. But is it really healthy? Studies have shown that a serving may contain up to 30 per cent of sugar requirement of an adult in a day, which means that it'll be on the higher side for children.[4]

This is again an example of how the media has sold a product not really healthy but passed off by enticing children with the flavour of chocolate and a toy. The television ads feature bears and other animated cartoon characters which are quite successful in capturing a child's imagination. Consumers need to be aware about their daily nutritional requirement for a child and how much a cereal really contains before buying the same. The media does not show or warn the consumers regarding the same, since the media is being paid to sell products and not actually educating the consumer or helping him make a smarter choice.

The Fizz in the Colas

Who puts the real fizz in the cola? It is the media of course. The key requirement for roping in the consumers to buy colas is to attract them by depicting the results of drinking that cola. Apparently it increases charm, attracts the opposite sex, allows you to be a star, and promises the world under bottle caps.

Since the very beginning colas have been associated with being macho by various ad agencies and the formula has always worked. When the consumer sees his favourite movie star drinking the same cola while performing insane stunts, it tempts him to give into such fantasies and buy the cola his icon drinks. A major advertising tactic is to rope in a celebrity to endorse the aerated drink and show him/her in various attractive poses sipping the cola. Sadly the uneducated consumer always falls for this over-publicized gimmick. Since he hardly knows what harm cola's might do health-wise, he unassumingly picks up his favourite bottle of cola whose advertisement he has just seen on the television. Though the media is supposed to state facts like the drink contains caffeine and a high amount of calories, but the print is so fine and the visuals so stunning that the consumer pays no heed to the warning. Thus, the media again fails to educate the consumer about the ill effects of the same product they are advertising. Without knowing both sides of the coin, the consumer tends to make an un-informed choice which ends up in a health trouble.

If we trace the marketing strategy of the McDonald's chain, or any soft drink or a cereal for that matter, we see that it relies solely on media channels like newspaper ads, television ads and bill board advertisements. The Government of India brought about strict policies, banning advertisements of alcohol and tobacco products in the late 1990s. It's time now that the government should focus on educating the urban consumer, who tops the list of unhealthy citizens, by running awareness campaigns regarding junk food and also by making it mandatory to print nutritional details on menus and soft drink bottles. It will make the consumers aware of the actual product they are consuming even after misleading advertisement by the media.

Deception Caused by Media in Garb of Advertising

Ever since the reach of media has increase companies have used this means of communications to inform people about their products. Further, it allows innovative ideas and concepts to be shared with others. However, as the years have passed, the sophistication of advertising methods and techniques has also advanced, enticing, shaping and even creating consumerism and needs where there was none. In fact it has turned luxuries into necessities.

Ben Bagdikian, a prominent media critic, and author of the well-acclaimed book *The Media Monopoly*, provides many more details and examples. In one of the chapters, Bagdikian describes in detail the pressure on media companies to change content (to "dumb down") and to shape content based on the demographics of the audiences. Slowly then, the content of media isn't as important as the type of person being targeted by the ads. He also shows that the notion of "giving the audience what they want" is also a bit misleading because, it is more about targeting those readers that can afford the products that are advertised and so it is almost like giving the advertisers what they want! The "dumbing down" of the content also acts to promote a "buying mood". Hence, as Bagdikian summarizes, "programming is carefully non-controversial, light, and non-political."[5]

The BBC aired a documentary called *Century of the Self* looking back at the rise of consumerism in the 20th century. Discussing the role of the media, it was pointed out how journalism also changed as big business started to gain more influence. Many, in order to get stories that would attract readers, had to agree to editorial content being dictated by business, such as placement of specific advertising in the pictures, placing certain sentences and paragraphs, and mentioning key products related to the story. The influence of advertising on magazines reached a point where editors began selecting articles not only on the basis of their expected interest for readers but for their influence on advertisements. Serious articles were not always the best support for ads. An article that put the reader in an analytical frame of mind did not encourage the reader to take seriously an ad that depended on fantasy or promoted a trivial product. An article on genuine social suffering might interrupt the "buying" mood on which most ads for luxuries depend. The next step, seen often in mid-twentieth century magazines, was commissioning articles solely to attract readers who had good prospects to buy products advertised in the magazine.[6]

Mass advertising is no longer solely a mean of introducing and distributing consumer goods, though it does that. It is a major mechanism in the ability of a relatively small number of giant corporations to hold disproportionate power over the economy. These corporations need newspapers, magazines, and broadcasting not just to sell their goods but to maintain their economic and political influence. The media are no longer neutral agents of the merchants but essential gears in the machinery of corporate giantism. And increasingly they are not only needed but they are owned by the corporate giants.[7]

Regulation of Media and Advertising

Advertising communication is a mix of arts and facts subservient to ethical principles. In order to be consumer-oriented, advertisement needs to be truthful and ethical. On the one hand, commercialisation has thrown open the need of a more well informed consumer, and on the other, there has emerged the *need of educating media,* the flip side to the commonly understood notion of "media-literacy". The following works on the principle that major industrial players must realise the ethical ways of functioning which ensures that the consumer is not mislead. If not instilled in them through a self-regulated code the same should be as a resultant of compulsion and fear that they might loose credibility, if unethical conduct comes within the scanner of administrators. Hence, there is a need for a *tri-partite* pressure mechanism through administrative action, legal reform and judicial activism.

Self-Regulation

At the onset, one of the best attempts of self-regulation was by the Advertising Standards Council of India (ASCI), through *ethical regulating code* inspired from the Advertising Standards Authority (ASA) UK. The following are basic guidelines in order to achieve the acceptance of fair advertising practices in the interest of the consumer:

- To ensure the truthfulness and honesty of representations and claims made by advertisements and to safeguard against misleading advertising;

- To ensure that advertisements are not offensive to generally accepted standards of public decency;
- To safeguard against indiscriminate use of advertising for promotion of products which are regarded as hazardous to society or to individuals to a degree or of a type which is unacceptable to society at large; and
- To ensure that advertisements observe fairness in competition so that the consumers are informed on choices in the market places and canons of generally accepted competitive behaviour in business are served.[8]

The Advertising Standards Council of India (ASCI) has the authority of issuing notice to a party for violating its code of advertising practices, and party is given a chance of presenting its case. The same is reflected in the case of Hindustan Liver Limited's Clinic All Clear Dandruff shampoo. It was claimed that ZPTO was the special ingredient in Clinic All Clear that stops dandruff. This claim was found to be untrue since ZPTO is a micro biocide, when in reality, dandruff is known to be caused by several other factors, besides, microbes. On enquiry it was found that HLL's multi-crore research wing 'clearly overlooked' this aspect. The advertisement has been withdrawn henceforth. Another case was that when Novartis India claimed that their disposable contact lenses ensure there is no protein build-up. This claim was found to be totally false. The truth is that build up is a natural biological phenomenon with all contact lenses. The advertisement was discontinued.

Regulation of Advertising

There is no single regulatory body in India for regulation of advertisements. Depending on the nature of the case, power to regulate may vary from the courts, State and Central Governments[9], tribunals[10] or other authorities like the Press Council of India. The Press Council is often regulated by its 'Norms of Journalistic Conduct' in regulation of its advertisements. The other legislations affecting the area of advertising are like the Drug and Magic Remedies (Objectionable Advertisement) Act, 1954, which was enacted to control the advertisements of drugs in certain cases and to prohibit the advertisements for certain purposes, remedies alleged to possess magic qualities and to provide for matters connected therewith. The following are a few cases which had come within the scanner of this Act. In Hamdard Dawakhana case the Supreme Court was faced with the question as to whether the *Drug and Magic Remedies Act,* which put restrictions on the advertisements of drugs in certain cases and prohibited advertisements of drugs having magic qualities for curing diseases, was valid as it curbed the freedom of speech and expression of a person by imposing restrictions on advertisements. The Supreme Court held that, an advertisement is no doubt a form of speech and expression but every advertisement is not a matter dealing with the expression of ideas and hence advertisement of a commercial nature cannot fall within the concept of Article 19(1)(a). However, in *Tata Press Ltd.* case.[11], a three-judge bench of the Supreme Court differed from the view expressed in the *Hamdard Dawakhana* case and held that 'commercial advertisement' was definitely a part of Article 19(1)(a) as it aimed at the dissemination of information regarding the product. The Court, however, made it clear that the government could regulate commercial advertisements, which are deceptive, unfair, misleading and untruthful.

Thus, it may be concluded that the age of consumerism and commercialisation has coincided and largely catalysed by the growth and spread of media, which has provided it the larger than life image. Though self-regulation within the advertising industry is an effective method of ensuring ethical advertising practices, still there is a growing need that the executive takes initiatives and develops a unified system of regulation by adequate reforms in laws and effective implementation of the same.

Media Literacy

Media literacy is the process of analyzing, evaluating and creating messages in a wide variety of media modes, genres and forms. It uses an inquiry-based instructional model that encourages people to ask questions about what they watch, see, and read. Media literacy provides tools to help people critically analyze messages to detect propaganda, censorship, and bias in news and public affairs programming (and the reasons for such), and to understand how structural features such as media ownership, or its funding model[12] affect the information presented.[13]

To understand and to work towards better Media Literacy there is need to look into its core concepts and help consumers understand the basis on which marketing and advertising are done to sell a product and what exactly they should be watching out for. The Centre for Media Literacy in Santa Monica, California, created the five core concepts of media literacy, using the Canada's eight "Key Concepts" for media literacy as a guide. The *Five Core Concepts*[14] are:

- All media messages are constructed.
- Media messages are constructed using creative language with its own rules.
- Different people experience the same media message differently.
- Media have embedded values and points of view.
- Most media messages are constructed to gain profit and/ or power.

All Media Messages are Constructed

This concept acknowledges that media texts are constructed by authors. The final product is not a natural or objective text; rather, it is made up of various elements that were created by authors (writers, photographers, directors, producers, etc.). Many decisions go into the creation of a text, and the consumer sees the end result. The consumer does not, however, get to see the ideas that were rejected along the way, which could have produced endless variations on the media text. By asking who created the message, consumers are able to conceptualize both the human element behind the media text and the process of actually piecing a text together. Each media text has its own language, which can be understood through careful consideration of the sounds and visuals that are employed to convey meaning. One of the ways in which consumers can learn to analyze the language of media texts is by creating their own.

Different People Experience the Same Media Message Differently

Because audience members all differ in backgrounds and life

experiences, they are positioned to interpret media texts in different ways. Two people who consume the exact same media text may come out with completely different meanings. Media texts are not objective, they all contain values that tell us who or what is important. By virtue of what is omitted, they tell us who and what is not important as well.

Most Media Messages are Constructed to Gain Profit and/or Power

Most media messages are made in order to create an audience so that advertisers can market their products. It is important for consumers to understand this financial motivation to discern whose interests are actually being served. The consumer can be made aware only to a certain level, but there is a point when the consumer has to ask question, why is the media so financially motivated instead of being motivated towards consumer welfare. This is a very fair and pertinent question and there is need to urge the media to create an awareness regarding the five core concepts stated above, so that both the media as well as the consumer can do their own work as well as create a balance by showing the consumer how the advertisers work and what they work towards.

An Oxford economist Paul Collier notes that most media—across regions and on any platform: print, radio, TV or online—aren't interested in serving the public good, because "there is no finance to that public-good role. Indeed far from there being finance for it," says Collier, "there is actually a hostile environment to it...."[15] Citizens derive the power to make informed decisions and the power of oversight from free and independent media. Media Literacy not only educates the general public, and policy makers but it also helps to show the importance of access to independent news and information and how essential the media can be in bringing transparency and accountability of government and the development sector.

Conclusion

The media is required to be slammed for thinking only about monetary gains instead of consumer welfare, but the third and the fourth issues bring out our real stand which says that there needs to be more regulations for the advertising industry and that media literacy need not be necessarily be telling the consumers that the media is out to get their money and nothing else. We believe that media literacy must focus on how advertising agencies and marketing agencies function in an instead of repeatedly slamming them for profiteering while seeing to it that the media stays within certain ethical boundaries with the help of legislation and self-regulation.

This will help the consumer understand the objectives of these advertising agencies and in turn help them to make wiser choices while buying, while not worrying that the advertisers are disseminating misinformation.

NOTES

1. http://hindu.com./2007/10/12/stories/2007101260940600.htm
2. http://www.financialexpress.com/news/mcdonalds-india-to-open-180190-more-restaurants-by-2015/466279/
3. http://www.pnwlocalnews.com/east_king/bel/news/37473779.html
4. http://latimesblogs.latimes.com/booster_shots/2009/09/smart-choices-sugary-cereal.html
5. Ben H. Bagdikian, *The Media Monopoly*, Sixth Edition, Beacon Press, 2000, p. 133.
6. *Ibid.*
7. *Supra*, p 150.
8. Madhavi Goradia Divn, *Facets of Media Law*, Eastern Book Company, Fifth Edition, 2006, p. 197.
9. Young Persons (Harmful Publication) Act, 1956.
10. Consumer Forum under Consumer Protection Act, 1986.
11. *Tata Press Ltd.* v. *Mahanagar Telephone Nigam Ltd.*, (1995) 5 SCC 139.
12. Funding model is Corporate media, a term which refers to a system of media production, distribution, ownership, and funding which is dominated by corporations, and is governed by the capitalist imperatives of maximizing profits for the investors, stockholders, and advertisers.
13. http://en.wikipedia.org/wiki/Media_literacy#cite_note-0
14. Thoman & Jolls, 2005, p. 186.
15. Susan Moeller, *"Media Literacy: An Avenue to Broader Citizen Participation & Good Governance"*, www.blogs.worldbank.org

REFERENCES

Ben H. Bagdikian, *The Media Monopoly*, Beacon Press, Sixth Edition, 2000.

Consumer Protection Act, 1986.

Drug and Magic Remedies (Objectionable Advertisement) Act, 1954.

Hamdard Dawakhana v. *Union of India*, AIR 1960 SC 554.

http://en.wikipedia.org/wiki/Media_literacy#cite_note-0

http://hindu.com./2007/10/12/stories/2007101260940600.htm

http://latimesblogs.latimes.com/booster_shots/2009/09/smart-choices-sugary-cereal.html

http://www.financialexpress.com/news/mcdonalds-india-to-open-180190-more-restaurants-by-2015/466279/

http://www.pnwlocalnews.com/east_king/bel/news/37473779.html

Madhavi Goradia Divan, *Facets of Media Law*, Eastern Book Company, Fifth Edition, 2006.

Susan Moeller, *"Media Literacy: An Avenue to Broader Citizen Participation & Good Governance"*, www.blogs.worldbank.org

Tata Press Ltd. v. *Mahanagar Telephone Nigam Ltd.*, (1995) 5 SCC 139.

www.blogs.worldbank.org

Young Persons (Harmful Publication) Act, 1956.

Index

AC Nielsen, research company, 284
Academic education, 121
Adjudication mechanism, 165
Administrative reforms, 3
ADR forums, 231
ADR mechanisms, 97, 103, 106, 228–30
ADR movement, 229
Adulterants, 130
Adulterated products, 178
Adulteration, 4, 16, 38, 113, 116, 128, 130, 133–35
    cases, 135
    of food stuff, 130
Advertising
    industry, 314, 317
    literacy, 26
    methods, 311
Advertising Standards Authority (ASA), 312
Advertising Standards Council of India (ASCI), 312–13
Agriculture Organization, 129–30
Alternate Dispute Resolution (ADR), 15, 72, 97–98, 100–107, 177, 228–29, 235–36, 293
Amnesty Scheme, 23, 278
Analytical methods, 172
Andhra Pradesh Legal Metrology Department, 194–95
Anti-Competitive Agreements, 76–78, 81, 83–84
Anticompetitive agreements, 77
Anti-trust laws, 85
Arbitration Act, 100
Arbitration and Conciliation Act, 100
Assam Electricity Regulatory Commission (AERC), 218, 223
Awareness programmes, 9, 71, 165, 180

Banking sector, 21, 124, 204, 226, 237
Bargaining powers, 4, 34, 299
Benevolent methods, 231
Bihar School Examination Board Act, 254
Bihar School Examination Board, 253–54, 256
Bill board advertisements, 310
Bill collection centres, 268
Board of Secondary Education, 248
Bureau of Indian Standards Act, 287
Business organizations, 101
Business-consumer relationship model, 34

California Public Utilities Commission (CPUC), 223
Canbank Mutual Fund, 52
Capacity building programmes, 69, 85, 180
C-Club projects, 119
Central Board of School Education (CBSE), 120
Central Bureau of Investigation (CBI), 122
Central Consumer Welfare Fund, 40
Central Electricity Regulatory Commission Act, 265
Centralized organization of infrastructure industries, 20, 215
Centre for Consumer Studies, 12, 171
Centre for Media Literacy, 315
Chit fund company, 47, 50
Chit Funds Acts, 50
Citizen Charters, 295–96

Civic and Consumer Literacy, 296
Civic and Consumer movement, 24
Civil society organizations, 8
Civil Supplies and Consumer Affairs Department, 53
Codex Alimentarius Commission, 130
Commission Advisory Committee (CAC), 219
Commodities Act, 111
Community empowerment, 98
Companies Act, 87
Comparative Analysis, 81
Competition Act, 14, 73, 75–77, 79–88
Competition Commission, 76, 80–83
Competition policy, 14, 75, 80, 85
Complaints handling mechanisms, 222
Comptroller and Auditor General of India, 123
Computer literacy, 69, 72
CONFONET scheme, 8
Consumer Action and Network Society (CANS), 110
Consumer assistance programmes, 113
Consumer awareness programmes, 70
Consumer Consultative Councils, 222
Consumer cooperatives, 117
Consumer disputes redressal forums, 42, 103, 114, 304
Consumer Education and Research Centre (CERC), 23, 218, 223, 237, 260–61, 264, 277
Consumer education, 7, 10, 16, 37, 39–40, 57, 112, 114–17, 120–21, 163–66, 176–78, 189, 303, 305
  formal, 117
  impart, 115
  informal, 117
Consumer empowerment, 40, 164
Consumer Forums and Commissions, 8, 96
Consumer forums, 19–22, 45–46, 48–49, 54, 61, 68–69, 71–72, 96, 109, 117–18, 201–2, 230–31, 270, 295–96, 303–4
Consumer Guidance Forum, 293–94
Consumer movement, 2, 8–10, 12–13, 16, 19, 24–25, 32, 38, 40–41, 47, 60, 67, 113–14, 116–18, 176–78
  global, 3
  responsive, 8
  sustained, 17
  vibrant, 6
Consumer Policy and Law, 12, 29
Consumer Protection Act, 6, 10, 12–15, 22–23, 60–61, 64–65, 67–70, 73, 82–84, 94–95, 109–10, 163–65, 207–8, 243–44, 303–5
Consumer Protection Councils (CPC), 49, 57, 64, 96, 103, 109, 122
Consumer protection rules, 56, 74, 224, 244
Consumer Protection, General Guidelines for, 3
Consumer redressal mechanism, 302
Consumer Rights, Education and Awareness Trust (CREAT), 220, 225
Consumer Unity and Trust Society (CUTS), 219–20, 225
Consumer Welfare Act, 85
Consumer Welfare Fund, 8
Consumer welfare model, 85
Consumer Welfare Rules, 8
Consumer welfare schemes, 175
Consumerism, 2–3, 10–12, 16, 19, 31–33, 37, 40, 94, 96, 108, 113, 116, 128, 163, 311
  components of, 12, 32
  defined, 2
  effectiveness of, 13, 32
  new era in, 33
Consumers Disputes Mediation Centres, 106
Consumers Information Centre, 104
Consumers rights education, 116
Cooperative
  bodies, 7, 60
  efforts, 154
  ownership, 154
  societies, 263
  super markets, 112
Corporate
  control, 152

giants, 312
governance, 75
grip, 156
houses, 162
law, 15
media, 149
profits, 148
Cosmetics Act, 38, 287
CREAT-USAID Model, 220
CUTS programme, 219–20

Deepthi Coaching Centre, 51
Delhi Electricity Reforms Act, 265
Delhi Electricity Regulatory Commission (DERC), 264, 267–68, 277
Delhi Legal Services Authority (DLSA), 21, 226–27, 232, 234, 236–37
Delhi Municipal Corporation, 274–75
Delhi Vidyut Board, 276
Department of Civil Supplies, 114, 294–95
Department of Consumer Affairs, 7–8, 53, 72, 119, 122, 124, 127, 179–80, 196
Department of Post, 10
Department of Power, 23, 277
Development Authorities, 255–56
Development organizations, 153
Disproportionate powers, 312
Dispute resolution institutions, 228
Distribution methods, 80
District Consumer Disputes Redressal Forums, 179, 304
District Consumer Protection Council, 296
District Forums and State Commissions, 8, 42, 116
Drug and Magic Remedies Act, 314
Drug industries, 148
Drugs and Cosmetics Act, 38, 287

Economic analysis, 85
Economic development, 101
Economic powers, 5
Economic reforms, 215
Education Departments, 119, 122
Efficiency models, 229
Electricity Act, 21, 23, 216–18, 221, 225, 262–63, 270, 273–74, 277–78, 303
Electricity Consumer Council, 222
Electricity department, 276
Electricity generation, 266
Electricity industry, 21, 216, 265–66
Electricity Reforms Act, 217
Electricity Regulatory Commission Act, 23, 216, 260, 262, 265, 276–77
Electricity sector reforms, 20, 215
European Competition Commission, 77
Exclusive Supply Agreement, 79

Facilitation-cum-Information Centres, 104
Federation of Indian Chamber of Commerce and Industry (FICCI), 10, 166, 284
Federation of Indian Chambers of Commerce and Industry, 284
FICCI Alliance for Consumer Care (FACC), 10
Financial institution, 47
Financial Sector, 204
First Press Commission, 152
Florence-Access-to-Justice-Project, 228
Fly-by-night operators, 101
FMCG industry, 169–70
Food Adulteration Act, 136
Food and Agriculture Organization, 17, 129–30
Food business operator, 137, 139
Food industry, 140–41
Food Safety and Standards Act, 17, 136, 140–41, 190
Food sector, 136
Four-part systemic model, 146
Friendly forums, 43
Fuel poverty, 223
Fundamental laws, 5
Fundamental principles, 208
Fundamental Rights and Directive Principles, 5, 297
Fundamentalist groups, 150

Gandhian concept, 1

Gas and Electricity Consumer Council, 222
Gas Consumers' Council, 222
Goa Non-Biodegradable Garbage Control Act, 297
Goodday Biscuits, 183
Grading and Marketing Act, 38
Grievance forums, 239
Grievance redressal mechanism, 20, 200–201
Gujarat Electricity Board, 49
Gujarat State Commission, 49

Hamdard Dawakhana case, 314
Haryana State Commission, 268
Haryana State Electricity Board, 268
Hazard Analysis and Critical Control Point, 138
Help Groups (SHGs), 24
Hydro projects, 263

Indian Medical Association, 54, 257
Indian Medical Council, 303
Indian Newspaper Society (INS), 154
Indian Oil Corporation Ltd, 113
Indian Penal Code (IPC), 38, 100, 287
Indispensable factor, 74
Industrial designs, 281
Industrial revolution, 108
Industrialization, 109
Industry-based schemes, 222
Industry-funded structures, 222
Informal education, 117
Inquiry-based instructional model, 314
Inspirational model, 167
Institutional arrangements, 6, 60, 163
Institutional buyers, 193
Institutional Consumers, 192–93
Institutional mechanism, 16, 60
Insurance Act, 204–5
Insurance Council, 205
Insurance Industry, 201
Insurance policy, 201, 208, 210–12
  double benefit, 210
  mediclaim, 212
Insurance Regulatory Development Authority (IRDA), 20, 201–5
Insurance sector, 20, 200, 204, 210, 214
Inter Ministerial Group (IMG), 196
Inter-corporate investments, 150
International cooperation, 4, 35, 80, 242
International Press Institute (IPI), 154
IRDA Act, 201
IRDA Annual Report, 203–4
ISI Certification Marks Act, 111

Jharkhand State Electricity Board and Anr, 270
Journalism, 9, 146, 152, 155, 311
  commercial, 146
  investigative, 150
Judicial activism, 122, 312
Judicial reforms, 229–30
Justice delivery mechanism, 53
Justice reform, 228

Karnataka Electricity Reforms Act (KERA), 216
Kellogg Company, 309
Kellogg's Revolution, 309
KERC and Assam Electricity Regulatory Commission, 223
Krishna District Forum-I, 47

Lanham Act, 74
Law Commission of India, 132
Law Department, 61
Law reformers, 110
Legal education, 231, 239
Legal Metrology Department, 47, 177, 186
Liberal democracy, 149
Liberal framework of development, 262, 277
Lok adalats, 227
Lucknow Development Authority, 43, 250–51, 255–56, 258

Magic Remedies Act, 314
Maharashtra State Commission, 47, 52
Mahatma Gandhi, 37
Marketing and Research Team (MART), 166, 284

Mass education, 117
Maximum Retail Price (MRP), 19, 111, 123–25, 127, 174, 183, 185–88, 191
Media campaign, 164
Media corporations, 18, 146, 150
Media education programmes, 26
Media reforms, 152, 155
Mediation Centre, 106, 177
Mediclaim policy, 212, 214
Merchandise Marks Act, 286
Ministry of Food Processing Industries (MoFPI), 136
Misrepresentation test, 74
Modern economic development, 1
Monopolies and Restrictive Trade Practices Act, 75, 82, 111
Motor Vehicle Act, 210
Multi-culturalism, 229
Multi-departmental control, 136
Multi-lateral trade, 149
Multi-media campaign, 8, 10, 19, 176
Multinational institution, 229
Municipal Council, 296
Municipal Solid Waste Management Rules, 297

National Commission for Women, 298
National Consumer Commission, 255
National Consumer Day, 8, 176–77, 180
National Consumer Dispute Redressal Commission (NCDRC), 7, 72, 210, 244
National Council for Applied Economic Research (NCAER), 168
National Council of Education, Research and Training (NCERT), 120
National Electricity Policy, 217, 263
National Human Rights Commission, 297
National Institute of Criminology and Forensic Science, 122
National Sample Survey Organization (NSSO), 129
Negotiable Instruments Act, 232
Nehru Yuva Kendras, 176–77
Neo-liberal economics, 149
New Delhi Municipal Corporation, 276
Northern India Tiles Corporation, 275

Office of Consumer Advocacy (OCA), 224
Office of Ratepayer Advocates (ORA), 223
Ombudsman, 204, 206, 264
Open forums, 305
ORG Centre for Social Research, 164

Pacification schemes, 229
Packaged Commodities Rules, 124, 127, 182, 184–86, 190–94
Panchayati Raj Institutions, 19, 176, 179–80
Party autonomy, 97–99
Patch tests, 291
Pharmaceutical sector, 121
Police Department, 52
Political empowerment, 301
Political powers, 3
Postal Department, 50
Posts and Telegraphs Act, 50
Poverty alleviation, 262
Power policy, 266
Power reforms, 260
Power Sector Reforms, 219–20
Power sector, 21, 216–19, 224, 262–63, 277
Powerless consumers, 11
Press Council of India, 154, 313
Prevention of Food Adulteration Act, 17, 111, 130, 132, 137–39, 287, 303
Price control mechanism, 37
Price movements, 162
Private hospital/health centres, 257
Prohibiting Anti-Competitive Agreements, 76
Public Grievance Rules, 204
Public Private Partnership (PPP), 122
Public sector undertaking, 50

Quality control mechanism, 140
Quasi-Judicial forum, 20, 201
Quasi-Judicial Powers, 82

Rajasthan State Electricity Regulatory Commission (RSERC), 220
Rajasthan State Industrial Corporation, 49
Rapid industrial development, 1
Redressal Agencies Dependent on Consumer Affairs Department, 53
Redressal Forums, 43, 82, 268
Redressal mechanism, 14, 19, 64, 69, 94, 98, 115, 175, 177–79, 201, 212, 293, 305
Regional agreements, 149
Regulatory commissions, 20, 217–19, 221, 223, 225, 261, 263–64
Residential welfare associations, 221
Revenue model, 299
Revenue Recovery Act, 51
Revenue/other departments, 48
Road Safety Patrols (RSP), 297
Roscoe Pound's theory, 80
Rule of laws, 94, 229, 252

Safety and Standards Act, 140
Sales of Good Act, 303
Saligao Civic and Consumer Forum, 295
Scheduled Castes, 231
Schiller, Herbert, 147
Second Press Commission, 152
Securities and Exchange Board of India, 40
Self-Help Groups (SHGs), 24
Social movement, 3, 32
Socio-economic factors, 102
Socio-economic programmes, 59
Standards of Weights and Measures Act, 111, 182–83, 186, 195–96
State Consumer Commission, 114
State Electricity Reforms Act, 216
State Electricity Regulatory Commissions, 260, 264
State Institutes of Rural Development, 177, 180
Statistical methods, 172
Statutory powers, 104, 222, 252, 274
Structural Adjustment Programmes, 229
Suo motu powers, 84
Supreme Court (SC), 22, 42–43, 99, 114, 123, 211, 246, 250–52, 254–57, 270, 314
Sustainable Development, 243
Systematic movement, 38

Telegraph Act, 123
Telephone departments, 111
Titan Industries, 195
Tourism sector, 294
Trade and Merchandise Marks Act and Copyright Act, 286
Trade associations, 284
Trademarks Act, 287
Tri-partite pressure mechanism, 312
Twenty-Point Programme, 6

UN Charter of Human Rights, 297
Unfair methods, 191
Unilateral decisions, 274
United Nations Conference on Trade and Development, 80
Unorganized food sector, 137
Urban centres, 178
Urban cooperative banks, 121

Value Added Tax (VAT), 121, 123–25, 127
Vertical Agreements, 78
Videocon Industries, 195
Vigilance Department, 297
Village forums, 295, 298–99
Voluntary Consumer Organisation (VCOs), 9, 24, 32, 36, 119–23, 127, 175, 293
Vulnerable products, 283

Weights and Measures Act, 195
World Consumers' Day, 38
World Earth Day, 294
World Health Organization, 129–30
World Trade Organization, 130

Young Civic and Consumer Movement, 298